AF352639

Idealism without Absolutes

SUNY series, Intersections:
Philosophy and Critical Theory

Rodolphe Gasché, editor

Idealism without Absolutes

Philosophy and Romantic Culture

Edited by
Tilottama Rajan and Arkady Plotnitsky

STATE UNIVERSITY OF NEW YORK PRESS

Published by
State University of New York Press, Albany

For information, address the State University of New York Press,
90 State Street, Suite 700, Albany, NY 12207

Production by Diane Ganeles
Marketing by Jennifer Giovani

Library of Congress Cataloging-in-Publication Data

Idealism without absolutes : philosophy and romantic culture / edited by Tilottama Rajan and Arkady Plotnitsky.
    p. cm. — (SUNY series, intersections—philosophy and critical theory)
    Includes bibliographical references and index.
    ISBN 0-7914-6001-0 (alk. paper).
    1. Idealism, German.   2. Romanticism—Germany.   3. Absolute, The—History.   I. Rajan, Tilottama.   II. Plotnitsky, Arkady.   III. Intersections (Albany, N.Y.)

B2745.I34 2004
141'.0943—dc21   2003050602

Contents

Acknowledgments

The editors would like to acknowledge the support of their respective institutions, The University of Western Ontario and Purdue University, for support that has made possible the completion of their research for this volume. Tilottama Rajan would also like to acknowledge the aid of the Social Sciences and Humanities Research Council of Canada, a grant from which, among other things, paid for research assistance for the editing, indexation, and preparation of the manuscript. We owe a great debt to our contributors, some of whom waited with great patience for this project to come to fruition.

An earlier version of chapter 10 was published as "Hegel Beside Himself: Unworking the Intellectual Community," *European Romantic Review* 13, no. 2 (2002): 139–45.

Introduction

~

Tilottama Rajan

In the past decade the philosophical tradition of German Idealism has come to be recognized as a rich and complex part of "Theory," while this field itself has been associated with a fundamentally interdisciplinary way of thinking and range of practices. Yet there has been little intensive consideration of either the disciplinary or interdisciplinary nature of Idealism itself. Nor has much attention been given to the ways in which philosophy—the discipline in which Idealism is anchored—is itself hybridized and de-idealized by its connections with other fields. This volume attempts to rethink the conceptuality and disciplinarity of post-Kantian philosophy across the full range of the long romantic period, from Immanuel Kant and the Schlegels at one end, through the post-Kantian Idealists, to Friedrich Nietzsche.

The volume is thus organized by three interconnected concerns. First, the essays share a sense that it is possible to have an idealism without the totalizing formulas often associated with post-Kantian philosophy, as represented by such concepts (conventionally interpreted) as G. W. F. Hegel's Absolute Knowledge or J. G. Fichte's Absolute Ego. The space for this idealism is created by a particular symbiosis between ideality and materiality. Second, this symbiosis often occurs through the contamination or extension of philosophy into other, more "material" disciplines such as psychology, history, or literature. At stake, then, is the very identity of philosophy as the host for a variety of other parasitic discourses that reciprocally reconfigure philosophy itself. In such circumstances it would be easy to read the intellectual tradition studied here through twentieth-century lenses. And indeed the essays all draw on contemporary theory: notably the work of Gilles Deleuze,

Jean-François Lyotard, Martin Heidegger, Paul de Man, Theodor Adorno, Jacques Derrida, and others. Yet in the end the revision of Idealism by materialism explored here results in a uniquely romantic mode of thinking. We suggest, therefore, that Romanticism's particular contribution is "an idealism without absolutes," rather than any kind of absolute materialism or idealism, and that it is this critical idealism that allows thinkers as different as Nietzsche and Hegel to inhabit the same conceptual space. It would also be appropriate (if beyond the parameters of this volume) to read others as belonging to this post-romantic configuration, as Richard Beardsworth intimates with reference to Karl Marx and Sigmund Freud in the final essay. Hence *finally* there is also a timeliness in rearticulating the significance of the Idealism-Romanticism juncture for the modern and postmodern intellectual scene.

To begin with, then, this volume hopes to initiate a rethinking of German Idealism in terms of how it brings materiality into conjunction with ideality (or phenomenality, as what can be made visible or expressible). That materiality is a concern of German Idealism has often been recognized. However, it is often seen—even by certain key representatives of Idealism itself (though against the grain of their most radical thought)—as playing a merely supplementary role in the discourse(s) of philosophy. Materiality is thus often identified with the traditional opposite of Idealism: the materialism of Spinoza or, differently, Marx. By contrast, the aim of this volume is to show the constitutive role of materiality in the work of the figures defining *Idealist* philosophy. In other words we suggest that Idealism is not only reconfigured by materiality but also itself reconstitutes the material: both "materiality" as a concept, and the material with which philosophy deals.

"Materiality" needs to be distinguished from the narrower notion of "materialism," whether it be metaphysical materialism as an idealism of matter, classical Marxism as an idealism of capital or class, or cultural materialism as an absolutism of the empirical. While these associations are important, *materiality* is not inevitably tied to matter or to matters of fact. Instead we use the term to indicate a field of concepts, theoretical and practical effects, and intellectual "events." As an analogue to *différance* or heterogeneity, materiality in this sense disturbs all absolutes: whether those of Idealism or materialism. It thereby proves to be a much more explosive concept than materialism without de-absolutization. Most important, then, materiality refers to a certain mode of the constitution of thought: one that involves a rethinking of conceptuality itself along the lines developed by Deleuze and Felix Guattari, who reconceive the very notion of the "concept" outside of its metaphysical and ideological closure. According to their view a "concept" is not an entity established by a generalization from or idealization of particulars. It is rather an irreducibly complex, multilayered structure: a multicomponent conglomerate of concepts, figures, metaphors, and particular (ungeneralized) elements.[1] Yet this notion of the concept (as materiality and creativity) is itself irreducibly romantic and idealist, as Arkady Plotnitsky suggests in his exploration of Hegel's use of the term *concept*, and as Tilottama Rajan suggests in her discussion of Kant's and Hegel's use of the term *idea* as a foundation for "Idealism." Hence the most critical materialism, and the most powerful weapon against the "romantic ideology," may paradoxically be Idealism itself, absolved from absolutes. This is true even if a provisional simplification of multiplex "ideas" such as Spirit or Freedom is sometimes necessary for the functioning of the broader aesthetic, ethical, or political visions emerging in Romanticism.[2]

Equally seminal for this conjunction of ideality and materiality is Leibniz, whose work is formative for Deleuze (in his reading of Kant as much as Leibniz). Indeed as Plotnitsky intimates in his essay, Idealism is just as much post-Leibnizian as post-Kantian. Kant works through separations, boundaries, and distinctions—whether in terms of concepts or at the level of the various disciplines that "contest" philosophy, and that he seeks to keep separate from philosophy. By contrast, Leibniz's thought is interactively constituted in a series of metaphoric transfers and contaminations between physics, biology, mathematics, metaphysics, and theology. Moreover, both Leibniz's materialist idealism, as a counter to Spinoza's materialism, and his specific concepts (in particular his monads), manifest and actively deploy the conceptual materialism described here. Indeed one could offer the "monad" as a figure for the concept as material plurality. Monads are, on the surface, units—and unities— of thought, like concepts in the conventional sense. Yet when considered microscopically, each monad is, arguably, infinitely subdivisible into further monads, smaller conceptual units, and is thus irreducibly nonsimple. Or to put it differently, the monad possesses a certain "architectural" unity, but on closer inspection unfolds into numerous smaller, not necessarily synchronic, rooms, spaces, and closets. Yet the architectural metaphor is itself only a rubric, as these smaller "molecules" do not simply coexist but also interact.

This interference of the "matter" of concepts with their ideality is, we suggest, paralleled on a larger scale through an opening up of philosophy by the subject matters with which it deals. Kant inherited from the medieval university an arrangement in which there were three "higher" faculties (law, medicine, and theology) and a lower (in effect undergraduate) faculty of "philosophy." This faculty—a faculty of "arts" in the older form that included science—taught philosophy in the narrower sense, but also everything else not covered by the professional faculties.[3] The Idealists therefore worked not just on philosophy, but also on aesthetics, ethics, history, anthropology, the natural sciences, psychology, and religion. At the same time the romantic period witnessed a professionalization of philosophy in the German university and a concomitant reflection on what constitutes "science" or knowledge. From this perspective the amorphousness of philosophy was a threat. Thus

F. W. J. Schelling writes that we now have a philosophy of agriculture, will soon have a philosophy of "vehicles," and that eventually there will be "as many philosophies as there are objects," so that we risk "los[ing] philosophy itself entirely." Like Husserl (who traced philosophy's loss of "rigor" back to Idealism), the early and more conventionally idealist Schelling saw this heterogenization as a "crisis" in the phenomenal identity of philosophy as "science." Yet the diversity of philosophy was also an opportunity, including for Schelling himself in the *Freedom* essay and in *The Ages of the World*.[4]

In *The Conflict of the Faculties* Kant tried to cope with the amorphousness of his faculty by defining it against the professional faculties as a space for speculation and research (empirical as well as conceptual). He further sought to separate philosophy (in a more restricted sense) from other areas that he taught, such as anthropology and geography. The internal economy of this philosophy is mapped by the three Critiques. In all of these cases Kant dealt with the problem of disciplinarity by using the model of conflict or "contest": a contest *(Streit)* rather than an intermingling of "faculties" (both administrative and cognitive faculties), and by extension a contest of disciplines. But as Deleuze argues, if Kant's faculties can "enter into relationships which are variable but regulated by one or other of them," together they must be "capable of relationships which are free and *unregulated*, where each goes to its own limit."[5] Hegel, who is the subject of several essays in this volume, in effect pushes these limits by imagining an "encyclopedia" of all of the philosophical sciences, wherein the concepts of individual sciences are recognized "as finite." Going beyond Kant, who tried to unify the liberal arts under the rubric of philosophy as method, Hegel claimed a greater specificity for philosophy by introducing "Idealism" into "all the sciences."[6] On one level this project may seem like an imperialism of philosophy, which becomes the macrosystem that contains microsystems of other disciplines as wheels within wheels. But Hegel also builds a profound reflectiveness into his encyclopedia through the doubling of "levels" as "spheres." In the subsumptive logic of his system each discipline is merely a level in the whole: thus "organics" is a level in the sphere of natural science, which itself is a level leading to the sciences of spirit. But conversely each level is also a sphere in its own right, a monad made up of further units that must be understood on their own terms as spheres. The encyclopedia project thus exemplifies Plotnitsky's notion of the Hegelian "baroque," as a constant folding and unfolding of disciplines into each other: a "superfold" that unravels the identity of particular disciplines.[7]

The encyclopedia project, in other words, is what Georges Bataille calls a "general economy" in which totality—as Absolute Knowledge—becomes de-absolutization. For while a certain *multi*disciplinarity on the regulated, Kantian model has often characterized philosophy, what is at issue here is rather an *inter*disciplinarity or intergeneration of discourses. Moreover, the deregulation of philosophy in particular, the move beyond philosophy as a "restricted economy,"[8] occurs because of the more general climate of "Romanticism."[9] Of relevance here are Friedrich Schlegel's conception of "Literature," his hybrid discourses of symphilosophy and sympoetry (as the philosophizing of poetry and the poetizing of philosophy), and Novalis's (Friedrich von Hardenberg's) principle of a general "versability" of disciplines that allows for a poetizing of science or even physics and mathematics. In this environment Philosophy (with a capital P) becomes itself the deployment of a multicomponent architecture of generals and particulars, rather than an abstract reduction from the particular. Yet the term *architecture* is provisional, as philosophy may also be contained by its components: a philosophy of history generates, in turn, histories of philosophy as Gary Handwerk argues in his essay. "Philosophy," in other words, comes to signify the general and reciprocal mediation occurring between and among philosophy and other fields of inquiry.

It is through this "folding" of discourses (to borrow Deleuze's figure) that this volume addresses not just philosophy, but the romanticism of philosophy, as each codefines the other. The essays gathered here thus show how romantic philosophy was engaged with a wide variety of fields from aesthetics, literature, and psychology, to history and histories of philosophy or culture. As important, there are clear analogies—though not identities—between philosophy in the interdisciplinary form explored here and the more recent field of "Theory." A setting in place of these analogies is a crucial goal of this volume. While the volume, then, hopes to rethink Idealism through its unique conjunction with materiality, these extensions also position the Idealism-Romanticism episteme as one crucial matrix for the historical-philosophical configuration that is our own.

Our first essay, by Jan Plug, focuses on the extension of philosophy "beyond" or "*between* itself" produced by Romanticism's invention of *Literature*, in the specific sense this term has from Friedrich Schlegel to Maurice Blanchot. The intimate connection of philosophy to Literature, as seen from both the idealist and romantic ends of the spectrum through Kant and the Schlegels, is one site for philosophy's opening onto the material. Kant, as suggested, was concerned not only with the relation between pure and practical reason, but also with philosophy's relation to other disciplines and domains. The very nature of his work in the university constructs philosophy as needing a referent, even if he saw a speculative distance from the empirical as also characterizing its stance. Plug suggests that it is the aesthetic—and the "symbol"—that best mediates this (dis)engagement. Because the symbol is not the material but its *sign*, the aesthetic involves an approach to the material that is idealist in being concerned with its forms and conditions of possibility, yet thereby critical of any absolutizing of ideas or concepts. At the same time, we should not think of the material as simply the raw material of philosophy. Rather the materiality that enters philosophy through the aesthetic (and Kant's notion of "aesthetic" ideas) continuously reconstitutes thought by deconstructing and reanimating it.

Kant's work discloses an interdisciplinarity at the heart of Idealism, which reworks the task of philosophy through the analogue of the aesthetic, in ways that extend to other forms of critical thinking such as the political. Yet Plug sees a related conjunction at work in "Romanticism." For the Jena Romantics also cross philosophy with the aesthetic, though for them it is more a question of a Literature that is the *theory* of literature, and thus a form of philosophy. That the Schlegels and Novalis gave this self-reflective Literature the prestige of philosophy is what Philippe Lacoue-Labarthe and Jean-Luc Nancy argue in *The Literary Absolute*. But for them Literature, despite and because of its reflexiveness, self-contains its own ironies as a form of absolute knowledge. Literature thus simply replaces philosophy as a form of absolute idealism. Arguing for a *literary* absolute rather than a literary *absolute*, Plug suggests instead that Literature is a mode of philosophy and criticism that precisely undermines the absolute in both literature and philosophy.

The materiality of the aesthetic that brings life to spirit for Plug is the death of a more absolutely idealistic spirit in Andrzej Warminski's reading of Hegel. Warminski focuses on the duplicity of the *Aesthetics* that narrates two histories: those of art-spirit and absolute spirit. The lectures correspondingly have two high points and two ends. On the one hand, art comes to an end with the dissolution of classicism which, as the adequate embodiment of the Idea and the high point of art-spirit, is inadequate for absolute spirit. On the other hand, the resulting post-art in the romantic, as the impossibility of embodying the Idea, comes to an end in a promise already suspended by the persistent remaindering of art. The problem is intensified by the difficulty of distinguishing one art from another. Only by an interpretive imposition can we say that what ends at the end of art is romantic and not symbolic, post- and not, once again, pre-art; only thus can we even say that the Idea has once been classically embodied rather than symbolically deferred. And insofar as art is a "mirror" in which the philosopher views "the inner essence of his own discipline,"[10] the history of art is also a repetitive allegory of Idealism's inability to attain its end in absolute spirit.

Tilottama Rajan deals with similar ambiguities, not however to deconstruct Idealism but rather to read Hegel beyond himself so as to make the *Aesthetics* an apparatus for the creation of new concepts (in Deleuze's sense). She thus returns to the intertextuality of the aesthetic and the philosophical also discussed by Plug. More specifically, she focuses on the cross-fertilizing of transcendental and cultural philosophy that occurs when Kant's distinction between the sublime and beautiful is transferred by Hegel into the triad of symbolic, classical, and romantic art. Kant's sublime calls for reflective judgments open to new "ideas" rather than determinant judgments that uphold existing "concepts." By reworking the sublime between the romantic and the symbolic (or oriental), Hegel turns the philosophical category of judgment toward the cultural category of "taste," thus allowing its ideal nature to be unsettled by the material of history. In other words, the *Aesthetics* is subject to a form of cultural materiality, in which philosophy is given a referent that reflects it back to create new determinations of philosophical concepts. Against the grain of his own philosophical taste, Hegel thus introduces new forms of judgment that challenge his classicist norms of aesthetic and philosophical identity. These forms respond to "inadequate" embodiments of the Idea in art, recognizing that every expression of the Idea has its own adequacy. The new forms (of art and judgment itself) also generate a reconceptualizing of such absolutes as beauty, freedom, and identity outside of the philosophical shape imposed on thought by Western culture. For Hegel, through the symbolic and romantic, rethinks not only the judgment of art but also the very nature of Idealism, which becomes a Romanticism associated with "the restless fermentation" by which spirit produces itself as its *nonidentity*.

For Jochen Schulte-Sasse, Hegel's thought is also the occasion for the formation of new epistemic practices, though in this case it is a question not so much of concepts as of cultural institutions that produce a self-critical "modernity." For Schulte-Sasse, then, de-absolutization and materiality result in the modernization, not the romanticization or postmodernization of Idealism. Schulte-Sasse begins with the notion of work in the *Phenomenology of Spirit* as the process by which consciousness externalizes, reflects on, and comes to know itself. Importantly, *Werk* in Hegel refers not to an activity so much as to the artifacts, the textual products (in a broad sense) that result from this externalization. In this sense Hegel may be said to have invented the domain of "culture" later elaborated by the post-Hegelian sociologist Georg Simmel, as well as the notion of mediality or what Simmel broadly defines as "technology."[11] For culture to progress individual consciousnesses must externalize themselves in readable artifacts and read the precipitates of other consciousnesses. Canons, intellectual histories, or historiographies (whether of art, religion, or philosophy) are thus among the practices that Hegel sees as necessary for the philosophical process of self-reflection. The phenomenology of mind, contrary to Bill Readings's claim that the post-Kantian university instituted philosophy as "pure process . . . the formal art of the use of mental powers,"[12] is mind's reflection on the history of its own work in the form of textual and discursive externalizations. Negativity, as the capacity to rethink the resulting technologies so that they do not ossify, is in part the hermeneutical reworking of culture through this externalization and reflection.

Gary Handwerk takes this focus on history as the medium of Idealism's self-reflection in a different direction, by tracing Friedrich Schlegel's work from his histories of classical literature to his later lectures on the histories of literature and philosophy. That philosophy and Idealism are at issue in Schlegel's work, though he may not seem a "philosopher," was already evident in Plug's essay. But by taking up Schlegel's *historiographical* writings, Handwerk reminds us that a key aspect of Romanticism's dialogue with Idealism is the engagement of philosophy with nonphilosophy. Indeed, as Schlegel says, it is through its encyclopedic engagement with *all* the "*sciences*" that Idealism itself becomes a "*critique of idealism.*"[13] Furthermore, since his histories include histories of *philosophy*, Schlegel invites us to rethink philosophy through the empirical problems—including that of history—to which it invisibly responds, however transcendentally. Indeed for Schlegel *history* is precisely the site for "transcendental" thinking, given that "transcendental" is whatever "relates to the joining or separating of the ideal and the real."[14]

The problem posed by history for idealist paradigms of "science" is that history does not yield universal patterns or certain knowledge. Withdrawing from metanarrative, the early Schlegel, according to Handwerk, seemingly returns to a *historia magistra vitae* in which the past persists into the present through the mimesis of historical *exempla.* But this is not any kind of straightforward classicism, since what is in these examples is a form of singularity expressed in Schlegel's use of the "Characteristic" as the form for exemplary history. Moreover, the past is a storehouse of *Urbilder,* archetypes, that like Kant's aesthetic ideas were never fully realized, and are contingently transformable into new fragmentary concepts within the infinite horizon of history. In his later work, the conservatism of which is similarly a deferral of absolutes, Schlegel further explores this contingent, nonlinear history open to the past and the future. He increasingly moves away from a grecophile history to an interest in non-European cultures that we have also seen in Hegel. This countermemory which, for example, leads Schlegel to explore the unacknowledged debts of Greek to Indian philosophy, is "determinedly vague." Nevertheless it inscribes cultural and intellectual history within a return and retreat of the origin, appropriately for someone who writes that the "feeling for fragments of the past" is indistinguishable from the "feeling for projects—which one might call fragments of the future."[15]

While Handwerk implicitly opposes Schlegel's work to a more linear dialectic in Hegel, Plotnitsky finds a different complication of science, and specifically mathematics, in the work of Hegel himself. Mathematics, as Derrida argues with regard to Husserl, seems indissociable from a certain ideality. Indeed, historically, the grounding of philosophy in "mathematics" has been a figure for its self-certainty. But as Plotnitsky argues, through notions such as differential calculus (as developed by Leibniz) and the Greek discovery of irrational magnitudes such as the diagonal of the square, this most ideal of sciences admits its own kind of materiality. Moreover, insofar as mathematics is the model for logic, these notions have a broader *philosophical* import that has a bearing both on the logic and on the architecture of thought.

In tracing these notions in Hegel's thought, Plotnitsky takes as his starting-point the idea of a "mathematical" Hegel, the logic of whose system no longer unfolds in a "Euclidean," homogeneous space. Plotnitsky, furthermore, repositions the mathematical in Hegel by connecting it to Deleuze's reading of Leibniz in *The Fold*, Leibniz himself being an important influence on Hegel. The Baroque fold is defined by Deleuze in terms of the interfold of the material and the conceptual/phenomenal, or in Plotnitsky's terms the trifold of matter, mind, and their interfold. In Hegel's thought the Baroque further acquires temporal, dynamic, and historical dimensions. Plotnitsky links the Baroque fold and the Hegelian Baroque, specifically in their mathematical aspects, to Deleuze and Guattari's view of philosophy as the creation of concepts and to their corresponding reconception of the "concept." Hegel's infinitely self-complicating system is topologically a manifold and temporally a spiral that unfolds and refolds itself through history. In the process it becomes a conglomerate of historico-political practices and conceptual-historical structures (including those of art, religion, and ethics): folds or spaces that are gathered up into a higher-level structure or "superfold." This superfold resembles Absolute Knowledge only in the sense delineated by Deleuze when he writes: "the Baroque invents the infinite work or process. The problem is not how to finish a fold, but how to continue it . . . how to bring it to infinity" in an idealism without absolutes.[16]

In our next essay, David Farrell Krell begins with an obvious difficulty: the Romantics and Idealists seem to elevate, not critique, the absolute. Krell takes up this problem by exploring the "ends" of the absolute in Schelling, Friedrich Hölderlin, and Novalis. Drawing on the multiple meanings of "end" as goal, termination, and deconstruction, he explores three subversions of the absolute: absolute inhibition, absolute separation, and absolute density. The de-absolutization of Idealism occurs because all three thinkers are as absolute in their commitment to the negative as to the positive elements of their thought. Moreover, in all three cases thought is unfolded by its unthought: by *Naturphilosophie* in Schelling, tragedy in Hölderlin, and chemistry in Novalis.

Krell begins with Schelling's development of the proto-Freudian concept of inhibition (*Hemmung*). Crucial here is one of the many materializations of philosophical ideas seen in this volume: in this case, the transfer of Fichte's dialectic of the I and Not-I from pure philosophy to nature, and thus to the realm of disease, sexuality, and death. De-absolutization occurs through a process of *absolutizing* not just the I but also its infinite inhibition. Indeed this paradox explains what is romantic in Schelling's *Destruktion* of Idealism through the infinitizing of *all* its elements. Krell finds a similar process in the work of Hölderlin and Novalis. Novalis conceives God as the absolute density of the in-itself: "infinitely compact metal—the most corporeal . . . of all beings." By pushing absolute identity to its limit, he allows the very concept of "god" to implode, seeking to access the materiality of some other life beyond the dead matter of spirit.

Krell discloses in Idealism a psychoanalytic materiality that is more centrally the focus of Joel Faflak's essay, which focuses on Arthur Schopenhauer's revisiting of Kant's missed encounter with the unseen/scene of reason. *The World as Will and Representation* subverts Kant's idealism by introducing into its own system the psychology of the philosophical subject, the "knower" who never actually knows itself. That Schopenhauer anticipates Freud is often noted. But less commonly discussed is the deconstruction of his philosophical corpus—even as deconstruction—by its own will. Faflak therefore does not stop at a reading that deals with the infiltration of philosophy by psychoanalysis through the *concepts* of representation and will. Such a reading would simply install Schopenhauer within an inverted Kantianism, an absolute nihilism or materialism. Instead Faflak reads the text as its own "autobiography": a conflicted process in which the explicit unsettling of Idealism is itself displaced by a resistance to this cognitive nihilism. The rationality of philosophy's complete telling of itself (albeit as absolute nihilism) is thus haunted by a further affective materiality, which Faflak calls the "telling *body* of philosophy." This body is both the corporealized will that discloses the unconscious of philosophy, *and* the philosophical corpus that repetitively speaks its own unconscious. The primal scene of Kantian Reason turns out to be Schopenhauer's missed encounter as well, leading to the trauma of a materialism without absolution. Thus even as he struggles to mourn it constructively, Schopenhauer is afflicted by an endless melancholy for the death of Idealism. This trauma is indeed written into the form of the text as an "analysis interminable": an analysis that repeats itself from book to book, and then through the years in Schopenhauer's revisiting and compulsive supplementation of his 1818 text (reissued in 1856).

The final three essays take up the persistence of the idealist problematic beyond Romanticism strictly defined, thus reflecting on the "futures of spirit." Reading between the work of Søren Kierkegaard and that of Adorno on Kierkegaard, John Smyth analyzes how the former, despite its putative anti-Hegelianism, still holds the possibility of an idealism without absolutes. Smyth unsettles the conventional positioning of the religious in Kierkegaard's corpus—and the field of Romanticism—as a form of metaphysics; instead he argues that by formulating the absolute as religious paradoxy, Kierkegaard avoids affirming it philosophically as a concept or dogma. The ethical and aesthetic, often opposed in discussions of Kierkegaard's corpus, thus prove to have a common structure in which Idealism, because it is dependent on a leap of faith, becomes subject to a deconstructive wager. Smyth then traces these deconstructive forces through the darker recesses of Kierkegaard's religious psychology in *The Concept of Dread*, which has as its primary focus a number of sacrificial aberrations and pathologies. Focusing on the anthropological ramifications of Kierkegaard's philosophy of the sacred, he raises the question of whether *The Concept of Dread* can generate a historical dialectic capable of reconciling Idealism and its psychic material, or whether its conception of history "leads down a more radical path indicated by de Man's reading of Schlegelian Romanticism." Smyth's response to this question, which sees dread as defining a space for speculation, makes the displacement of Idealism into religion and then the mediation or refraction of religion through psychology into the basis for a form of negative dialectics. This dialectic, generated by reading Kierkegaard through the resistances to/of his idealism, is more radical than Adorno's own dialectic, and thus discernible in the sacrificial logic of Adorno's aesthetic theory rather than in *Negative Dialectics* itself.

The sacrificial demands of what Hegel calls "Objective" Spirit and the dialectical unrest provoked by the pathologies of spirit are, differently, the subject of Rebecca Gagan's essay. Beginning with the university, which after Kant was conceived under the aegis of "philosophy," Gagan asks how philosophy is affected by the romanticism of the "university," conceived not just as an institution but also as the subject's relation to knowledge. Does the romantic university become a "sign" for the future, or should it be placed within the closure of metaphysics? To explore this question, Gagan takes up Bill Readings's account of the post-Kantian university as a university of "spirit" (in the conventional sense) and of a certain *Bildung* or "aesthetic education" accomplished through philosophy. Focusing on Hegel (rather than, as Readings does, on Fichte and Humboldt), Gagan suggests that the intellectual work of which this *idealist* university is an institutional image finds itself troubled by a more *romantic* relation of the community-subject to knowledge played out in Hegel's actual relation to the "work" of philosophy. Gagan returns to the question of discursive externalizations raised by Schulte-Sasse in his discussion of Hegel. Unlike Schulte-Sasse, she suggests that the work thus embodied as always vanishing, even if Hegel sees the need for a certain habit/habitus to facilitate this work. The work of art is perhaps the form of mediality that most (in)adequately embodies this work. The work of philosophy, of the university, can likewise be seen as aesthetic, given all the ambiguities that attend the discourse of the aesthetic in Hegel's own *Aesthetics*.

In our final essay, Richard Beardsworth also concludes by turning to the space of the university. Taking up a different position from Gagan's, that of the public intellectual, Beardsworth asks how the work of the university might be transformed by recovering the cultural and ethical potential of an idealism that we should not too readily relegate to the closure of metaphysics. He starts with a near axiomatic opposition between Hegel as the philosopher of Reason, system, and teleology, and Nietzsche as a thinker of force, antisystem, and contingency. The ensuing construction of Nietzsche contra Hegel as the father of Theory has led to a dismissal of the idealism of "Reason" through a refusal to credit it with an *ethical*, as distinct from epistemological, sensitivity to difference. The result has been a loss of contact, in our own time, with the project of critical philosophy, and an impoverishment of materialist thought, especially in its emphasis on economics. Yet through a reading of Hegel's early *Spirit of Christianity*, Beardsworth shows that the "differential alterity" of the gift and death (in Derrida and Levinas) can be found at the heart of "spirit." Beardsworth's disclosure of an ethical core in critical philosophy itself involves a profoundly ethical reading of Idealism beyond metaphysics: a demythologizing of Hegel's early theological writings that tries to get at their "spirit." This spirit, Beardsworth argues, then becomes the basis, in *The Phenomenology of Spirit*, for "the 'speculative' nature of thought" itself, in the self-difference of its responsibility to "the manifold unity" of life.

Building on this transvaluation of Idealism, Beardsworth then discloses a greater proximity than we assume between Hegel's idealism of reason and Nietzsche's materialist genealogy which, among other things, involves a progressive spiritualization of force from the biological to the sovereign. He nevertheless sees an "aporia" between the two, which compels us to think not just with but also between Hegel and Nietzsche, and then beyond them to Marx and Freud, who must themselves be rethought and recomplicated between Nietzsche and Hegel. Beardsworth stages these differences in the form of dialectic as described by Julia Kristeva, who insists on the necessity of marshaling " 'terms,' 'dichotomies,' and 'oppositions' " so as not to lose the force of the critical project in the grammatological movement of traces.[17] Yet the condition of possibility for this strategy is a continuous differencing of the dialectic, through a "spiral of complexification" that proceeds forward by returning to the past. According to this logic, which is similar to Plotnitsky's superfold, different thinkers, historico-political practices, and conceptual-historical structures fold into, unfold, and refold each other. The resulting epistemic realignments open up new possibilities for a culturally engaged and interdisciplinary philosophy that finds an enabling ground in Idealism's implicit practice of philosophy as "general economy."[18] Which is to say, as other essays in this volume argue albeit with different interdisciplinary stakes, that it is now time to think of Idealism romantically as its own future rather than poststructurally as the past.

Notes

1. Gilles Deleuze and Felix Guattari, *What Is Philosophy?* trans. Hugh Tomlinson and Graham Burchell (New York: Columbia University Press, 1993), 11–12, 16, 24.

2. Julia Kristeva points to this role of Idealism in materialism when she re-introduces G. W. F. Hegel into the postmodern, by arguing that the microtextural movement of traces in grammatology "absorbs . . . the 'terms' and 'dichotomies' " that Hegel "reactivates, and generates" (Kristeva, *Revolution in Poetic Language*, trans. Margaret Waller [New York: Columbia University Press, 1984], 141). While Kristeva is arguing against Derrida here, grammatology arguably reabsorbs the Hegelian dynamic so as to deploy rather than dissolve or "reduce" it.

3. Immanuel Kant, *The Conflict of the Faculties*, trans. Mary J. Gregor (Lincoln: University of Nebraska Press, 1992), 35, 43. According to Kant, the "philosophy faculty consists of two departments: a department of *historical knowledge*" and one of *"pure, rational knowledge"* (45).

4. F. W. J. Schelling, *The Philosophy of Art*, trans. Douglas W. Stott (Minneapolis: University of Minnesota Press, 1989), 14; Edmund Husserl, "Philosophy as a Rigourous Science," in *Phenomenology and the Crisis of Philosophy*, trans. Quentin Lauer (New York: Harper, 1965), 77. Schelling, *Philosophical Investigations into the Essence of Human Freecdom and Related Matters,* trans. Priscilla Hayden-Roy, in *Philosophy of German Idealism* (New York: Continuum, 1987), 217–84; Schelling, *Ages of the World,* trans. Jason M. Wirth (Albany: State University of New York Press, 2000).

5. Deleuze, *Kant's Critical Philosophy*, trans. Hugh Tomlinson and Barbara Habberjam (Minneapolis: University of Minnesota Press, 1984), xi–xii.

6. G. W. F. Hegel, *Encyclopedia of the Philosophical Sciences in Outline*, ed. Ernst Behler, trans. Steven A. Taubeneck (New York: Continuum, 1990), 54. The project of introducing idealism into all the sciences is articulated by Schelling in *Ideas for a Philosophy of Nature*, trans. Errol E. Harris and Peter Heath (Cambridge: Cambridge University Press, 1988), 272 n.

7. I develop these points further in Tilottama Rajan, "System and Singularity from Herder to Hegel," *European Romantic Review* 11:2 (2000); 137–49; Rajan, "(In)digestible Material: Disease and Dialectic in Hegel's *Philosophy of Nature*," in *Eating Romanticism: Cultures of Taste/Theories of Appetite*, ed. Timothy Morton (New York: Palgrave, forthcoming); and in Rajan, "In the Wake of Cultural Studies: Globalization, Theory and the University" (*Diacritics*, forthcoming). In using the term *encyclopedia project* here, I mean to indicate an encyclopedic reorganizing of the disciplines (e.g., in the *Aesthetics*) that exceeds and complicates, in its details, the more limiting and totalizing digest actually presented in the three volumes of the work titled *Encyclopedia of the Philosophical Sciences* (and consisting of the *Logic, The Philosophy of Nature* and *The Philosophy of Mind*).

8. I refer here to Georges Bataille's distinction between "general" and "restricted" economies in *The Accursed Share*, vol. 1, trans. Robert Hurley (New York: Zone Books, 1991). Restricted economy studies *"particular* systems . . . in terms of particular operations with limited ends" (22). By contrast, general economy has two

aspects: (1) a radical organicism wherein an individual phenomenon or discipline cannot be studied as "an isolatable system of operation" (19); and (2) a disseminative "energy" arising from this interconnectedness, the result of which is an excess "used for the growth of a system" (21).

9. I use "Idealism" to denote a specifically philosophical movement committed to dialectical totalization, identity, and system. However, "Romanticism" is the larger literary-cum-philosophical context within which Idealism emerges as no more than an "idea" continually put under erasure by the exposure of Spirit to its body. For further discussion of this *différance* see Philippe Lacoue-Labarthe and Jean-Luc Nancy, *The Literary Absolute: The Theory of Literature in German Romanticism*, trans. Philip Barnard and Cheryl Lester (Albany: State University of New York Press, 1988), 39–40, 122–23; and Ernest Rubinstein, *An Episode of Jewish Romanticism: Franz Rosenzweig's The Star of Redemption* (Albany: State University of New York Press, 1999), 8–12,18–19.

10. Schelling, *Philosophy of Art*, 8.

11. Georg Simmel, *Schopenhauer and Nietzsche*, trans. Helmut Loiskandl et. al. (Amherst: University of Massachsetts Press, 1986), 3–4.

12. Bill Readings, *The University in Ruins* (Cambridge: Harvard University Press, 1996), 67.

13. Friedrich Schlegel, "Introduction to the Transcendental Philosophy," in *Theory as Practice: A Critical Anthology of Early German Romantic Writings*, ed. Jochen Schulte-Sasse (Minneapolis: University of Minnesota Press, 1997), 255.

14. Schlegel, *Atheneum Fragments*, in *Philosophical Fragments*, trans. Peter Firchow (Minneapolis: University of Minnesota Press, 1991), 21.

15. Schlegel, *Philosophical Fragments*, 21.

16. Deleuze, *The Fold: Leibniz and the Baroque*, trans. Tom Conley (Minneapolis: University of Minnesota Press, 1993), 34.

17. Kristeva, *Revolution in Poetic Language*, 141. See also note 2.

18. Richard Beardsworth's criticisms of the current narrowed emphasis on economics clearly evoke Bataille's project of thinking this discipline in particular within a more expansive framework (Bataille, *Accursed Share*, 19–26).

Romanticism and the Invention of Literature

~

Jan Plug

This is no—or hardly any, ever so little—literature.

Jacques Derrida, Dissemination

I

Contrary to Derrida's provocative assertion, Philippe Lacoue-Labarthe and Jean-Luc Nancy's seminal *L'absolu littéraire* maintains not only that there *is* literature but that its conception can be dated rigorously as the advent of Romanticism. But what can it mean that Romanticism marks the "*invention* of literature"? That it "constitutes, very exactly, the inaugural moment of literature as the *production of its own theory*—and of theory thinking itself as literature"?[1] As Lacoue-Labarthe and Nancy's discussion of the literary absolute will make clear, even to speak of the invention of literature is in effect to describe a metaphysics in which literature's self-conceptualization is identical with its very "being" as literary. As long as literature "is" as its own theorization, its ontology will be indistinguishable from that of thinking. Literature's theorization of itself closes it off as self-contained, in effect excluding all difference in its relation to itself, the (self-) identity of literature as its own thinking. The literary *absolute* recuperates difference for identity, establishing itself as the ultimate identity of being and thinking, reality and ideality. As such, it ultimately maintains the structure of absolute idealism with the "difference" that the absolute now finds its ultimate fulfillment in the literary.[2]

15

As long as literature is thought as self-production and self-theorization, there can *be* no literature where there is no thought, literature as the thinking of itself. How to think literature without already being implicated in its ontological and metaphysical claims? Lacoue-Labarthe and Nancy would seem to bypass precisely this critical question. For them the literary absolute not only justifies but necessitates a "properly philosophical" reading of Romanticism because of an "inherent necessity in the thing itself" that is, however, properly neither philosophical nor literary, but rather their absolute identity.

> Die ganze Geschichte der modernen Poesie ist ein fortlaufender Kommentar zu dem kurzen Text der Philosophie: Alle Kunst soll Wissenschaft, und alle Wissenschaft soll Kunst werden; Poesie und Philosophie sollen vereinigt sein.[3]

> L'histoire toute entière de la poésie est un commentaire suivi du bref texte de la philosophie; tout art doit devenir science, et toute science devenir art; poésie et philosophie doivent être réunies. (AL 95)

> (The whole history of modern poetry is a running commentary on the following brief philosophical text: all art should become science and all science art; poetry and philosophy should be made one.) (CF 115)[4]

Absolutely crucial for an understanding of the literary absolute, this fragment nonetheless reveals that the identity of poetry and philosophy is hardly unproblematic. Translating *dem kurzen Text der Philosophie* as "the *following* brief philosophical text," the English identifies the text of philosophy as *a determinate* text.[5] It is not that *philosophy* itself or as such is a brief text that is commented upon by modern poetry; rather, the *philosophical* text says that art should become science, science art, and that poetry and philosophy should be united. By (over)determining the text of philosophy, the translation reduces the desired unity of philosophy and poetry to a brief philosophical text and sublates the apparent unity, thereby reasserting the priority of the philosophical over that alleged unity. Insofar as it is philosophy that announces the desirability, if not the present reality, of that unity, philosophy takes precedence over art and even over the unity of art and science. As long as this relation is maintained and philosophy usurps its ostensible unification with poetry in a dialectical movement, that unity will remain merely apparent.

Lacoue-Labarthe and Nancy's argument for a *philosophical* reading of the literary absolute would seem justified by such a (re)imposition of a philosophical ascendancy over poetry, but it also risks becoming complicit in philosophy's metaphysical claims. Their own translation presents the possibility of another reading. While the German speaks of "running," *fortlaufen*, the French, though idiomatically perfect, introduces the ambiguity of a commentary that can be read as "running," *un commentaire suivi*, or as "followed by," *suivi du*, the brief text of philosophy. The difference is crucial, if imperceptible, since what is at stake is whether commentary is continuous, consequential, running, as we say, running along, side-by-side, or whether it is rather followed by philosophy, in which case philosophy would clearly be lagging behind in the race. This ambiguity, however unintentional, might best render the German, in which the running commentary, as Carol Jacobs points out, seems to be "running" *away*—fort*laufen*.[6] Far from justifying a "properly philosophical" approach to Romanticism, this would mean that commentary, poetry, is at once running away and following, and in its position as both before and after resists the dialectical movement of thought, even its own thinking of itself. Poetry's positing of itself as absolute is thus also what resists this same gesture and interrupts its resolution in thinking. This would suggest a *literary* absolute that, while it completes the absolute, as Lacoue-Labarthe and Nancy point out, also reintroduces a critical difference that resists that very completion. And that difference is none other than the literary. Language and poetry will emerge as the *material* that Idealism can never fully assimilate or marginalize in its formation of an absolute.

If a "properly philosophical" approach to this fragment is demanded by its presentation of philosophy's attempt to reassert its claim over its own unification with poetry at the same time that it is jeopardized by a poetry that belies that claim, no less does poetry reverse these roles and attempt to reassert its rightful claims to criticism. Any attempt to "criticize" poetry, understood as the production of its own theory, would have to come to terms with the fact that such a criticism would itself have to come from poetry. "Poetry can only be criticized by way of poetry. A critical judgment of an artistic production has no civil rights in the realm of art if it is not itself a work of art, either in its substance, as a representation of a necessary impression of its form and open tone, like that of the old Roman satires." (CF 117: 14–15) Poetry's status as absolute is guaranteed by a reflexive structure in which criticism, even were it to question the absolute, would do so by recuperating this questioning and sublating it under the absolute of poetry as self-criticism. The conjunction of poetry and philosophy that Friedrich Schlegel calls for in his elaboration of the literary absolute would thus appear to articulate the self-criticism of the literary in terms not so much of a crossing or bridging of distinct realms as the sublation of their autonomy.

Despite the unity of poetry and its theory, the fragment leaves open the possibility for another realm independent of, and distinct from, that of art, a critical judgment that could exercise its civil right to be not art but criticism, perhaps that, even *by* exercising its rights, would establish itself *as critical*.

What is at stake here, therefore, is a mode of commentary that would establish itself as critical to the extent that it does not submit to the rule of poetry. Such criticism would not conform to Schlegel's ideal, to be sure, and it would surrender its poetic rights, but in so doing it would establish itself precisely by not partaking of the very poetic it is to critique. What this possibility will entail is a conception of the symbol and of a poetic materiality as the resistance to the dialectical and totalizing thrust of thought, even of poetry's thinking of itself, a conception of materiality that will necessitate a rethinking of the ontological claims of the literary *absolute*.

II

While a poetic materiality would seem remote from Immanuel Kant's concerns, especially given the necessary disinterest in the potentially beautiful object, any consideration of the question of criticism, particularly in the context of Romanticism, would seem to have to pass by way of his aesthetics. It has become something of a commonplace to note that the transition in Kant from the first *Critique* to the second is ensured only after the fact in a sense, by the third *Critique*.[7] The transition is guaranteed by "establishing the causal link between . . . a purely conceptual and an empirically determined discourse," occasioning "the need for a phenomenalized, empirically manifest principle of cognition on whose existence the possibility of such an articulation depends," this principle being the aesthetic.[8] The question of this third *Critique* that situates itself between the first and second, of this inter-*Critique*, is the question of how aesthetics as a philosophical discipline ensures the transition from theoretical to practical philosophy and thus secures the unity and completion of the system of critical philosophy by way of a particular mode of cognition. Aesthetics describes the possibility of the unification of philosophy, but this is a unity that at the same time extends philosophy beyond, or better, *between*, itself, a between that is never fully contained by the philosophy it unifies.

The figure of this third that is not quite third therefore refuses to close philosophy off as the thinking of its own completion. If, as Cathy Caruth puts it, "Kant might be said to represent, in the history of philosophy, the attempt to deal rigorously with the referential problem by founding his theory on the very knowledge of its independence from empirical referents," then the recourse to an instance at once within or between philosophy and (thus) "outside" it will be problematic for philosophy's understanding of itself.[9] A theory that could *know* its independence from the empirical would mark its difference from any materiality doubly. Not only is the knowledge offered by this theory independent of the empirical but the theory is itself the knowledge of that independence—the knowledge, then, of the irreducible difference between knowledge and the empirical. Theory would reinscribe in itself its difference from the empirical as the knowledge that constitutes it as such, as theory, reinscribing its difference from the empirical as its own self-knowledge.[10]

While Kant never theorizes a literary absolute that would unify thinking and being in the mode of literature, his does turn to poetry and to the symbol in the elaboration of aesthetic ideas. There, however, poetry will be conceived as a materiality that remains irreducible to either the purely material, the purely formal, or an ideal. In fact, anticipating and enabling Jean-François Lyotard's formulation of a political criticism, Kant's poetics might be read as the practical symbol of philosophy, a poetics that might fulfill that task adequately insofar as it represents the very symbol of symbolization. This implies not only that philosophy is unable to think itself as independent of other fields even as it attempts to think its independence from the empirical, but that philosophy's relation to materiality will have to be rethought in terms of a particular understanding of poetry and language. The spirit and soul of this art will be a rather singular stuff.

> *Spirit*, in an aesthetic sense, is the name given to the animating principle of the mind. But that by means of which this principle animates the soul, the material (*Stoff*) which it applies to that, is what puts the mental powers purposively into swing, i.e., into such a play as maintains itself and strengthens the mental powers in their exercise.
>
> Now I maintain that this principle is no other than the faculty of presenting *aesthetic ideas*. And by an aesthetic idea I understand that representation of the imagination which occasions much thought, without however any definite thought, i.e., any *concept*, being capable of being adequate to it; it consequently cannot be completely compassed and made intelligible by language.[11]

In the double history of its animation, "spirit" is the animating principle of the mind but only by means of a material or stuff (*Stoff*) whose materiality would seem foreign to it. Yet spirit in Kant is not in strict opposition to the material.[12] The figuration of *ideas* and the aesthetic as material apparently describes the materialization of the nonmaterial as the *necessary* means toward the maintenance and strengthening of spirit. Figuration, rhetoric, would therefore provide a materiality essential to a spirit that cannot maintain itself without it. Rather than threatening the ideality of spirit and necessitating a dialectical (in the Hegelian sense) sublation of the material by the idea(l), the ideal must be made material, stuff. Prefiguring Kant's own introduction of rhetoric later, such a figurative reading of the material in effect either dematerializes its materiality or, alternatively, materializes spirit. In either case, the

animation of the mind resides upon a figurative materiality, that is, a materiality that is neither material nor nonmaterial, but rather rhetorical: a *linguistic* materiality. The very impossibility of determining whether or not such a
figuration holds sway here, whether the material animating spirit is literal or
figurative, only serves to reconfirm the indeterminate status of this *Stoff*.

Aesthetic ideas thus represent a principle not of cognition (that would
resolve the philosophical tension presented to the third *Critique*) so much as of
its frustration, and its frustration, moreover, precisely by the figure of intuition.

> In the most universal signification of the word, ideas are repre-
> sentations referred to an object, according to a certain (subjective or
> objective) principle, but so that they can never become a cognition
> of it. They are either referred to an intuition, according to a merely
> subjective principle of the mutual harmony of the cognitive powers
> (the imagination and the understanding), and they are then called
> *aesthetic*; or they are referred to a concept according to an objective
> principle, although they can never furnish a cognition of the object,
> and they are called *rational ideas*. In the latter case, the concept is
> a *transcendent* one, which is different from a concept of the under-
> standing, to which an adequately corresponding experience can al-
> ways be supplied and which therefore is called *immanent*.
>
> An *aesthetic idea* cannot become a cognition because it is an
> *intuition* (of the imagination) for which an adequate concept can
> never be found. A *rational idea* can never become a cognition be-
> cause it involves a concept (of the supersensible) corresponding to
> which an intuition can never be given. (CJ 187, KU 283–84)

The relationship between intuition and the concept described by ideas is
inverted, though perfectly symmetrical: aesthetic ideas are intuitions without
an adequate concept; rational ideas imply a concept for which there is no
intuition.[13] The apparently perfect totalization of the chiasmus (intuition-
concept/concept-intuition) figures the closure of their relation. But this is a
closure upon an absence: the impossibility of cognition arising from the ideas
because of the irreducible *a*symmetry of intuition and concept. Insofar as they
excite "much thought, without any determinate thought, i.e., any *concept*,
being capable of being adequate" to them, so that they cannot be "completely
compassed and made intelligible by language," aesthetic ideas frustrate any
attempt to articulate them in a figurative system. Not only do they resist
determination and adequation in a given concept, even as such they constitute
a *thinking of excess*, thought *as* excess. An excess of thought, *too* much
thought to be circumscribed or made intelligible by language.

It is not simply a case here of the "sad incompetence of human speech,"[14] not just the inadequacy of language in face of thought, but of language's inability to make that thought *intelligible*. Language might well be up to the task of coming to terms with this excessive thought, then, but what it will never be able to do is reduce it to a concept. Language describes an intentionality which, far from expressing the absolute (as the) unity of thought and being in the form of a cognition that would claim to reduce being to knowledge, rethinks the relation between language and consciousness. In so doing it resituates the empirical in relation to both the absolute and cognition. The privilege of art, including "poetry and rhetoric [*Dichtkunst und Beredsamkeit*]" (CJ 158, KU 252), is to set in motion a process in which the concept can no longer be compassed by language, such that language apparently fails as the intention of consciousness.

> [Poetry] expands the mind by setting the imagination at liberty and by offering, within the limits of a given concept, amid the unbounded variety of possible forms according therewith and that which unites the presentation of this concept with a wealth of thought to which no verbal expression is completely adequate, and so arising aesthetically to ideas. It strengthens the mind by making it feel its faculty—free, spontaneous, and independent of natural determination—of considering and judging nature as a phenomenon in accordance with aspects which it does not present in experience either for sense or understanding, and therefore using it on behalf of, and as a sort of schema for, the supersensible. (CJ 170–1, KU 265)

Freeing the mind from determination, absolutely, freeing it *tout court*, and thus permitting a judgment of nature that no longer refers to the laws of experience or understanding, poetry makes possible the bridging of the gap to the supersensible. It opens the possibility for the phenomenal to stand as a schema for the nonphenomenal. Irreducible to any concept, poetry is the source of the excess of thought over language and thus emerges as a language in excess of language.

It was perhaps inevitable that another conception of language should emerge from the third *Critique*. For as long as poetry and rhetoric are the source of the surpassing of language by thought, not only can they no longer be described in terms of cognition, but they will always be more than language. Rather than describing a failure in the epistemological claims of language, the understanding of poetry as the source of the excess over the concept describes it as a noncognitive and nonintentional instance of language. Language would no longer be the intention of a structure of conceptuality but rather of a thinking that would be irreducible to it. The intentionality of language would thus be that of thought, much thought, not determinate thought, concepts, but their very surpassing. Predictably, given his apparent view of its inadequacy in the face of thought, Kant elsewhere describes language as "the mere letter," that which "binds up spirit" (CJ 160, KU 253). But as was the case of the *stuff* that animates spirit, the materiality of language is difficult to contain, and Kant's own attempt to reduce language to a restrictive materiality will ultimately emerge not as the constraint upon a spirit independent of matter but as its very life. Poetry and rhetoric unleash spirit from its bonds, enliven it, or make it live. On the one hand, then, language is dead and constraining. On the other, in the forms of poetry and rhetoric, it is the very unbinding and enlivening of spirit. Other than the dead *letter* in both their very figurativeness and their *be-leben* (en-livening) of spirit, poetry and rhetoric are therefore also something other than a strict materiality.

Rather than merely being caught up in the contradiction of two opposing conceptions of language, Kant's aesthetics can equally be read as a history, the history of life and death, of their difference, and of the movement between them. On the one hand, this history can be described as that of a resurrection. While poetry allows the mind to experience its own freedom and to establish the schematic link between nature and the supersensible, phenomena and the nonphenomenal, it is already *other than* phenomenal. In fact, poetry leaves behind the corpse of its materiality in order to become so and thus figures the resurrected form of a merely literal and material language, its spirit, so to speak. Poetry would therefore describe the nonmaterial and nonphenomenal opening of, and to, the supersensible. If, as A. W. Schlegel puts it, the supersensible is nothing other than the "absolute, the unconditioned, the infinite, "[15] then poetry marks the opening of and to the absolute. The literary absolute, again. The absolute is thus brought back to life by a material, a stuff, which is never properly that. Its life depends upon a linguistic materiality which, while it resists complete idealization, also can never be fully reduced to the material. Poetry and rhetoric figure the material life of spirit, its resurrection, which will never be merely bodily or material.

But, on the other hand, the spiritualization of language and its enlivening of spirit and surpassing by thought signify language's very death *as* material, no longer a resurrection, therefore, but a sacrifice, or perhaps a resurrection that also and at the same time demands a sacrifice. In order for spirit and figure to live, that is, the body of language must be *declared* dead. But the dead body of language is never fully laid to rest. It can and must return to enliven itself and spirit, to live and make live—again. The history described here, then, is that of the *repeated* sacrifice and resurrection in which the material, the dead letter, gives life to spirit only to be killed off in so doing. This history in effect refuses to reduce language to a strict materiality just as it refuses to implicate it in a teleological history that would resolve it in spirit. Language figures the source of its own surpassing, a kind of self-transcendence, which gives life to spirit, although not by instantiating it or sacrificing its materiality. Rather, as a self-surpassing materiality that never relinquishes itself as such, language figures the very life of the absolute.

III

By turning to poetry and to the symbol at a key juncture in the aesthetic, Kant elaborates a theory of language which, while it would not live up to the name for either Idealism or its reading in contemporary theory, nonetheless anticipates the literary absolute. Kant's literary absolute is never that because it never achieves the status of a self-theorizing poetry, which alone has the right to the title. But in a perhaps even more profound sense, it could never be considered a literary absolute not because of a failure so much as because the notion of poetry that allows that absolute to emerge also refuses to reduce it to the mere letter, to a materiality the absolute would leave behind on its dialectical trajectory.

These two poles are the possibilities taken up by the Romantics. And with them and the extension of the theoretical scope of the aesthetic they enable is taken up also the vexed question of language, the symbol, and materiality. In his reading of Kant, A. W. Schlegel extends the aesthetic beyond the realm of art insofar as he sees the "acknowledged inadequacy of language" in relation to aesthetic ideas at work in "everyday life" (TA 205). If language "can never completely exhaust even a single individually determined representation of an external object," then "every such representation . . . would be an aesthetic idea" (205). The aesthetic can therefore no longer be confined to the surpassing of language by much thought occasioned by a poem, for instance, but rather describes representation in general, such that the aesthetic emerges not as one discipline among others but as the discipline of disciplines.

F. W. J. Schelling, as opposed to Kant, who for Schlegel "stopped halfway in his elaboration of a transcendental idealism" (TA 205), articulates just such a conception of art, making it tantamount to transcendental philosophy,[16] when he claims that the philosophy of art (and thus his *Philosophy of Art*) "is actually general philosophy itself."[17] He thus expresses the absolute identity of philosophy itself and what would appear to have been a branch of that philosophy, except that in the philosophy of art philosophy is "presented in the potence of art." The philosophy of art thus differs from general philosophy only in that it takes art or works of art as its object.

> Thus we will understand the way in which art lends objectivity to its own ideas in the same way we understand how the ideas of individual real things become objective in the phenomenal realm. Or we might put it thus: our present task, which is to understand the transition of the aesthetic idea into the concrete work of art, is the same as the general task of philosophy as such, namely, to understand the manifestation of the idea through particular beings. (PA 99)

The relationship between the philosophy of art and philosophy as such, like that between art and phenomena, is one of strict analogy: The rule of the objectification, manifestation, and realization of aesthetic ideas into works of art is "the same" as those for ideas into particular beings. Art is the phenomenalization of (aesthetic) ideas. In fact, it might be that what defines art *as art* is not so much a category like the beautiful, or a matter of technique, for instance, not its deployment of symbols to allow access to the supersensible, or even its own phenomenalization of aesthetic ideas, so much as it is its very functioning as symbol, precisely the *symbol of phenomenalization*. The symbolization that art presents is necessarily double: it is the phenomenalization of aesthetic ideas and, by reflecting on itself, this very phenomenalization, by symbolizing it in turn, provides the self-closure of art as ideal(ism).

Schelling defines the symbol as the synthesis of the schematic and the allegorical, that "representation in which the universal means the particular or in which the particular is intuited through the universal," on the one hand, and that representation in which "the particular means the universal or in which the universal is intuited through the particular," on the other (PA 46). As the synthesis of these two modes of presentation, the symbolic is the *unity* of universal and particular and as such constitutes the only *absolute* form of representation. The embodiment of this unity, art, is symbolic.[18] Yet even that ideality is double and as such might be called into question.

> *Representation of the absolute with absolute indifference of the universal and the particular **within the particular** is possible only symbolically.*
>
> *Elucidation.* Representation of the absolute with absolute indifference of the universal and the particular *within the universal* = philosophy—idea—. Representation of the absolute with absolute indifference of the universal and particular *in the particular* = art. (PA 45)

In effect Schelling here separates philosophy from art, for philosophy is aligned with the idea while art is articulated in terms of particularization. While the symbol, art, is meant to express the absolute unity of the universal and the particular, while it represents the absolute itself, it does so always within the particular, just as philosophy does so in the universal. The indifference of the universal and the particular therefore does not resolve their difference absolutely, for it is achieved as a representation in one or the other. Consequently, the absolute, in art, will always be symbolized, but the symbol, even as the particularization of the indifference of the universal and the particular, will always be a *certain* absolute, the representation of absolute indifference, but a *particular* one. A particular absolute, at once absolute and particular.

Not surprisingly, then, the symbol will be articulated precisely in terms of difference and, significantly, materiality.

> *To the extent that its symbol is the real unity as particular unity, the idea is matter.*
>
> The proof of this proposition is given in general philosophy. Matter that actually appears is the idea, but from the perspective of the simple informing of the infinite into the finite such that this informing is only relative, not absolute. Matter as it appears is not the essence, it is only form, symbol; yet it *is—only **as form, as** relative difference. . . .*
>
> *Hence, insofar as art takes up the form of the informing of the infinite into the finite as particular form, it acquires matter as its body or symbol.* (PA 99)

The symbol is here conceived as the *materiality of the idea*. Not merely the particular instantiation of the ideal, but the idea *as* matter—"the idea is matter." It is matter as long as the informing of the infinite in the finite is relative and not absolute, such that the persistence of materiality will always be the sign of relative difference. The sign or, perhaps better, the symbol. For the symbol can here no longer claim absolute *in*difference and informing of universal and particular, form and matter, but rather only difference, relative difference, and matter *as* form. In art, matter thus emerges as the em*bodi*ment of that in*form*ing. A. W. Schlegel similarly appeals to a conception of the "ideal" as a poem or work of art in which "matter and form, letter and spirit have penetrated each other to the point of being completely indistinguishable" (TA 201), but insofar as his conception of a real-ideal[19] relies upon the body it too will necessarily be frustrated by such a difference. Here too a material body is articulated as a symbol—for the unity it embodies. Yet the body stands not so much as the figure for the symbolic unity of idea and matter, particular and universal, as it does for its very resistance to symbolization. The figure of difference.

Schelling sets overcoming the opposition between idea and matter in an inverse and symmetrical movement of the resolution of the particular into the universal, the resolution, he states mostly clearly, of "being into knowledge." If such a resolution offers the promise of an absolute, rather than (relative) indifference, it is still in art. This is, once again, the promise of a *literary* absolute. For this resolution *"becomes objective in **speech** or **language**"* (PA 99), which Schelling juxtaposes with "the other form of art, matter" (99). Language enables the resolution of the absolute and the particular to take place without endangering the ideality of their unity; the particular appears as matter only when it takes place relatively and as a *particular* unity.[20] However, Schelling introduces a kind of second-degree symbolism according to which this particular unity, so long as it "functions as the form of the idea— in the real world" (100), does not lose its ideality. The ideal must assume a body that will not jeopardize its ideality, "and *this* symbol is language, as one can easily see" (100).

As one can easily see, language is the reality of the ideal, its symbol, but a symbol that embodies the ideal without rendering it merely bodily. Only thus, it would appear, can the objectification of the resolution of being into thought that language represents pose no insurmountable difficulty. Thus, *"verbal* art is the *ideal* side of the world of art" and "art insofar as it assumes the ideal unity as its potence and form is verbal art" (PA 102). Language therefore allows Schelling to save the absolute from becoming a mere particularization that lacks ideality. The *Philosophy of Art* can be read as the ultimate embodiment of the literary absolute in that it articulates an idealism that lives up to its name and that would no longer be a mere subcategory of philosophy as such. To the extent that it conceives of verbal art as real ideality, *The Philosophy of Art* provides the linguistic symbol for the ideal, unifying ideality and materiality and reducing what might have been difference to the unity of the same.

Needless to say, perhaps, this entire development depends upon a singular conception of language. For the absolute (and it bears repeating that we have good reason to speak of a *literary* absolute here) to be maintained, language must be "something real without ceasing to be ideal." The very ideality of the ideal, the resolution of being into thought, demands the negation of the materiality of language, of a materiality, more precisely, which would resist negation by leaving a remainder that could not be subsumed to or recuperated by the ideal. Schelling's literary absolute is founded on the exclusion of just such a materiality. Yet contrary to the thrust of Schelling's own argument, this very exclusion at the same time renders linguistic materiality the source of the interruption of the literary as absolute. If the literary absolute can be constituted only by way of a notion of language, then the irreducible materiality of language will inevitably return to frustrate the absolutization of the literary. Materiality here no longer figures the symbolic embodiment of the idea; rather, it will permit no symbolization that is not also an embodiment of its very materiality.

Not only does Schelling's system have difficulty fitting the materiality of works of art into his system, therefore, but the materiality of language can never be reduced to the system. Since this philosophy of art is always also the symbol of philosophy itself, the symbolization that should provide the fulfillment of Idealism will have to come to terms with its inability to overcome this irreducible materiality in a work of art. If, as Friedrich Schlegel claims, Schelling's philosophy "concludes in earthquake and ruins" (AF 105: 30), it may be that it is the materiality of language and of its own analyses that bring it down to earth, as it were, to matter. Yet this earthquake and these ruins need not be read simply as a criticism of the absolute failure of Schelling's philosophy or of the absolute. If one keeps in mind that this commentary is itself expressed in the form of a *fragment*, it would seem that being ruined by, and into materiality, might be what saves Schelling from his own system.

IV

What we are moving toward here is a conception of the symbol which, even while it offers the possibility of the fulfillment of the absolute, repeatedly turns to a linguistic materiality which, linked with the figure of the body, refuses the embodiment of the ideal. The *necessary* fulfillment of Idealism in a materiality which, as linguistic, remains irreducible to both ideality and materiality, at the same time interrupts that fulfillment. At once not only real and ideal, but also fulfillment and its interruption, language remains what is left over after the (in)completion of philosophy as Idealism.

A. W. Schlegel's reference to Schelling's conception of art in the *System of Transcendental Idealism* (developed more fully in the *Philosophy of Art*) as the corrective antidote to a Kantianism that fell short of realizing the full potential of Idealism could hardly seem further removed from such a conclusion. Schlegel, like Schelling, calls for the recognition of the "spiritual in the material" (TA 210). As was the case for Schelling, he conceives of this manifestation "symbolically, in images and signs," and of poesy as "nothing but an eternal act of symbolization" that brings everything to life by seeking an outer shell for something spiritual" or by relating "an exterior to an invisible interior" (210). If Schlegel's development of poetic symbolization corresponds to Schelling's insofar as it articulates poesy as *nothing but* symbolization, this restriction of the poetic runs up against his own development of what he calls "the poetic view."

> According to the unpoetic view, sense perception and understanding determine things once and for all; the poetic view, on the other hand, continually reinterprets things and sees a figurative inexhaustibility in them. (Kant speaks at one point of a cipher-writing through which nature figuratively speaks to us in its beautiful forms.) (TA 209–10)

In contrast to the unpoetic view, the poetic view resists all determination in figurative inexhaustibility and perpetual *re*interpretation. Poetic symbolization offers the matter for these interpretations, but is itself determined absolutely as a "nothing but," without remainder. The determination of poesy as nothing but symbolization and thus as the inexhaustibility of the figurative, which remains indeterminate, the determination of the indeterminate, then, unleashes an inexhaustibility that can no longer be determined. The indeterminate has as its condition of possibility an absolute determination, and the inexhaustible is unleashed by an initial exhaustion.

Leaving aside the by now passé question of figuration and writing, a writing that speaks, the reference to Kant's cipher-writing (*Chriffreschrift*) is crucial, as it reintroduces the passage from aesthetic judgments to moral feeling.[21] For A. W. Schlegel, it is not a matter of a schematization of nature in terms of the supersensible, however, but of "an *absolute act* that is not grounded in our experiences and logical conclusions" as the means of the material revelation of spirit or recognition of the spiritual in the material: "it is through the *deed* that we immediately, or unconsciously, acknowledge the original oneness of spirit and matter, which can only be speculatively demonstrated" (TA 210, emphasis added). As in Kant, Schlegel's development of the symbol as *act* or *deed* articulates what would appear to be a strictly aesthetic category in terms of the practical and ethical, especially insofar as it will be cited as the possibility of the full development of human "talents" (210), the orientation toward perfection as the destination of man.

And yet, by articulating the absolute thus, *as* act and as beyond both experience and cognition, Schlegel makes the absolute the *enactment* of the symbol, its *performance*, and formulates a theory of communication, community, expression, and representation.

> Without this [the absolute act, the deed] communication among human beings, through which the development of all their talents first becomes possible, could never have occurred; for not even the desire to communicate could be communicated if human beings did not always already understand each other prior to any agreed-upon mode of communication. (TA 210)

To try to understand communication in terms of convention and a theory of arbitrary signifiers would be to fall into an abyss in which the founding of the convention itself can never be situated. All subsequent communication must rather be grounded in the immediacy of an understanding and in a communication *prior* to the mediation of conventions, prior even to experience and cognition, and in fact making all of these possible. The absolute act, the deed through which the material and spiritual mutually inform one another, is communication. Not so much a *speech* act, then, as the *act of communication*, the expression of "emotive sounds and passionate gestures" (TA 210), constitutes the absolute. As a deed before experience and understanding, before *communication* and *community* as we generally understand those terms, the absolute act can be reduced to neither matter nor spirit, neither being nor knowledge; rather, it describes their enactment, a performative that constitutes both in its very deed.

The theoretical power of the deed is to perform the possibility of experience and cognition in general. Understanding and communication are founded on the absolute act as the already understood and communicated, the absolutely pre-understood, the enactment of a community of understanding as community *of desire*: what grounds all subsequent communicative acts is the originary communication of the desire to communicate. This absolute act is the act of (self-) symbolization, expression, which for Schlegel is the act at the basis of language as representation: "the inner is, so to speak, ex-pressed [*herausgedrückt*: literally "squeezed out"] as if by a power unknown to us; or the expression is an imprint on the exterior emanating from the inside" (TA 210). Despite this conventional exposition of symbolization as manifestation, the development of the absolute as act and performance would suggest that symbolization does not take place merely as the revelation of a preexisting spirit in a preexisting matter, but is that act by which matter and spirit posit themselves as unity. Accordingly, we are to the extent that we express ourselves, not least because we cannot but express ourselves, expression being "involuntary," no longer the matter of a free will or an intentionality. Schlegel's aesthetic and linguistic translation of the implicit performative claims of Fichte's absolute proposition I = I[22] in a theory of language as a philosophy of community therefore refigures the subject as always already (in) community. Human beings are necessarily communitary beings, not because they naturally seek out the company of others (to communicate with them), but rather because their very performance of themselves is that of a communication. Always already expressing ourselves, our "being" is to be in communication, to be the expression of ourselves, exteriorization.[23]

The *bodily* enactment of this self-symbolization in language as the "linkage of certain sounds to certain inner sensations as their immediate signs" (TA 210) also articulates the body with a larger body politic. But as the arbitrary or representation, which for Schlegel takes place as the positing outside the subject of what is to be signified, takes over, as signs are formed upon the immediate signs of expression, as language develops "from mere expression to representation" (211), not only the relation to the body but the relation between "sign and referent" disappears. No longer bodily or symbolic, "language . . . becomes nothing more than a collection of logical ciphers [*logische Ziffern*] suitable only for performing the calculations of the

understanding" (211). Once again, it is clearly a question of ciphers—
Chiffreschrift, logische Ziffern. But whereas Kant's cipher-writing stands as
the model of a figurative language at the disposal of aesthetic judgment, these
ciphers signify not the connection between nature and the supersensible but
its dissolution—and the absence of figure. The difference, then, is that Kant's
ciphers are never *only* writing but also figurative speech. Logical ciphers, in
order to reinscribe themselves as a writing, must be more than merely logical
and more than writing. They must be refigured. And language must have "its
figurative quality restored" (211).

While Schlegel rather predictably sees the "boundless transpositions of
poetic style" as renewing the symbolic origins of language, leading back to
the "great truth, that one is all and all is one" through the introduction of a
fantasy that overcomes divisive reality (TA 211), the refiguration of language
gives it a figure again, and not only figuratively, since language is linked to
the bodily production of sound. Poetic style takes language back to figure and
the body, its very symbolization returning to the bodily source of the unity
of spirit and matter.

Yet style also speaks another language that in the end might not conform to the fulfillment of Idealism as literary *absolute.* Schlegel raises the
issue of style in the general context of the imitation of nature. Beginning with
the premise that "the particular forms itself [*sich bildet*] out of the general by
limiting and opposing" and that art "must be regarded as something general
and valid for all" (TA 221), the question becomes, How is it possible for our
individuality not to limit the universality of art? In Schlegel's own words,
"How is it possible not to be mannered in art, indeed, even to notice that we
have a manner of our own?" (221). The answer: "It is possible because we
are not just individuals, but also human beings" (221). In other words, it is
that which we share in common that must be brought forth in art. In order
for this to take place, art must transform nature.

> There is something between art and nature that keeps them apart.
> It is called *manner* if it is a colored or opaque medium that throws
> a false light on all represented objects; it is called *style* if it does not
> impinge on the rights of either art or nature, which is only possible
> through a declaration that is, as it were, imprinted on the work itself,
> namely, that it is not nature and has no desire to pass itself off as
> such. (TA 222)

Whereas manner is a mere "subjective opinion, a bias," style is a "system of
art, derived from a true fundamental principle" (TA 223). What distinguishes
style is its respect for the rights of nature and art, as well as its refusal of the
"material error" (214) in which spirit is overburdened by reality or the necessary and laudable difference of art from nature is dissolved.[24]

Crucial to Schlegel's development of this concept and prefiguring its ultimate fulfillment is that this difference should take the form of a declaration that is *imprinted* on the work. The work of art carries the declaration of its own difference as a certain writing. It could not be otherwise, in fact, for the question of style will always have been precisely the question of the instrument of writing.[25] Thus, while we are not confronted with actual poetry here, art and the symbolic never escape the question of language.

> The judgment of style and manner, especially of the point where the former passes over into the latter, the object into the subject, the general into the individual, is one of the most difficult points of expertise and it is for the sake of presuming to make these judgments that these words are used so frequently, and often incorrectly. Furthermore, I would like to draw attention to how extraordinarily fitting the images are that underlie both of these terms. *Maniera* apparently derives from *manus* and originally from the guidance of the hands. These are part of our person and thus it is easy for physical habits to take over the process. *Stylus*, on the other hand, is the slate pencil with which the ancients wrote on tablets of wax: it is not part of us, but rather is the tool of our free activity. To be sure, the nature of the stylus determines our strokes, but we have chosen this stylus of our own free will and could trade it for another. (TA 224)

Everything comes together here: the objective becoming subjective, the general individual, both analogously to the symbol or explicitly in relation to judgment and the work of art and to the ultimate question of freedom. For if the body is crucial here, it is insofar as it figures the *limitation* of freedom. Manner in art, a mannered art, is inferior, perhaps not quite art at all, precisely because it never escapes the body, more precisely the habits of the hands. The body has no hand in style, however, the stylus being an instrument of writing which, while it leaves its particular marks, can always be put down in favor of another. Style will always be a kind of inscription in wax or the imprinted declaration on the work of art—that it is precisely art and not nature. Style will always be the *writing of difference and freedom*, not because writing remains undetermined but because its determination is always subsumed to an act of free will. Freedom, the freedom of art (from nature), is predicated upon a declared independence from the body. As though the stylus, "on the other *hand*," as the English translation rather felicitously has it, were being held by something other than a hand.

The stylus will always be "on the other hand," as it were, the hand that is other than the hand. One can chose one's style and stylus, but not with one's hand, lest style become manner, the "stylus," *maniera, manus.* One would do well to learn to write differently, even to have one's hands cut off, that is, if the aim is to be an artist—or a work of art. Thus, while the tracing of poetic and symbolic style back to writing apparently privileges language as such in distinction to the figurative arts in which matter and the hands figure prominently, earlier A. W. Schlegel ridicules those whose reductive mimeticism stops them from finding a "resemblance in a bust because a real person has hands and feet" (TA 214). The ultimate work of art, and perhaps even the ultimate artist, might well be this mere bust, the dismembered body whose very lack of hands and difference from nature make it the work of style.[26] It figures the possibility of writing without hands (or feet, for that matter), of choosing one's style and stylus freely precisely because one has no hand in it, choosing freely and freedom, because style is here the informing of the work of art not by an instrument, no matter how freely chosen, but by free will. Schlegel's stylus would ultimately have to be put aside or cut off, handed over, that the work of art might be the instantiation of a free will in which the body would have no hand.

An act, a deed. Style as absolute act. The positing of the free will, free of the body.

V

Taking art out of the artist's hand and locating it in the will would literally cut off any material embodiment of the idea. The disfiguration of the symbolic embodiment of the idea in an adequate figure, the bust A. W. Schlegel turns to is an embodiment, but of the figure of the artist of style and stylus, rather than of an idea. If Kant allows for a reading of poetry as the material life of spirit, and if Schelling can be read as the completion of Idealism precisely because he makes the absolute literary, with the same gesture excluding a linguistic materiality from the absolute, Schlegel would here seem to be riddled by two opposing tendencies. His theory of art argues for poetic style as the completion of the ideal and the expression of the ethical imperative of the freedom of the will from (bodily) constraint. The "Theory of Art" thus situates itself within the general purview of Schelling's philosophy as the completion of what Kant is said to have left undone in that it attempts to belie the philosophy intimated in its own title, a theory that would give the rule to art. Yet that same theory and its *de*-idealization of the work of art in the figure of the body enacts the disfiguration of the figure of the coincidence of form and matter, idea and body, thinking and being.

This implies not only a bracketing of the question of being as the philosophical question par excellence,[27] but also that of the very identity of literature with thinking, in particular literature's thinking of itself. To the extent that it can be shown to resist this coincidence, even in its enactment as the literary absolute, literature refuses to submit fully to the metaphysical and ontological claims of the philosophy that it at the same time embodies.

Unlike a simple refusal of the absolute in the form of a denial of its claims, which could always be recuperated dialectically as a moment of negativity, this apparently self-contradictory position enacts the interruption of the absolute. And since what is implied in that coincidence is also that of literature and its thinking in philosophy, a fusion in which both risk losing their integrity, what is stake is also the end of a certain disciplinarity. The resistance to totality takes place, then, as the *simultaneous* completion and interruption, embodiment and disfiguration, of the absolute.

While it has almost become a critical cliché to state that an aesthetics of immanence of the kind we are reading here constitutes the "Romantic ideology,"[28] Walter Benjamin, for one, has argued that this same formulation allows the Romantics to avoid dogmatism and to overturn the major aesthetic ideologies prevalent at the time.[29] The elaboration of the literary absolute allows for a reformulation of philosophy in nondogmatic, nonfoundational terms: "*Philosophy* (in its proper sense) has neither foundational principle nor object, nor determinate task."[30] What is *proper* to philosophy, then, is to have no principle, foundation, or object *proper*, which means that philosophy will necessarily be the indetermination of any fixed principle, including that principle it itself formulates, even the principle of the nonprinciple. Rather than being caught in a double bind, philosophy emerges in precisely the terms we have seen at work in the "Theory of Art," for instance: as an act, deed, or performance; as the "communitary" that stands as the condition of possibility for all community and communication; as an embodiment that does not subsume the body to an idea.

Philosophy now emerges as *process*, one that Friedrich Schlegel describes in chemical terms and as composed of "living, fundamental forces" (AF 304: 60). Necessarily always in a state of becoming (54: 24), philosophy "always must organize and disorganize itself anew" (304: 60). If it is by necessity unfinished and divinitory, this is not in the sense that there is still more to be done, whether one conceives of that "more" as a real possibility, infinitely deferred, whatever. Rather, philosophy must remain divinitory in its relation to an absolute that it can never know or verify and thereby marks its very difference from the absolute. The *literary* absolute I have tried to elaborate would therefore not *be* the fulfillment of the absolute in its embodiment of the idea, so much as it would equally mark the absolute *as absolute*, as that which cannot be embodied in any conventional sense. In the *literary* absolute the absolute remains absolute. The disfiguring of the absolute coincidence of thought and being by materiality, the dismembering of the embodied idea, resists the materialization of the idea or what Benjamin might call the "sobering of the absolute."[31]

It will no doubt be argued that such a reading imposes poststructural (and postidealist) concerns on a text that clearly wants to say something else, or that it tries to make A. W. Schlegel a Paul de Man or a Jacques Derrida.

But to read these texts with and against their own figurative movement, especially in the case of A. W. Schlegel, who articulates a writing that can only be read *as figure,* is not to disfigure their intentions and place in the history of aesthetic theory so much as it is to disclose a movement they perhaps *cannot but* set in motion, one that immediately reaches beyond them and that enables much contemporary theory.[32] Such a movement in fact allows one to account for the way in which we still belong to the era of Romanticism, as Lacoue-Labarthe and Nancy put it, a belonging that is also the questioning of Romanticism's ostensibly absolutizing claims.

> [T]he literary Absolute aggravates and radicalizes the thinking of totality and the Subject. It *infinitizes* this thinking, and therein, precisely, rests its ambiguity. Not that romanticism itself did not begin to perturb the Absolute, or proceed, despite itself, to undermine its Work. But it is important to distinguish carefully the signs of this small and complex fissuring and consequently to know how to read these signs in the first place—as signs of a romantic, not romanesque, reading of romanticism.[33]

If at the same time that it completes the absolute Romanticism makes that completion its interruption, then our debt to Romanticism, our inevitable positioning in Romanticism, is also that of the questioning of its most totalizing claims. This too would be part of the genealogical link to Romanticism, a history in which the self-theorizing literary absolute is the theorization of its incompletion by that same "absolute."

Notes

1. Philippe Lacoue-Labarthe and Jean-Luc Nancy, *L'absolu littéraire: théorie de la littérature du romantisme allemand* (Paris: Éditions du Seuil, 1978); hereafter cited as AL, translations mine. These phrases are taken from the back of the book's dust jacket. As such, they no doubt have a certain programmatic quality, but that is precisely the point here. It no doubt bears noting that Jacques Derrida is also well aware of the invention of literature in the eighteenth century. See, for example, Derrida, *Acts of Literature*, ed. Derek Attridge (New York: Routledge, 1992), 40–41.

2. For an account of how self-reflection enables self-constitution and self-containment and recuperates difference for identity, see Rodolphe Gasché, *The Tain of the Mirror: Derrida and the Philosophy of Reflection* (Cambridge: Harvard University Press, 1986), in particular 14–34. For instance, Gasché describes how in the philosophy of identity and in G. W. F. Hegel's philosophy "being and thinking are one, only moments in the objective process of self-developing thought" (24).

3. Friedrich Schlegel, *Kritische Friedrich-Schlegel-Ausgabe*, ed. Ernst Behler, vol. 2, ed. Hans Eichner (Munich: Verlag Ferdinand Schöningh, 1967), 161.

4. Friedrich Schlegel's *Lucinde and the Fragments*, trans. Peter Firchow (Minneapolis: University of Minnesota Press, 1971), 157. The same translation is reproduced in the more recent *Philosophical Fragments* (Minneapolis: University of Minnesota Press, 1991), 14. All further references are to this more recent edition; the Critical Fragments are hereafter cited as CF, the Athenaeum Fragments as AF.

5. Simply as a point of reference, however, a more recent translation of this fragment drops the word *following*: "The entire history of modern poesy is a running commentary on the short text of philosophy: all art should become science and all science should become art; poesy and philosophy should be united," in *Theory as Practice: A Critical Anthology of Early German Romantic Writing*, eds. Jochen Schulte-Sasse et al., hereafter cited as TA (Minneapolis: Minnesota University Press, 1997), 319.

6. Carol Jacobs, *Uncontainable Romanticism: Shelley, Brontë, Kleist* (Baltimore: Johns Hopkins University Press, 1989), 192.

7. On this transition and the question of the relation of the faculties and of the three *Critiques* in general, see Gilles Deleuze, *La philosophie critique de Kant* (Paris: Presses Universitaires de France, 1963), 5–17, 67–107.

8. Paul de Man, "Phenomenality and Materiality in Kant," in *Aesthetic Ideology* (Minneapolis: University of Minnesota Press, 1996), 73.

9. Cathy Caruth, *Unclaimed Experience: Trauma, Narrative, and History* (Baltimore: Johns Hopkins University Press, 1996), 77.

10. Caruth states this thus: "pure philosophy defines itself as that which does not depend for its meaning on the empirical world; it knows itself *as* that which does not directly know the empirical object" (ibid., 78).

11. Immanuel Kant, *Critique of Judgement*, trans. J. H. Bernard (New York: MacMillan, 1951), 157; Kant, *Kritik der Urteilskraft* in *Werkausgabe, Band X*, ed. Wilhelm Weischedel (Frankfurt am Main, Germany: Suhrkamp, 1974), 249–50. All further references are to the editions, hereafter cited as CJ and KU respectively. (English translations have sometimes been modified slightly.)

12. See de Man, "Phenomenality and Materiality in Kant," 83.

13. On aesthetic ideas in Kant, see the fine accounts by Gasché, "Foreword: Ideality in Fragmentation," in *Philosophical Fragments*; Tilottama Rajan, "Toward a Cultural Idealism: Negativity and Freedom in Hegel and Kant," in this volume; and Deleuze, *Philosophie Critique de Kant*, 81–83.

14. William Wordsworth, 1850 *Prelude*, vol. 6, eds. Jonathan Wordsworth, M. H. Abrams, and Stephen Gill (New York: Norton, 1979), 150.

15. A. W. Schlegel,"Theory of Art," in *Theory as Practice*, 206, hereafter cited as TA.

16. It is to F. W. J. Schelling's *System of Transcendental Idealism* that Schlegel refers here. There, Schelling writes,

> if aesthetic intuition is merely transcendental intuition becomes objective, it is self-evident that art is at once the only true and eternal organ and document of philosophy, which ever and again continues to speak to us of what philosophy cannot depict in external form, namely, the unconscious element in acting and producing, and its original identity with the conscious. Art is paramount to the philosopher, precisely because it opens to him, as it were,

the holy of holies, where burns in eternal and original unity, as if in a single flame, that which in nature and history is rent asunder, and in life and action, no less than in thought, must forever fly apart. Schelling; *System of Transcendental Idealism*, trans. Peter Heath (Charlottesville: University Press of Virginia, 1978), 231.

There is implicit here a conception of a certain kind of performative that I will go on to develop in Schlegel. For a fuller development of the place of Schelling's philosophy of art in philosophy in general, see Bernhard Barth, *Schellings Philosophie der Kunst: Göttliche Imagination und ästhetische Einbildungskraft* (Freiburg, Germany: Verlag Karl Alber, 1991).

17. Schelling, *The Philosophy of Art*, trans. Douglas W. Stott (Minneapolis: University of Minnesota Press, 1989), 98. All further references are to this edition; hereafter cited as PA.

18. Although some arts are more ideal than others, since even within the realm of poetry, for instance, lyric is allegorical, epic schematic, and only drama symbolic (ibid., 48).

19. For a good account of this notion of the real-ideal, see Andreas Michel and Assenka Oksiloff, "Romantic Crossovers: Philosophy as Art and Art as Philosophy," in *Theory as Practice*, 167–73.

20. Given that Schelling goes on to postulate an *absolute* rather than merely relative informing, it would seem that he sees it as falling short of the literary absolute conceived in terms of a theory, of the fragment as the occurring of the absolute. See Gasché, "Ideality in Fragmentation," *Philosophical Fragments* xxix–xxx. This relative unity is not yet fully the particular as the enactment of the absolute, then, which only takes place symbolically in language. The very necessity of this final move to language, however, as I will argue in the next section; also depends upon an act of marginalization or exclusion that puts the absolute into question.

21. Derrida takes up this very question in "Economimesis," *Diacritics* 2:2 (1981): 3–25.

22. See Werner Hamacher, "Position Exposed," in *Premises: Essays on Philosophy and Literature from Kant to Celan*, trans. Peter Fenves (Stanford: Stanford University Press, 1999), 222–60.

23. Such an understanding of community might be read as anticipating that of Nancy in *La communauté désoeuvrée* (Paris: Christian Bourgois, 1990).

24. Schelling speaks similarly of style and mannerism, although the final and crucial turn to an etymology of style in the instrument of writing is never made in his *Philosophy of Art*:

> *Style* thus does not exclude particularity, but constitutes rather the *indifference* between the universal and absolute art form on the one hand, and the particular form of the artist on the other; indifference is so necessary to style that art can express itself only within the individual. Style would thus always and necessarily be the true form and to that extent the absolute, mannerism only the relative. This assumed indifference does not, however,

determine that it be posited through the informing of the universal into the particular or, vice versa, through the informing of the particular into the universal form. (94–95)

25. For a rethinking of the relation of style and stylus, see Jacobs, "The Style of Kleist," in *Uncontainable Romanticism.*

26. Two of Schlegel's contributions to the fragments are especially relevant here: "There's nothing ornamental about he style of the real poet: everything is a necessary hieroglyph" (*Athenaeum Fragments* 173: 40); "It's as if women made everything with their own hands, and men everything with tools" (133: 35).

27. On literature as the resistance to philosophy, see, in particular, Gasché's readings of Derrida and Maurice Blanchot in *The Tain of the Mirror* and *Of Minimal Things: Studies on the Notion of Relation* (Stanford: Stanford University Press, 1999), respectively.

28. See Jerome McGann, *The Romantic Ideology* (Chicago: Chicago University Press, 1984).

29. See Walter Benjamin, *Der Begriff der Kunstkritik in der deutschen Romantik,* in *Gesammelte Schriften,* eds. Rolf Tiedemann and Hermann Schwepppenhäuser, 7 vols. (Frankfurt am Main, Germany: Suhrkamp, 1974–89), 1:1, 71. For an excellent reading of Benjamin's thesis, see Gasché, "The Sober Absolute," in *Walter Benjamin: Theoretical Questions* (Stanford: Stanford University Press, 1996), 50–73.

30. PF 36 in *Theory as Practice,* 338.

31. See Gasché, "Sober Absolute," 72–74.

32. Schlegel himself spoke of such surpassing of intention as his greatest accomplishment, although this very rich fragment would also put that very statement in question:

What am I proud of, and what can I be proud of as an artist? Of the decision that separated and isolated me forever from everything ordinary; of the work that divinely surpasses every intention, and whose intention no one will ever probe entirely; of the ability to worship the perfection I have encountered; of the awareness that I can stimulate my fellows to do their best, and that everything they create is my gain. See Schlegel, *Ideas,* 136, 107.

33. Lacoue-Labarthe and Nancy, *Absolu littéraire,* 26; *The Literary Absolute: The Theory of Literature in German Romanticism,* trans. Philip Barnard and Cheryl Lester (Albany: State University of New York Press, 1988), 15.

Allegories of Symbol:
On Hegel's *Aesthetics*

Andrzej Warminski

G. W. F. Hegel's double, ambiguous and ambivalent if not downright duplicitous, attitude toward art is legible in his *Aesthetics* from one end to the other, from the beginning and to the end*s*. All we need to know both about the philosophy and the history of art (according to Hegel) is there to be read already in the introduction. As Hegel goes through the three main types or forms of art according to the different relations between sensuous form and spiritual content proper to each—*from* the ("symbolic") pre-art of the East and the Egyptians in which there is an inadequation between sensuous form and spiritual content on account of the *abstractness* of the latter *to* the ("classical") art, art properly speaking, of Greece in which there is a full adequation of form to content, and on to the ("romantic") post-art of Christian Europe in which there is again an *in*adequation between form and content, this time on account of the *concreteness* of the latter—a first doubleness and ambiguity comes to the fore. Namely, there are two high points, two "highest" stages, classical and romantic: if the classical form of art has arrived at the highest (*das Höchste*) that the embodiment or making sensuous (*die Versinnlichung*) of art can achieve, then the romantic form in its fullest development (i.e., romantic poetry) is the highest stage (*die höchste Stufe*) at which art transcends itself "in that it leaves behind the element of reconciled embodiment of the spirit in sensuous form and passes over from the poetry of the imagination [or, better, representation] to the prose of thought" (*indem sie das Element versöhnter Versinnlichung des Geistes verläßt und aus der Poesie*

39

der Vorstellung in die Prosa des Denkens hinübertritt)" (A 13:123, 89).[1] Of course, this first "ambiguity" is easily enough resolved by reference to Hegel's system and to the place of art *in* that system.

Let us recall, quickly and very schematically, that, according to the articulations of Hegel's "mature" system—that is, the "Encyclopaedia-system"—the Idea is first of all the logical Idea or, in Hegel's vocabulary, the Idea in itself (*an sich*), then it is the Idea outside or up against itself, in nature, or the Idea for itself (*für sich*), and, last, it is the Idea as spirit (*Geist*), or the Idea in and for itself (*an und für sich*). Hence the three divisions of Hegel's *Encyclopaedia of the Philosophical Sciences*. Now "spirit," *Geist*, in turn realizes itself as, first, subjective spirit—as the objects of the "sciences" of anthropology, phenomenology, and psychology respectively (i.e., what Hegel calls the soul [*Seele*], consciousness [*Bewußtsein*], and mind or spirit [*Geist*])—then objective spirit—the domains of abstract right, morality, and "social ethics"—and, last, absolute spirit, which appears in art, religion, and philosophy. As the manifestation of absolute spirit, art occupies a very high place indeed, in this regard as high as religion and philosophy. It is, writes Hegel in the introduction, "the first reconciling mediating term (*das erste versöhnende Mittelglied*) between pure thought and what is merely external, sensuous, and transient (*Vergängliches*), between nature and its finite reality and the infinite freedom of conceptual thinking" (A 13:21, 8). But as the *first* mediating link between senses and intellect, nature and mind, transience and infinitude, necessity and freedom, and so forth, art is also a merely *preliminary* appearance of absolute spirit, absolute spirit only *an sich*, and thus *not* the fully developed manifestation of absolute spirit in the "medium" or the element proper to it. The reason is self-evident. In art, absolute spirit has, by definition as it were, to appear in sensuous form, and the sensuous can never be a medium or a form or an element proper enough for that which is by definition *spirit*, spiritual and *not* sensuous, and *absolutely* spiritual at that. In other words, it is indeed very much a question of "definition" and "determination" here—as in *de-finire* or *de-terminare*, to "limit," to "border off"—as is always the case for Hegel. As "the sensuous appearance of the Idea" (the Idea in and for itself), art allows absolute spirit to appear all right, but to appear only as *determined* in and by the form of art which, in turn, is by definition determined as the form of the sensuous—again, the sensuous appearance of something essentially spiritual, the sensuous appearance of the Idea (*das sinnliche Scheinen der Idee*). And since in Hegel, as in Spinoza, *omnis determinatio est negatio*, this means that the determination of absolute spirit in art, by the sensuous form of art, is a negation of absolute spirit that would limit it and render it dependent upon that sensuous form. Absolute spirit, being spiritual, obviously cannot rest, cannot be "at home," *chez soi*, in that which is sensuous and must in turn negate the negativity of this determination that limits its freedom—that is, its freedom precisely to be itself, to be what it is in and for itself, namely, absolute spirit. Spirit, absolute spirit, is restless; it can get no rest and no satisfaction, and must pass on and over from the medium of representation, sensuous or otherwise, to the element of thought thinking itself absolutely, again, from the poetry of representation (*Vorstellung*) to the prose of thought (*Denken*).

Given the simultaneously exalted and yet merely preliminary position of art in Hegel's system, it comes as no surprise, then, that there should be *two* high points, two "highests," when it comes to art: classical and romantic. In relation to what Hegel calls the "ideal" of art, classical art is clearly "the highest" insofar as it is the *only* one of the three types of art that attains that ideal: namely, the perfect fusion, coalescence, and adequation of sensuous form and spiritual content. Since this is what art is and does, only an art that is and does it can be truly art as "beautiful art" or "fine art," as the translators put it, *schöne Kunst* (which, for Hegel, is a redundancy). And such is the case of Greek art—in the particular plastic form of sculptures of the gods of Greece who constitute an authentic spiritual *content* for the sensuous form of an art perfectly adequate to it. It is the *only* art in which the art-spirit (*Kunstgeist*) can be at home. But, needless to say, what makes the *art*-spirit happy can never satisfy the needs of *absolute* spirit, of spirit as such, since spirit, again, wants to appear not in sensuous form, not imprisoned in stone or marble (like a Sphinx-like human head on top of an animal body), but as itself, spirit, in spiritual form. The spiritual content that can enter adequately into sensuous form is necessarily a determined, limited content and, as such, a spiritual content that represents only a certain restricted extent and stage of the truth (*nur ein gewisser Kreis und Stufe der Wahrheit*) (A 13:23, 9). Hence insofar as romantic art constitutes a further stage in the progressive spiritualization of art—that is, *its* spiritual content is one more suited to a more "spiritualized" sensuous form like the colors of painting, the tones of music, and the linguistic signs of poetry—it represents a further and "higher" stage of art—an art "higher" than classical art, despite and (dialectically) *because of* its status as essentially a *post*-art. In short, classical art is "the highest" because it is appropriate for the needs of art-spirit; whereas romantic art is "the highest" because it is *more* appropriate (more than classical art) for the needs of absolute spirit.

But if the ambiguity of high points, of "highest" arts, can be resolved, and resolved apparently without remainder, by reference to the system, then a second, other ambiguity that the first one necessarily brings along with itself is not so easily dispatched and opens up a problematic most troublesome not only for Hegel's philosophy (and history) of art but also, and inevitably, for the system itself—for Hegel's philosophy (and history) of philosophy, as it were. If art has two high points, then quite clearly it also has two ends or, as one likes to call it in talking about the so-called death of art in Hegel, two *deaths* of art.[2] The first end of art would be relatively unproblematic. It is the end of art as such, of art properly speaking, in the dissolution of classical art. The end of classical art is of course foreordained, predetermined, in its very essence. The human bodily form of Greek sculpture so appropriate and so essentially adequate to mind or spirit is at the same time classical art's defect, lack, and (as such) self-negation because in it spirit is "determined as particular and human, not as purely absolute and eternal" (A 13:110, 79). Or, as Hegel summarizes: "The classical form of art has attained the highest that the embodiment ["rendering sensuous," *Versinnlichung*] of art could achieve, and if there is something lacking (*mangelhaft*) in it, it is only art itself and the limitedness of the sphere of art" (13:110, 79). And this lack or defect, limitedness or restrictedness (*Beschränktheit*), of art itself is, of course, the fact that it "takes as its object the spirit (i.e., the *universal*, infinite and concrete in its nature) in a *sensuously* concrete form," which means that in it "spirit is not in fact represented in its true nature" (13:111, 79). Thus the lack (*Mangel*) of classical art brings about its dissolution and "demands a transition to a higher form, the *third*, namely the romantic" (13:111, 79). So: the dissolution of classical art would be the *one* end of art, and provide one way to read Hegel's famous dictum: "art, considered in its highest vocation (*ihrer höchsten Bestimmung*), is and remains for us a thing of the past (*ein Vergangenes*)" (13:25, 11).

Now romantic art too has to dissolve; it too has its dissolution in-scribed, as it were, within its essence. But this second, other end of art is different, other, first of all on account of what it is that dissolves in the case of romantic art: namely, not so much *art* as a no-longer art, a post-art, an "art" whose spiritual content is no longer capable of being adequately repre-sented in sensuous form. The reason for this inadequation is Christianity's conception of the unity of human and divine natures: no longer, as in the case of the Greek gods, as "the sensuous immediate existence of the spiritual in the bodily form of man, but instead [as] self-conscious inwardness" (A 13:112, 80). In other words, the spiritual content of romantic art is too inward, too self-conscious, too spiritualized, too concrete—that is, already too self-consciously self-differentiating and self-negating—to be adequately repre-sented in sensuous form. Such a content withdraws itself, inward, from the externality of artistic expression. If this is so—if romantic art in its essential determination is an art that is already always passing away and passing over into a form of expression that is no longer artistic—then what ends with the end of romantic art is, again, not so much art, as the *ending* of art, what dissolves is the dissolving of art—the progressive inadequation and disjunc-tion between sensuous form and spiritual content. A certain wavering or suspensiveness, a "remaindering" (my translation of Jacques Derrida's *restance*), of the end seems to characterize the second end, or rather end*ing*, of art in the dissolution of romantic art, and it is no doubt this ending without end that introduces a hesitation into Hegel's otherwise apparently unambiguous pronouncements about the end of art. For instance, at the very end of the introduction Hegel seems to put the full completion, the complete ending, of art into the future:

> Now, therefore, what the particular arts realize in individual works of art is, according to the Concept of art, only the universal forms of the self-unfolding Idea of beauty. It is as the external actualization of this Idea that the wide Pantheon of art is rising. Its architect and builder is the self-comprehending spirit of beauty, but to complete it will need the history of the world in its development through thousands of years (*das aber die Weltgeschichte erst in ihrer Entwicklung der Jahrtausende vollenden wird*). (13:124, 90)

It is as though in rereading his own pronouncement that art is and remains for us a thing of the past, Hegel were putting the stress on the *remaining* of art for us *as* a thing of the past, as a pass*ing* thing, not *ein Vergangenes* but *ein Vergehendes*—as though art's ending without end were the repetition of art's pastness and passing. A repetition perhaps not unlike one that can be heard, or rather read, in Hegel's words of the end: *in ihrer Entwicklung der Jahrtaus-ende voll-enden, -ende -enden.*[3]

The full import of the double end of art—or rather the self-redoubling end*s* of art—and its necessary remaindering comes starkly into view once we juxtapose romantic art with the case and the end of *symbolic* art. Such a juxtaposition is authorized by the text, for in his discussion of the specificity of romantic art Hegel cannot help but bring up, and compare it to, symbolic art again and again. Indeed, according to Hegel, romantic art marks a certain reversion to, and repetition of, symbolic art insofar as in it "the separation of Idea and shape, their indifference and inadequacy to each other, come to the fore again, as in symbolic art. . . ." (A 114, 81). Just as the spiritual content of romantic art is *no longer* suited to being expressed in the sensuous form of art, so the spiritual content of symbolic art is *not yet* suitable for art. If in romantic art the spiritual content withdraws from the externality of sensuous form into inwardness, then in symbolic art the spiritual content in a sense removes itself into a sublime externality far above all natural, sensuous form that remains insignificant in relation to it or is violently yoked to and charged with the task of signifying the absolute idea. If romantic art is a *post*-art, then symbolic art is a *pre*-art (*Vorkunst*), a mere seeking (*bloßes Suchen*) or yearning for sensuous configuration (*Verbildlichung*), not the power of genuine representation. Of course, for Hegel, there is an essential difference between symbolic art and romantic art—the enigmatic, sublimely stony spirit signified in Egyptian architecture (pyramids and sphinxes) and the sounds as mere signs of spirit in romantic poetry—and he summarizes it as follows:

> Thereby the separation of Idea and shape, their indifference and inadequacy to each other, come to the fore again, as in symbolic art, but with this essential difference, that, in romantic art, the Idea, the deficiency (*Mangelhaftigkeit*) of which in the symbol brought with it deficiencies (*Mängel*) of shape, now has to appear *perfected* (*vollendet*) in itself as spirit and heart (*Geist und Gemüt*). Because of this higher perfection (*Vollendung*), it withdraws itself from an adequate union with the external, since its true reality and manifestation it can seek and achieve (*suchen und vollbringen*) only within itself. (A 114, 81)

The essential difference, then, is clear and especially legible (in German) in the oppositions between the lack (*Mangelhaftigkeit, Mängel*) of the Idea in symbolic art, and its fullness (*vollendet, Vollendung,* and *vollbringen*) in romantic art. The *lack* in symbolic art's spiritual content is its *abstract*, one-sided nature—its lack of sufficient determination or its vicious and untrue, and thus equally abstract and one-sided, determinacy. If the spiritual content is too abstract and one-sided, so will be the sensuous form. The "perfection," completedness, finishedness, or *fullness* of romantic art's spiritual content lies in its *concrete*, self-differentiating, self-conscious, and self-negating nature— its fullness, indeed excess, of determinateness, and a true, spiritual determinateness at that.

Nevertheless, both symbolic and romantic arts do come down to the same thing: just as the spiritual content of symbolic art is *too abstract* for the sensuous form of art, so the spiritual content of romantic art is *too concrete* for it. The former's excess (of abstraction) issues in a pre-art; the latter's excess (of concreteness) in a post-art. As such, both in fact arbitrarily yoke or bind a sensuous form to a spiritual content, both *impose* a meaning onto a material substance of nature. To the extent that they do so, both are arts of the *sign*—it's just that the one would be the sign of a *lack*, the other would be the sign of a *fullness*, a lack and a fullness of spirit. That romantic art in its fullest, most developed (i.e., self-dissolving) form—that is, in the form of romantic poetry—is an art of the sign is explicit in Hegel's introduction. As much as the romantic spiritual content may want to withdraw itself from the externality of the sensuous form that is inadequate to it, it nevertheless still needs "an external medium [or vehicle] of expression" (A 13:113, 81), as the translators put it: "Inwardness celebrates its triumph over the external and manifests its victory in and on the external itself, whereby what is apparent to the senses alone sinks into worthlessness. On the other hand, however, this romantic form too, like all art, needs an externality for its expression (*bedarf auch diese Form, wie alle Kunst, der Äußerlichkeit zu ihrem Ausdrucke*)" (13:113, 81). In romantic poetry, this in itself worthless medium or vehicle or externality of expression is what Hegel calls the sign, mere signification (*bloße Bezeichnung*), a sign for itself without meaning (*ein für sich bedeutungsloses Zeichen*) (13:122, 88), a sign for itself worth—and contentless (*als eines für sich wert- und inhaltloses Zeichen*) (13:123, 89). The worthlessness, contentlessness, and meaninglessness of the sign of romantic poetry is such that Hegel does not hesitate to call its external material (*das äußere Material*) a mere letter (*bloßer Buchstabe*): in romantic poetry "the sound or tone may as well be a mere letter, for the audible, like visible, has sunk down into being a mere indication of spirit (*zur bloßen Andeutung des Geistes*)" (13:123, 89). (This reduction of the sensuous vehicle, medium, or externality of romantic art to the status of a mere sign, a mere inscribed letter, is most appropriate for a context in which the poetry of representation (*Poesie der Vorstellung*) passes over into the prose of thought (*Prosa des Denkens*). For in Hegel's *Philosophy of Spirit*, in the section on "subjective spirit," the transition from the "faculty" of *Vorstellung* (representation, picture-thinking), to the "faculty" of thought (*Denken*) also takes place by means of an account of the sign, arbitrary linguistic signs—which manifest the mind's freedom from, and mastery over, the sensuous (which is still too preponderent in the case of the motivated relation between the *symbol* and what it symbolizes). The full ability to manipulate signs and exercise dominance over them is manifested in a "subfaculty" of *Vorstellung Gedächtnis*, a merely mechanical memory by rote, memorization, which reads and writes (for such a memory always requires some notation, some inscription) signs as though they were mere letters[4]).

But let us not forget about symbolic art, as much as Hegel's *Aesthetics* would indeed seem to want to have us forget it as irretrievably, mysteriously, enigmatically, and sublimely of the past, as an art which, unlike classical and romantic, could never be conceived as "the highest." And yet as soon as we comprehend the full extent of romantic art's essential nature as an art of the sign, as an art of the mere inscribed letter, we cannot help but notice, we cannot help but read, that, as such, romantic art is essentially the same as symbolic art: that is, the structure of the relation between a "sensuous form" reduced to the status of a mere sign or a mere letter and the "spiritual content" that it can only signify or indicate is the same in romantic art as it is in symbolic art. However much Hegel may want to insist upon the "essential difference" between them— one is a sign or letter that means or indicates a lack; the other is a sign or letter that means or indicates a fullness—on the level of the sign, of the letter—or, if you like, as far as their rhetorical structure is concerned—the two are the same. If both are signs, how do you tell the difference, how do you know that one is the sign of an excessive lack of spiritual meaning, whereas the other is the sign of an excessive fullness of spiritual meaning? If both are inscribed letters, how do you know that one is the indicator of a spirit too abstract, whereas the other is an indicator of a spirit too concrete? Again, and very brutally, given an Egyptian symbolic work of (pre-)art and a Christian romantic work of (post-)art to see—or, rather, to *read*—how can you tell that the one is the product of an artistic intention whose conception of the absolute was too abstract and one-sided to allow successful expression in art, whereas the other was a product of an artistic intention whose conception of the absolute was too concrete and self-differentiating to allow successful expression in art? How can you tell that the one artist tried and failed to arrive at art, tried and failed to have the absolute spirit *appear* in sensuous form, whereas the other artist didn't even try for an artistic representation of the absolute but instead only meant to signify the spirit in a sign or to inscribe it in a letter? You are looking at two pyramids, and you can tell that the one pyramid is the container of a mummified corpse that only commemorates the death of spirit, whereas the other pyramid is an empty tomb of no body into which a "foreign soul," a living spirit, has been introduced, so that it may signify the eternal life of spirit. But, of course, it is easy. We can tell, we must be able to tell, the difference between sign and sign, letter and letter, for otherwise we will not be able to tell whether we are coming or going, dead or living, on the way to art or way past art, we will not be able to tell, we will not be able to remember, to remember, who we are. This is why we need the Greeks, the classical art of Greece, the one moment in the history of art when absolute spirit *did appear* in sensuous form and was not merely deposited in the irrevocable externality of signs and letters. If the Greeks did not exist, we would have to, we *have* had to, invent them—to remember, rather than just *memorize*, who we are. Otherwise, again, we could not, cannot, tell whether we are pre-Greek Egyptians or post-Greek Christians.

The ultimate trouble is that the collapse of romantic art and symbolic art into indifference—into the same indifference and disjunction of sensuous form and spiritual content—has inevitable consequences for the classical art of the Greeks, for how do we know, how do we recognize, *art as art*—that is, neither as pre-art nor as post-art—when we see it? How do we know that the sculptured body of a man is the sensuous *appearance* of the spirit and not itself some kind of pyramid or sphinx, some kind of sign or letter? Can we be so sure that it is not a mummified corpse or an empty sarcophagus? In fact, we don't *see* the Greeks or Greek classical art; we instead perform an ideological imposition of a "classical" meaning upon a sensuous form and thereby press it into service as an arbitrary sign—while pretending that what we will have to read there, to have *read* there, is the necessary, motivated relation between a symbol and what it symbolizes. If the Greeks are invented and have to be invented in order that the history of art—and history as such—may make sense, then the consequences of our not being able to *recognize* them, remember them, except in the mechanical memory by rote of inscribed signs, markers, and letters are dire. For starters, the history of art—and hence the history of spirit's progressive drive back to itself through and beyond the element of sensuous appearance and representation—becomes instead a repetitive allegory of how the spirit tries, but cannot, ever appear except in signs or letters that are, by definition, *not* appearances but commemorative markers of the death and dissolution—or, rather, the dying and the dissolving—of spirit. (Rather than absolving itself, absolute spirit winds up dissolving itself!) Rather than a history of the progressive spiritualization of art from symbolic, through classical, and on to romantic, the story of the *Aesthetics* would be a repetitive allegory of spirit's inability to appear, from symbolic to symbolic to symbolic or from romantic to romantic to romantic, Egyptian, Egyptian, and Egyptian again, or Christian, Christian, and Christian still again—but *never* classical and *never* Greek. What gets dissolved in such an allegory is not art or the different types of art—art does not end or dissolve; it is always ceaselessly ending and dissolving—but rather spirit. *Spirit* undergoes the progressive, ceaseless erosion of time, by time, in time. And it will take much time, thousands of years, for it to reach its completed end—which is, in fact, no end at all but a remaindering of ending. In that sense, *all* "art" would be symbolic (or romantic) art, an art of the sublime in a sense more Kantian than Hegelian: the striving and the failure to make the absolute appear.[5]

One final irony of this allegory is that the very word *symbol*—which would want to indicate some kind of motivated, necessary, adequate relation between symbolic expression and its meaning (as in *sun + ballein*)—should in fact be the name for an art of the *sign* when used by Hegel to denominate a (putatively) historical period of art (as in "symbolic art"). In other words, what Paul de Man calls the "nonconvergence of the apparently historical and properly theoretical components of the *Aesthetics*" takes place already in the word *symbol* insofar as it names both the ideal of art, the paradigm of art *as* art—that is, adequation between sensuous form and spiritual content—and also a "historical" art that is essentially an art of the sign—that is, one in which there is an arbitrary yoking of sensuous form and spiritual content, an imposition of "substantive idea" upon natural objects as their meaning. In short, the symbol is itself always riven by the division between sign and symbol, and this is legible right at the outset of Hegel's discussion of the symbolic form of art (*Die symbolische Kunstform*) when he "defines" the symbol as such (*Vom Symbol überhaupt*): "1. The symbol," writes Hegel, "is first of all a *sign*" (*1. Das Symbol ist nun zunächst ein Zeichen*). In other words, there is first of all an arbitrary linking between meaning and its expression, and it is only in the *second* place that the symbol is . . . a symbol!— that is, bears a motivated relation between expression and its meaning insofar as the expression already possesses the properties of the meaning it is to express ("The lion . . . as a symbol of magnanimity, the fox of cunning, the circle of eternity, the triangle of the Trinity"): "2. Therefore it is otherwise with a sign that is to be a *symbol*" (*2. Anders ist es daher bei einem Zeichen, welches ein* Symbol *sein soll*) (13:394–95, 304).

This doubleness of the symbol—that is, again, (1) the symbol is *first of all*, immediately, a sign, and (2) the symbol is *second of all* a symbol— is most peculiar (and a bit bizarre) because it at least implies that in the symbol's first, initial, immediate definition as sign, there is in fact a symbolic—that is, "natural," immediate, motivated—relation between subject and predicate; whereas in the symbol's *second*, derived, definition *as symbol*, there would in fact be a relation of arbitrary designation between subject and predicate. In short, the implication is that in order for the symbol to be *defined*—delimited, determined—*as* a symbol, there has to be a difference between the symbol and symbolized and a disjunction between the symbol and "itself" *as* the disjunction between sign and symbol. This primary, originary difference of the symbol from itself is, one could say, what programs Hegel's *Aesthetics*—and the divergent imperatives of absolute spirit and art-spirit (*Kunstgeist*)—from beginning to end and what turns it into an allegory of (the impossibility of reading) the symbol. It also gives "new meaning," as one says, to Hegel's more well-known insistence a bit later on the essential ambiguity of the symbol: "From this it follows that the symbol, according to its own concept, remains essentially *ambiguous*" (*Hieraus folgt nun, daß das Symbol seinem eigenen Begriff nach wesentlich zweideutig bleibt*) (A 13:397, 306). No doubt it is this essential, irreducible, and unsublatable (*unaufhebbare?*), ambiguity that makes Hegel's *Aesthetics*, in de Man's words, "a double and possibly duplicitous text." Although de Man's itinerary in "Sign and Symbol in Hegel's *Aesthetics*" goes through different texts (and mostly *not* the *Aesthetics*), his summary can serve our purposes as well:

> No wonder, then, that Hegel's *Aesthetics* turns out to be a double and possibly duplicitous text. Dedicated to the preservation and the monumentalization of classical art, it also contains all the elements which make such a preservation impossible from the start. Theoretical reasons prevent the convergence of the apparently historical and the properly theoretical components of the work. This results in the enigmatic statements that have troubled Hegel's readers, such as the assertion that art is for us a thing of the past. This has usually been interpreted and criticized or, in some rare instances, praised as a historical diagnosis disproven or borne out by actual history. We can now assert that the two statements "art is for us a thing of the past" and "the beautiful is the sensory manifestation of the idea" are in fact one and the same.

To the extent that the paradigm for art is thought rather than perception, the sign rather than the symbol, writing rather than painting or music, it will also be memorization rather than recollection. As such, it belongs indeed to a past which, in [Marcel] Proust's words, could never be recaptured, *retrouvé*. Art is "of the past" in a radical sense, in that, like memorization, it leaves the interiorization of experience forever behind. It is of the past to the extent that it materially inscribes, and thus forever forgets, its ideal content. The reconciliation of the two main theses of the *Aesthetics* occurs at the expense of the aesthetic as a stable philosophical category.[6]

Notes

1. All references to G. W. F. Hegel's *Aesthetics* will be given by volume number and page number for the German (vols. 13, 14, and 15 of the *Theorie Werkausgabe* of Hegel's works) and then to the English of T. M. Knox's translation, hereafter cited as A. See Hegel, *Vorlesungen über die Ästhetik* (Frankfurt am Main, Germany: Suhrkamp, 1970; and Hegel, *Aesthetics,* trans. T. M. Knox (Oxford: Oxford University Press, 1975). (Translation has sometimes been modified.)

2. That the "death of art" interpretation is certainly questionable is argued by Curtis L. Carter, "A Reexamination of the 'Death of Art' Interpretation of Hegel's Aesthetics," in *Selected Essays on G. W. F. Hegel,* ed., Lawrence S. Stepelevich (Atlantic Highlands, NJ: Humanities Press, 1993), 11–26.

3. Cf. Knox's suggestive essay, "The Puzzle of Hegel's Aesthetics," in ibid., 2–10.

4. On the passage from *Vorstellung* to *Denken*, on symbol and sign, and on memory as interiorization versus mechanical memory by rote in the third part of Hegel's *Encyclopaedia*, see Paul de Man's "Sign and Symbol in Hegel's *Aesthetics*," in *Aesthetic Ideology,* ed. Andrzej Warminski (Minneapolis: University of Minnesota Press, 1996), 91–104. See my quotation and use of de Man's essay later.

5. On the mind's striving and failure to present the ideas of reason—which, according to Immanuel Kant, is *itself* a presentation (not of the ideas of reason, which cannot be presented, but) "of the subjective purposiveness of our mind, in the use of our imagination, for the mind's supersensible vocation," see Kant's "General Comment on the Exposition of Aesthetic Reflective Judgments" at the end of the Analytic of the Sublime in Kant, *Critique of Judgment,* trans. Werner S. Pluhar (Indianapolis: Hackett, 1987), 128. Kant, *Kritik der Urteilskraft* (Frankfurt am Main, Germany: Suhrkamp, 1974), 193–94. See also Andrzej Warminksi, " 'As the Poets Do It': On the Material Sublime," in *Material Events,* eds., Barbara Cohen, Tom Cohen, J. Hillis Miller, and Warminski (Minneapolis: University of Minnesota Press, 2001), 3–31; and Warminski, "Returns of the Sublime: Positing and Performative in Kant, Fichte, and Schiller," *MLN* 116 (December 2001): 964–78.

6. Paul de Man, "Sign and Symbol in Hegel's *Aesthetics*," in *Aesthetic Ideology*, 102–3. The ultimate *in*difference of symbolic art and romantic art—as well as

the radical pastness of art as such (in its status as material inscription)—is corroborated by the genre, in fact the *poetic* genre, which Hegel places at the end, at the point of dissolution, of *both* symbolic art *and* romantic art: namely, the epigram, the inscription. The longer version of the present essay uses Hegel's remarks on epigram and inscription as a transition to a reading of Keats's "Ode on a Grecian Urn" as an example of the "genre" of *inscription*—and *against* the poem's apparent subscription to the two main these of Hegel's *Aesthetics*: (1) art is the sensory appearance of the idea; (2) art is for us a thing of the past.

Toward a Cultural Idealism: Negativity and Freedom in Hegel and Kant

Tilottama Rajan

I

German Idealism is often seen as transcendentally indifferent to history. When it is recognized that these theorists are not "pure" philosophers, their cultural and historical concerns are seen as emerging within a totalizing imperialism of philosophy. Yet it is the very idealism of post-Kantian philosophy, intersected as it is by a certain Romanticism, which has made possible our appreciation of aesthetic alterity. For whatever its local prejudices, philosophy after Immanuel Kant introduces new values and forms of judgment seminal for the reception of otherness. Within this context I focus on the opening created by the transposition of the Kantian sublime into the historical framework of G. W. F. Hegel's *Aesthetics*. More specifically, I focus on the excessive place of the symbolic and romantic within an art history whose classical totalization is torn open by its displacement from the end to the middle of Hegel's project.

Kant and Hegel are often opposed, the work of Slavoj Žižek being an exception.[1] But the *Aesthetics* shares certain cultural and philosophical *topoi* with Kant, while performing them differently. It transfers his distinction between the sublime and the beautiful from a philosophical context that elides their conflict to the historicized scene of their cultural competition. It is studded with references to the *Idea* and *freedom*—terms with a prehistory in Idealism and also in Kant's Critiques. As important, Hegel's work assumes

Kant's analytic apparatus: his distinctions between ideas and concepts, reflective and determinant judgment, and pure and practical reason. Not only is Kant more post-Kantian than we think ("reason" being not unlike Hegel's Spirit); Hegel is more Kantian than he appears. To read Hegel with Kant rather than J. G. Fichte is to recover a (self-)critical Hegel. More specifically, it restores the context of the *Aesthetics* in "judgment," an activity that reconstitutes thought as critique.

"Judgment" for Kant involves assessing how and whether concepts apply to experience. Determinant judgments interpret an object in terms of an a priori concept. But the aesthetic is, rather, the object of reflective judgments that are relative, not absolute.[2] While such judgments are less certain, they are also more innovative. For by generating a rule from a case for which there is no rule, they open knowledge to new epistemic material. Aesthetic, unlike logical, judgment does not "subsume [its object] under any concept," thus responding to the autonomy of imagination, whose "freedom . . . consists in the fact that it schematizes without any concept" (CJ 128–29). Kant's bipartite construction of judgment thus creates a space for the questioning as well as the description of what we might call "Aesthetic Reason." Ostensibly he limits the subversiveness of judgment by discussing it in a treatise confined to the aesthetic. But as David Carroll points out, judgment in the third Critique is not specifically aesthetic. This vagueness in its reference allows the judgment specified as aesthetic to become a revisionary paradigm for judgment in general—aesthetic, legal, or social.[3]

The most radical test of judgment occurs in the reflective process that Kant names the sublime, which confronts the mind with an excess it cannot grasp synthetically. The sublime causes a crisis in judgment, not only because it resists accepted canons of beauty, but also because it concedes that judgments are really "sensations considered to be judgments." In letting this judgment be nonsynthetic, moreover, Kant sees that there are cognitions that cannot yet be reduced to concepts because there are no concepts to convey them. He creates a *philosophical space* for material that had previously fallen outside the sphere of judgment: forms that lack form, and more recently, moods such as hysteria or melancholy. This material has not been "domiciled" within discourse, thus functioning—albeit negatively—on the side of "freedom."[4]

Kant's linked concerns with art, freedom, and judgment form a background for reading the *Aesthetics*. For not only is Hegel too concerned with the role of judgment in the formation of culture, he also extends Kant's discussion of the aesthetic as the "unformed" rather than the adequate embodiment of the Idea. Among Hegel's many contexts is Friedrich Schiller's *On the Aesthetic Education of Man,* in which the aesthetic is conceived as the beautiful, as Western culture. If the *Letters* convinces Kant to provide an education in which freedom is defined in terms of the beautiful and the *sensus communis*, Hegel's *Aesthetics* is (reluctantly) their sublime counterpart, a breach in the project of consensus and unification. It plays the same unsettling role in Hegel's corpus as the third Critique does in Kant's. What this means is that Hegel can no longer be cast as a figure for the end of art who absorbs art into philosophy. For Jean-François Lyotard, who more than anyone has brought out Kant's importance for contemporary theory, political judgment must be rethought through the aesthetic because art is a force that "depends on the . . . forms to *be* invented, rather than [on] what has already been formed or performed" (P 155). Lyotard's preoccupation with Kant has to do with the ways in which the sublime creates a space for his own use of the avant-garde: a use that Carroll calls "paraesthetic" in that it privileges art for critical rather than aestheticist purposes. But this sense of art as experimenting with new forms without knowing "where they will lead" (167) is also present in Hegel's analysis of the symbolic. Indeed this is why Hegel, having failed to recuperate the symbolic through the romantic, must defer, through the figure of the end of art, the very problem posed by the aesthetic to the unification of Subjective and Objective spirit.

At the core of the *Aesthetics* is the judgment of art-forms that fail to fit classical and Objective standards of beauty. Hegel distinguishes three ways of relating "inwardness" and its "externalization," "theme," and "execution," or the "Idea" and its "embodiment." In the earliest symbolic or oriental phase, art fails to achieve identity with itself because of a deficiency in self-consciousness that results from the Idea still being "indeterminate." This problem is overcome in classicism as art becomes "the adequate embodiment of the Idea."[5] But in the romantic, form and content are again sundered, this time because of a deficiency in matter that repeats and reverses symbolic inadequacy, external forms now being insufficient to present the Idea. Ostensibly Hegel's triad charts a philosophical and cultural progress in which the romantic is the West's dialectical redemption of the *différance* inscribed in the symbolic. But the narrative of the *Aesthetics* is highly overdetermined, most obviously in the fact that its "progress" displaces synthesis from the end to the middle, as if synthesis and identity are *not* progress. For it is classicism that most clearly conforms to Hegel's proclaimed view of art as a "free totality" in which the "content" is united with its "entirely adequate shape" (A 431). And yet Hegel finds this unity dull, revisiting through the romantic the disfiguration of the Idea abjected in his dismissal of the symbolic.[6]

At issue is the disfiguration of Hegel's own "idea" through a process in which theme and execution differ within the materiality of history. On the one hand Hegel follows the Enlightenment in making classical ideals of beauty and mimesis normative. On the other hand he cannot but be aware of the revaluation of oriental culture by Friedrich and A. W. Schlegel, Friedrich Creuzer, and Joseph Görres. Hegel's valorization of the romantic, moreover,

is the scene of a powerful attraction to the symbolic as the abjected form of
the romantic. And given the wider provenance of judgment, Hegel's aesthetics has paraesthetic ramifications for the assessment of judgment in terms of
its own cultural adequacy.

Since the *Aesthetics* thinks philosophy through art, it implicates not
only art but also philosophy in the problem of "taste." This move, though
implicit in Kant, is curtailed by his elision of the empirical referents of taste
and judgment in a purely "transcendental" treatment (CJ 6). *Symbolic* and
romantic are, however, terms from cultural history with a genealogy in the
work of Creuzer and A. W. Schlegel. By syncretizing them with the sublime,
Hegel inflects Kant's arguments with the rethinking of cultural difference
begun by Johann Gottfried Herder, who points out that what one nation
"holds as good," "beautiful," or "true" may be judged useless by a different
"taste."[7] To be sure Hegel, like Kant, is a philosopher rather than a critic of
culture. But like other German Romantics he is a hybrid thinker who fails
to respect the purity of the philosopical genre. In this respect his philosophy
is closer to "Theory," as a mixing of disciplines unsettled by the contest of
faculties. In crossing Kant with Herder and Creuzer, the *Aesthetics* thus not
only generates new categories of philosophical thought, but is drawn into the
rethinking of philosophy itself through culture.

II

In reading Hegel with Kant I shall focus on the paraesthetic functioning of
judgment on the border between the aesthetic and the cultural. Kant's analysis of judgment is a way of keeping knowledge open to new epistemic material. Since *determinant* judgments interpret the particular in terms of existing
concepts (CJ 15), if we had only such judgments we would have no new
forms of knowledge. But Kant also admits that "the forms of nature are so
manifold . . . that there must be laws for these [forms] also," which are the
object of *reflective* judgment (16). Kant thus provides tools for the critique as
well as for the constitution of rationality. Despite its radical potential, however, he still constructs reflective judgment according to an Enlightenment
model in which additions to knowledge are cumulative rather than ruptural.
Indeed the suggestion that exceptions are already there in "nature," the
marginalizing of the social and historical sphere of art, and the domestication
of reflective judgment through the beautiful, all mark this conservatism.

The revolutionary potential of reflective judgment nevertheless emerges
in the sublime. Lyotard approaches Kant as a "sign" so as to read his work
in terms of what it *indicates* for the future rather than strictly in terms of what
it expresses (S 407). In the beautiful Kant found an idea adequately embodied
in the discourse of his time; but "the sublime is a sudden blazing" that

"acquired a future" only later and "addresses us still" (L 55). The sublime is connected with Lyotard's own project of displacing an *aesthetics* by an *energetics* of form: "an aesthetics of what is not strictly visible . . . where the work on form, the deformation of form" is more fundamental than its "formation" (P 39). In addition Lyotard considers the sublime not simply in relation to art but also to the political. His linking of the sublime to the French Revolution makes it a figure for the political unconscious, in his particular sense of "figure."[8] Lyotard credits Kant with a fourth *Critique of Political Reason*, dispersed in "phrases" throughout his corpus (S 396). Kant's phrases are the figures that disturb Hegel's discourse of totality, generating through the symbolic a prefiguration of the political unconscious that is not so much in Kant or Hegel as between them, or between them and us.

Lyotard identifies the sublime as the site of a new kind of judgment. As important, this deconstructive and nonsynthetic judgment emerges within the romanticism of the *Idea*—a term that forms a crucial link between Kant and Hegel. The "sublime feeling" occurs when the mind is faced with something that exceeds its powers of presentation. Negatively, it involves a confrontation with "the formless and figureless" (S 404), which "denies the imagination the power of forms" (L 54). More positively, the sublime conveys a " 'presence' that exceeds what imaginative thought can . . . *form*" (53). Initially the result is a suspension of judgment: the indeterminacy of the sublime means that it cannot be grasped synthetically and domiciled cognitively. The sublime thus plunges the mind into the hermeneutical vortex of having to judge " 'before' knowing what judging properly is" (31–32). This crisis has to do not only with the disruptiveness of the sublime but also with its status as mood or feeling—a category increasingly important in German Romanticism.[9] But this is not to say that the sublime is the end of judgment. Whereas for Edmund Burke sensation is an end in itself, for Kant insofar as a sensation is a judgment it is an alternative form of cognition.

That the sublime is the material (and mode) of "judgment" pushes Kant to find an alternative to the "concept" still allied with thought. Crucial to this reconstitution of rationality is the distinction of ideas from concepts, which parallels that between reflection and determination. This distinction will be explored in the next section, which will unpack the figural and discursive operation of the term *idea* through the difference between its use in the first and third Critiques. Suffice it to say that while concepts are produced by the understanding in terms of what we know, ideas have to do with the faculty that Kant curiously calls "reason." On the one hand concepts therefore provide certain knowledge, while ideas are hypothetical. On the other hand Kant's ideas have an expansive role noted by Karl Jaspers when he comments that reason "makes things too big for the understanding," while the understanding "make[s] them too little for reason."[10] Anticipating Hegel's discontent with the adequate embodiment of the idea in classicism, Kant in the third Critique associates ideas with the indeterminacy, the obscurity that makes thought possible. Ideas in this sense resemble the sublime. Moreover, because they do not correspond to anything present, they also institute a historical sublime, a freedom generated in the gap between signifier and signified.

The radicality of ideas stems not just from their futurity but also from their obscurity. In the third Critique, Kant outlines two kinds of ideas. "Aesthetic" ideas are representations that cannot be expressed in concepts or "language." Conversely "rational" ideas are concepts that cannot be represented (CJ 157), but since they fall short of expressibility or visibility, they too are marked by a certain obscurity. In effect ideas are between concepts and sensations—the idea of "freedom" being less a precise definition of freedom than an intimation of, or a desire for, freedom. That ideas are a reflection on (and of) feelings is a point made more explicitly by Arthur Schopenhauer when he deconstructs *Vorstellung* as a representation produced by the will. But Kant's deployment of ideas in a network that includes "reason" and "freedom" marks his Hegelian difference from Schopenhauer: his inscription of ideas not simply as a deconstruction of concepts but also as a bridge between feeling and mind. Kant intimates the possibility of transferring figure into discourse or (in Julia Kristeva's terms) of transferring the semiotic into the Symbolic. Yet Kant does not really make this link. He could not address us as he does now without a transposition of the theoretical into the empirical that he would dismiss as "dialectical," and for which we need a different sign: that of Hegel.

III

At first Hegel's distinction of the Idea from the concept seems different from Kant's, and not simply in the reduction of plural to singular. While Kant's idea exceeds the concept, Hegel's seems to be its teleological fulfillment. But the issue is more complicated. The Hegelian "concept" is not fixed but is like the plant encoded in the seed: an immanent potentiality.[11] It is because he conflates the Hegelian concept with its Kantian namesake that Lyotard refers to an "absolute hegemony of the concept" in Hegel, accusing him unlike Kant of limiting thought to what can be "taken into intelligibility" through existing concepts.[12] But Hegel's concept is more unstable than Kant's, and closer to Kant's "idea." On the other hand, Hegel's *Idea* purports to be more logocentric than Kant's. The Idea is "the real existence of the Concept," objective as well as subjective (A 106–7, 110). One might say that Hegel refigures the Idea so as to evade the trouble he has got himself into through the concept, and that the Idea recontains the sublime within the beautiful. Indeed Hegel describes the Idea as "beautiful" and "immediately one with the objectivity adequate to itself" (107).

Yet this *concept* of the *Idea* cannot be objectified in the *Aesthetics*, where the separation of the terms collapses. For Hegel's use of "Idea" associates it with potentiality rather than with totality, with the *Streben* linked by his Jena colleagues to the romantic and the sublime: in the forms of art "the Idea presses on to representation and reality" without always finding an adequate embodiment (A 299). Perhaps the difficulty in which the Idea finds itself is merely temporary. But though Hegel valorizes the classical as "the adequate embodiment of the Idea" over the symbolic, he also says that the Idea is "only truly Idea as *developing itself* explicitly by its own activity" (A 299; emphasis added). As important, though it is clear that the Idea fails as the salvation of the concept, what is signified by "concept" is itself unclear. For Hegel distinguishes dizzyingly between "the Concept without its objectivity" and the "Concept rebuilt as Concept within its objective realization" (143). For a distinction *between* concept and idea he substitutes a distinction *within* two terms that have now drifted dangerously together, rendering their distinction superfluous: thus there is a "Concept without its objectivity" that "is not genuinely Concept," and an "Idea outside its actuality" that "is not genuinely Idea" (143). Struggling to desynonymize the two, Hegel oscillates between defining either the *concept* or the *Idea* as achieved totalities, but can do neither. Instead the terms double each other, trading places in a process of mutual supplementation that produces only the phantasm of totality.

What should be evident is the enormous influence on Hegel of Kant's "ideas," which infiltrate *both* the concept and the Idea in Hegel. Hegel's notion of the Idea as not having achieved "representation and reality" (A 299) recalls Kant's notion of rational ideas as concepts that cannot be given sensuous presentation. Indeed Hegel's development of the symbolic and romantic refigures Kant's elaboration of the two ways ideas exceed concepts. As an art that tries to imagine "a meaning for the shape" (440), the symbolic resembles Kant's aesthetic ideas; for its part the romantic, as an Idea that has defined itself but cannot be sensuously represented, corresponds to the rational idea (302). But what matters here is not this distinction, which Hegel cannot sustain. What matters, as in Kant, is the inscription of the Idea as *difference* through the marking of a disparity that can be seen now in one way and now in another, and that is, because of this recurrence, inescapable.

Crucial for Kant's legacy to Hegel are the cultural ramifications of the distinction between ideas and concepts. Concepts are governed by the understanding, which subsumes an object or intuition "under a conception" that neither exceeds nor falls short of what it schematizes.[13] Since it judges according to a priori representations, understanding produces knowledge according to the *sensus communis*. Plato, by contrast, sees an *idea* as something that "far transcends" the understanding "inasmuch as in experience nothing perfectly corresponding" to it can be found (CPR 219). In Kant's romantic rendering, an idea is thus "the *feeling* of a much higher vocation than that of merely spelling out phenomena" or replicating things as they are (CPR 219, emphasis added).[14] An idea is an *ideal*, as when Kant speaks of the "idea of humanity" as a "*maximum* [or] archetype" with which people will "never be in perfect accordance" but which is still not "chimerical" (220–21). This definition of "idea" is picked up by post-Kantians such as Schiller to intimate both the disparity between, and the desired reconciliation of, the *Formtrieb* [Form drive] and *Stofftrieb* [Sense drive]. Of relevance also is Friedrich Schlegel's use of "idea" as another word for fragment,[15] and the use of the term in "The Oldest Systematic Program of German Idealism." This anonymous fragment—attributed variously to F. W. J. Schelling, Friedrich Hölderlin, and Hegel—makes the idea "the object of *freedom*," by insisting that it be "aesthetic" or that it bring together "mythology" and "reason."[16]

There is nothing surprising in the equation of "idea" with "ideal." Kant's contribution, however, is a *critical* idealism that emerges between the first and third Critiques, becoming in Hegel a semiotics of the idea as the difference between form and content. Briefly, in their "transcendental" form as described in the first Critique, ideas project the reconciliation of the disparity that characterizes the aesthetic or rational ideas of the third Critique. But transcendental ideas do not exist, or exist only immanently as a difference from themselves. The "transcendental" idea(l) of humanity in the first Critique is what mobilizes "freedom" as a resistance to being bound by existing conceptions. But the immanent functioning of ideas in the third Critique as what Jacques Derrida calls *différance*, as the deferral of the concept by its presentation or of presentation by the absence of the concept, is what constitutes Idealism as self-critical.

We can phrase this differently, to emphasize its ramifications for the place of judgment in culture. In the first Critique Kant deals only with transcendental ideas, thus focusing not on difference but on the *distance* between the idea(l) and actuality. Since idea(l)s here are a kind of logos, criticism does not occur within the ideas themselves. Instead Kant concentrates on two things: on the idea as operating on the side of freedom because it transcends experience, and on the dangers of hypostatizing this idea through an identification of representation with reality that would convert an idea into what Francis Bacon calls an "idol." For ideas, as Kant says, are "the parents of irresistible illusions" that necessitate "the severest and most subtle criticism" to avoid fanaticism. To assume that an idea corresponds to an actual object or to apply it "to an object falsely believed to be adequate" to it constitutes a "*subreption*" or "misapplication." Ideal(s) are regulative and not constitutive, and involve a "hypothetical exercise of reason" in which they are "employed as problematical conceptions" (CPR 373–75). Thus an idea such as "the good" must remain an empty signifier if it is not to be shackled to "what is done." Insofar as practical reason deploys it as "immanent and constitutive,"[17] this constitution of the good in praxis is a symbolic or imaginary resolution that must remain open to the possibility raised by speculative reason of the good being other than what convention or ideology make it.

In the first two Critiques, then, criticism emerges *rationally* from the asymmetries between theory and practice. The third Critique differs in ways connected with the introduction of the sublime. To begin with, criticism arises less from the difference between actual and transcendental ideas, or present and future, than from the self-difference of the idea in the present. As important, though the "rational" idea as a concept with no adequate object is consistent with the "transcendental" ideas of the first Critique, the aesthetic idea is not strictly speaking an idea at all. Rather it is a "representation of the *imagination* which occasions much thought, without any definite thought, i.e. any *concept*, being . . . adequate to it" (CJ 157, emphasis added). The aesthetic idea develops more fully Kant's description of an idea as a "feeling," and points toward such contemporary categories as Kristeva's "genotext," which names a process that "can be seen in language . . . [but] is not linguistic."[18] Moreover, as in the genotext, the process of the sublime is negativity. As Hegel says in quoting Kant, the ideas of reason cannot be adequately represented, and insofar as they are "aroused" it is precisely by an "inadequacy" that still "admit[s] of sensuous representation" (A 363, CJ 84). For Hegel, then, the transference of the sublime into the scene of history can lead only to a negative dialectic, as distinct from the dialectic of enlightenment that he wrests from the transition of art into philosophy.

But this is not to make the third Critique incompatible with the project of rationality in the first two. If the sublime marks a break with the first two Critiques, its association with "reason" reconnects it to the *Critique of Pure Reason*. My reading of the sublime thus differs from that of Lyotard, who sees it as falling outside "the project of philosophical unification" undertaken by the Critiques (L 52). More pertinent is Gilles Deleuze's account of the intertextuality between them, resulting in an "unregulated exercise of all the faculties":

> This might be the fourth formula of a deeply romantic Kant in *The Critique of Judgement*. In the two other Critiques, the . . . faculties had entered into relationships [which] were rigorously regulated in so far as there was always a dominant or determining faculty. . . . [But] if the faculties can, in this way, enter into relationships which are variable but regulated by one or other of them, it must follow that all together they are capable of relationships which are free and *unregulated*, where each goes to its own limit and nevertheless shows the possibility of some sort of harmony with the others.[19]

Deleuze suggests the limits of reading Kant through any single Critique. To emphasize only pure reason would make him a formalist, neglecting his concern with ethics and conduct. To emphasize the second Critique would be to trace back to Kant the ascendancy of practical reason evident in cultural studies today. Insofar as Kant would critique this positivism, he remains seminal for theorists such as Derrida and Lyotard, who have always constituted theoretical and practical reason in a relationship of deferral by keeping their philosophical work apart from their strategicaly occasional political writings and actions. It is this ascendancy of practical reason, moreover, which has led to a partial understanding of Hegel based on a reading of his more historical works as misguided cultural criticism rather than philosophy. But finally, to emphasize only the complementarity of the first two Critiques would be to produce an Enlightenment Kant for whom the self-examination of reason occurs only on the ground of rationality. For it is only through the discussion of the *sublime* in the third Critique that we can grasp the latent *romanticism* of the figure of "ideas" as a form of imagination in the first.

The Idea as imagination is part of Kant's legacy through Jena Romanticism to Hegel. Yet there is a further aspect to the intertextuality of the Critiques that is pertinent to Hegel. For the Kant so far described can be found in the first Critique, even if it takes the third to make us recognize him. Ideas in the first Critique are still positive: they still posit, if hypothetically. Schiller's *On the Aesthetic Education of Man* attributes this positivity to Kant in describing the idea as something that is not given "by experience but is the necessary result of [man's] rationality."[20] For Schiller the idea figures a perfectibility, and projects the reconciliation of the *Formtrieb* and the *Stofftrieb* as an unattainable but approachable goal. But the sublime deconstructs such reconciliation. The sublime does not posit: it is rather the negativity of reason.

The third Critique therefore lays more emphasis than the first on the *indeterminacy* of the idea. While the idea still plays the role of a teleological signifier, this "higher finality," as in Søren Kierkegaard's notion of infinite absolute negativity, is the absence of the idea as *fixed* signifier. With this shift the very notion of "freedom" is radically altered. Freedom is not the utopian striving for what can be imagined but not substantiated; rather it is the space opened up by the failure of (re)presentations and discursive formations—a more radical, if radically contingent, "freedom." Freedom, as realized through the negativity of ideas, is conceived not positively but critically in a manner that leads after (but through) Hegel to negative dialectics.

IV

Kant, according to Jaspers, "forgoes richness of content" to convey a "pure consciousness of the 'forms' ": "Forms are superior to philosophical embodiment, because, if I think them through, they make me produce my thinking. They act upon my nonobjective inwardness, my freedom" (K 145–46). This asceticism is absent from Hegel, who seems to deal with knowledge rather than with its forms, thus supporting the claim that German Idealism develops from an (ab)use of Kant in which practical gains ascendancy over theoretical reason. For the *Aesthetics* is rich in "content," and it is this (often Eurocentric) content that preoccupies us, to the detriment of the forms Hegel introduces. To approach Hegel through Kant is thus strategic. It reminds us that Hegel must be read in the Kantian framework he assumed: that his figures of dialectic and teleology are ideas, and that the judgments they produce are subject to a dialogic relay between theoretical and practical reason. Moreover, it is through this dialogue that the idea of freedom is developed in accord with reason rather than statically imposed by the State. Finally, such a reading also reminds us that Kant entered the historical and cultural arena through Hegel, who goes far beyond Kant in developing paradigms for the operation of criticism *in culture*. Cultural criticism, it is fair to say, develops in the space between Kant and Hegel, which is also a space (and a difference) within "Hegel."

Put differently, it is difficult to generate a "practical" aesthetics from Kant. As Derrida suggests, Kant's "critique of taste does not concern production" or "culture" but "formal conditions of possibility."[21] Kant's formalism is important in separating principles from their historically contingent practice. But he also held that ideas have an application, and it is in the resulting problematic that Hegel extends Kant. On one level Hegel's conversion of the theoretical into the practical leads to "misapplication": his judgments of oriental art make his own prejudice constitutive. On another level, however, Hegel's (ab)use of Kant is what Stanley Corngold calls an "error" rather than a mistake: a creative translation by which the practical incipiently reconstitutes the theoretical against its own grain.[22] For the "concepts" that allow Hegel to judge symbolic art generate a process in which his principles are dialectically reformulated by the difference between the concept of judgment and its more expansive "Idea." This process is left unfinished in the *Aesthetics*, and in the case of oriental art its continuation awaits later art-historians such as Alois Riegl and Wilhelm Worringer. The "critical historians of art" who comprise the Hegelian aftermath offer the first *practical* examples of a cultural idealism (rather than materialism) that adapts judgment to the cultural other.[23] Nevertheless, it is Hegel's extension of Kant into the sphere of culture that allows a revaluation of Hegel's prejudices that occurs under the "sign" of Hegel. Moreover, it is Hegel rather than his successors who inscribes "from a transcendental point of view" the *ideas* necessary to value art as a form of negativity.[24]

That the genealogy of a certain kind of cultural criticism (albeit not current cultural studies[25]) might include Hegel is a controversial claim, given his attacks on Indian art and his view that the symbolic is deficient in self-consciousness. Hegel offers culturally constructed judgments as determinant, or rather uses classical principles as determinant while dealing with material that cannot be subsumed under these concepts. But Kant too is guilty of misapplication. Kant criticizes the monstrous and uses neoclassical norms to dismiss the sublime as less "important" than the beautiful (CJ 91, 84). Because he develops a formal apparatus for the critique of such abuses, we separate his principles from their expression. But it is just as reasonable to extract the formal contribution made by Hegel's analysis of the symbolic from the local prejudices that accompany it. Indeed this possibility is inscribed by his own metacritical apparatus, which allows for culturally explicable discontinuities between "theme" and "execution," or between the constative and performative effects of texts, including his own.

From this perspective Hegel's achievement is to extend judgment to material that by his norms is unaesthetic. Moreover, in this process he is split between determination and reflection, evaluation and thought, and indeed Objective and Subjective spirit. Hence, although he dismisses the symbolic on the level of "taste," on a philosophical level it leads him to perceptions that reconstitute the very criteria of judgment. As is well-known, Hegel approaches the three major art forms as "different ways of grasping the Idea as content" or "different relations of meaning and shape" (A 75). Moreover, for Hegel form is not an empty container but the symptomatic site of a content different from itself. This deferral of content by form and of form by content is part of a psychological narrative about the history of art as the story of spirit's attempt to become clear to itself through the forms in which it "produces" or writes itself. The *topoi* for this story about spirit, as Hegel says, come from Kant (56). But Hegel's use of narrative rather than taxonomy is the space for a new kind of judgment that is historical rather than transcendental. Through narrative Hegel, on the one hand, moves away from Kantian abstraction. On the other hand, as history, narrative is the never-ending process of the accomplishment of the Idea, and thus not the unification but the mediation of concept and reality.

As already noted, the *Aesthetics* transposes the distinction between the beautiful and the sublime into a cultural history compounded from A. W. Schlegel and Creuzer, thus confronting more openly a crisis in philosophical taste elided by Kant. Inheriting Kant's divided loyalties to the beautiful and the sublime, Hegel also takes over his precursor's commitment (a) to the normative, synthetic judgment elicited by classical beauty, but (b) to the nonsynthetic critical judgments elicited by the symbolic and the romantic. Hegel's intense anxiety about the symbolic reflects his more acute sense of the incompatibility between these standards, and their consequences for how we conceive history, rationality, and freedom. But as troubled as he is by forms that do not cohere, he is also bored by their opposite: an art whose form is the embodiment of its content, eliciting no thought, no discontent. On the level of its plot the *Aesthetics* recovers the crisis in representation that mobilizes it along a cultural axis that protects West from East. It constructs the romantic as the *Aufhebung* or sublation of the symbolic, so that the problems disclosed in oriental art are dialectically resolved in the "noncorrespondence" of matter and spirit in Christianity. In another sense, however, the lectures are organized by repetition rather than by dialectic. For the romantic is a way of revisiting the symbolic, an alibi for reconsidering excess. This is all the more true because the opposition between the two keeps collapsing, thereby making it difficult to judge in intrinsic rather than chronological terms what would be "symbolic" as distinct from "romantic." At one point, for instance, Hegel describes how the symbolic artist "strives to imagine . . . a meaning for the shape" (A 440), thus following his concept of the symbolic as a figure whose "idea" is indeterminate. But in the same sentence he describes the symbolic artist as struggling "to imagine a shape for the meaning" (440), thus linking him to the greater inwardness of the romantic artist, who has an idea but cannot embody it in the discourses available to him.

Hegel's lectures are the conflicted transcript of a process in which the very nature of art and judgment are being rethought. His ambivalence to the symbolic can be traced to his desire for an art based on classical perfection as the paraesthetic support for synthetic judgments and for an alliance between art, reason, and the state. But his reservations about the symbolic also come from an almost opposite direction, reflecting his commitment to a critical aesthetics, and his sense that the symbolic is an inadequate embodiment of that aesthetic, whose essence is itself inadequacy. On one level, then, the symbolic is condemned for its "deficiency" and "indeterminacy," but on another level it is not deficient enough and claims a premature positivity.

Hegel's complex attitude toward the claims of negativity and positivity can be traced through his revision of Creuzer, whose *Symbolik und Mythologie* (1810) had made the "symbol" an object of cultural competition by transposing it into comparative religion.[26] Johann Wolfgang von Goethe and Schelling distinguish between symbols as the manifestation of the universal in the particular, and allegory as their separation. Hegel's own use of "symbol" is almost the opposite, but is mediated by Creuzer in two ways. To begin with, Creuzer associates the symbolic as the presencing of the infinite in the finite with India, thus explaining why Hegel (in contrast to Schelling) makes the symbolic the earliest phase of art. Second, Creuzer distinguishes two kinds of symbol: "plastic" and "mystic," corresponding to the beautiful and the sublime or the classical and the romantic. Though he wants the aura of symbol for both forms, he verges on deconstructing the traditional concept, by conceding in the "mystic" symbol a mutual inadequacy of form and content, an excess or lack absent from the more conventional "plastic" symbol.

The *Aesthetics* reworks Creuzer in conflicting ways. By defining the symbol as malformed, Hegel takes aim at the prestige conferred by Creuzer on oriental culture. Yet Creuzer is not the only one to discuss symbol, which is not used only with reference to the East. Thus it is just as likely that Hegel's target is the *concept* of symbol, of art as the presentation or *Darstellung* of the Idea.[27] Since this concept for Hegel is represented by classicism, on the level of *discourse* he upholds its privilege. Yet his demotion of the signifier "symbolic" to a (presyn)thetic phase of art is a *figure* for the deconstruction of an incarnational aesthetics, prefiguring his deconstruction of presence through the romantic.

As important, Creuzer despite himself had disclosed in the *symbol* tensions seminal for Hegel, which is why the term retains an originary privilege in the *Aesthetics*. In Creuzer's symbol there is already an " 'indeterminacy' as between essence and form" or "an 'excess' (*Überfulle*) of content as compared with its expression."[28] This excess is at odds with the manifestation of spirit in nature figured in the plastic symbol, thus leading Creuzer to the supplementary notion of the mystical symbol. For Hegel the symbolic is thus the aporia between these forms, a confusion of mystic with plastic—a confusion that Hegel seeks to transcend through the romantic. Moreover, this ambiguity of the symbol is already present in Goethe, who links the distinction between symbol and allegory to the difference between ideas and concepts. In allegory "the concept [is] captured definite and complete in the image," but in symbol the "idea remains infinitely powerful and unattainable in the image."[29] Hegel, it would seem, denies the symbol as *Darstellung*, but retains its mystic link to ideas.

Hegel's fascination with the symbolic thus has to do with a negativity that Creuzer uncovers but fails to theorize. This unrecognized negativity is at the heart of Hegel's criticism of oriental art, which we can approach through Kant's analysis of the relation between sublimity and visibility as traced through the distinction between the dynamic and the mathematical sublime. In a passage Hegel cites, Kant explains that the physical presentation of the sublime (as in a raging ocean) is merely "horrible" (CJ 84), because it violates the nature of the sublime as what Hegel calls an "invisible meaning without shape" that has no adequate objective correlative in phenomena (A 363). Kant goes on to argue that unlike the true or dynamic sublime, the physical sublime is merely mathematical, involving an immense but measurable magnitude (CJ 86–89). As a result the sublime is not to be found either in art or nature but only in the mind (91, 95). Hegel's condemnation of symbolic forms such as the grotesque that involve a hyperactive visual surface has its source in these comments by Kant, and despite its Eurocentric motivation, it is also generated by a philosophical argument against visibility as the premature foreclosure of negativity. Indeed his valorizing of the romantic as the inwardness of the Idea continues Kant's critique of the attempt to posit the absolute in phenomena through a subreption or premature positivity that Hegel also finds in the symbolic. This deconstruction of positivity is pervasive in the *Aesthetics*: in the privileging of literature and music over sculpture, and in the negation of the idealist concept of art as *Darstellung* through the rewriting of the term *symbolic*.

Yet the situation is not so simple, for Hegel locates the sublime in the symbolic and not the *romantic* phase, there being two kinds of symbolic art: the "positive" art of India and Persia and the "negative" art of the sublime (A 364). One could argue that by localizing the sublime in the oriental Hegel contains the threat posed to *Bildung* by a category Kant does not restrict historically. But this is to ignore the symptomatic significance of identifying the symbolic with the sublime, and thus metonymically associating even its more positive forms with the projects of reason and freedom. The division of the symbolic has two consequences. It blurs the boundary between the symbolic and romantic: the sublime-symbolic is already romantic, thus making the "romantic" an excuse for recuperating an art Hegel is required to condemn within the discourse of his time. But as important, this division points to a major difference between Kant and Hegel, who after all criticizes the "infinite absolute negativity" of romantic irony as comprising only "*one element* in the speculative Idea" (69). The Idea for Hegel is not transcendental, not removed from culture, formation, and thus "error." The fascination of the symbolic lies precisely in its confusion of negativity with positivity.

Ostensibly the romantic corrects the symbolic. Its Idea is determined and "free" where the symbolic Idea is still indeterminate and open to reflection. Moreover, the romantic mode of signification is purely mystical, where the symbolic forces what cannot be expressed into plastic form, thus conveying the negativity of the Idea through a form that is deformed, disabled from being identical with itself. There is no question that the romantic is more aesthetic than the symbolic and lends itself more easily to judgment. Yet the romantic also "fails" for the simple reason that art must present the Idea sensuously "and not in the form of thinking and pure spirituality" (A 72). As pure inwardness the romantic "still needs an external medium for its expression," and must be judged defective if it resists this exteriority that would, however, compromise its freedom. Put differently, the romantic "reverts, even if in a higher way" to the problem posed by the symbolic (79). This problem involves a disparity between Subjective and Objective spirit, a resistance of the first to being subsumed into the second on the way to Absolute spirit. Hegel gets out of this problem through the deus ex machina of the end of art. But this liquidation of a cultural form that has preoccupied him for a thousand pages can be no more than an imaginary resolution of underlying contradictions. Thus the problem of "difference and opposition" posed by the symbolic remains Hegel's legacy to us and a "sign" for the future.

V

Through the symbolic and romantic Hegel inscribes a space for an art that he is compelled to judge defective in terms of his own determination that "the highest" art unites "Idea and presentation" (A 79, 74). Yet by his own standards this art is not defective, since "defectiveness of *form* results from defectiveness of *content*" (74), so that symbolic forms are indeed expressions of their content. As Hegel himself concedes, such forms are deficient only in "beauty," but in terms of adequacy "the specific shape which every content of the Idea gives to itself in the particular forms of art is always adequate to that content" (300). An art in which "meaning and shape present, equally with their affinity, their mutual externality, foreignness, and incompatibility" (300) poses an obstacle to judgment, because it is difficult to have a unified conception either of the artwork or of the criteria that a successful judgment would reinforce. Such art remains troublesome as late as Virginia Woolf, who complains that the cultural constraints on women writers introduce "distortion[s]" that are unaesthetic.[30] At the same time such distortions have been seminal for certain kinds of feminist criticism that believe that the work on form, the deformation of form, is more crucial than its formation. Such criticism often focuses on affect as a strategy of dis-figuration by which the artwork resists socio-aesthetic standards of "adequacy." In this emphasis on disfiguration, it takes up what is also at issue in the structural deformations uncovered by a Marxist criticism that reinscribes history as a negative dialectic.

But the challenge posed to aesthetics by material that resists judgment is faced long before by Kant and Hegel. While Kant deals with this material only in nature, Hegel confronts it as an aspect of culture. He thus casts in doubt the very notions of *Bildung* and (self-)development contained in models of "aesthetic education" as a form of governmentality designed to produce the "synthesis" of Subjective and Objective spirit. The *Aesthetics* indeed fails to produce such "education." For the radical consequences for taste of saying that aesthetic shapes are always adequate to their content can hardly be overemphasized. In the *Aesthetics* "deficiency" and the "dissociation . . . of meaning and shape" border on being valorized, and require that we invent new standards of judgment.

At the heart of these standards is the issue of *freedom*, a recurrent term in the *Aesthetics* that follows a larger oscillation between Enlightenment and Romanticism first figured in the difference between the beautiful and the sublime. On the one hand, freedom is associated with clarity and self-identity. Symbolic art is not free because spirit is "not yet inwardly clear to itself" but is overdetermined by factors it neither understands nor controls (A 352). Classical art, by contrast, is a "free totality" in which content has found an adequate shape such that the artwork "display[s] in its existence nothing but itself" (427, 431). The classical artist is a "clear-headed man" who "*knows* what he wills*," "*can* accomplish" it, and is not "unclear about the meaning and the substantial content which he intends to shape outwardly" (438). On the other hand, classical freedom is allied with the state in a way that is reflected in the precedence of the signified over the signifier. The classical artist receives his "content" as "cut and dried," so that his work consists "only" of "reproduc[ing]" what is "already present in the creeds and . . . religious ideas" of his culture (439). For this reason the very adequacy of the classical proves inadequate as Hegel seeks for "absolute freedom" through the romantic: subjectivity "withdraw[s] into itself because in the previous shapes it can no longer find its adequate reality, [but] has to be filled with the content of a new spiritual world of absolute freedom and infinity" and seek "new forms of expression for this deeper content" (442).

That the judgment of form raises social issues is far clearer in Hegel than in Kant. Because the classical artist inherits a content decided by "national faith [and] myth," he is "free" to concentrate on the rhetoric of fiction in the service of Objective spirit. The symbolic artist is caught in a more organic disintegration of form and content. He "tosses about in a thousand forms," and his imagination "runs riot without proportion and definition" as it "adapt[s] to the meaning sought the shapes that ever remain alien" (A 439). Though Hegel's specific judgments of symbolic excess are classically dismissive, more important is his introduction of a new metasignifying possibility. Through the symbolic he creates a space for art as an intuition without definite shape, or for art as a "shape" that has meaning, "yet without being able to express it perfectly" (372).

This possibility of signification without representation is also present in Kant, who locates in the aesthetic a genotextual excess that allows mind to think, "in an undeveloped way," more than is "comprehended in a concept and . . . a definite form of words" (CJ 159). But Hegel adds a historical dimension to Kant's acceptance of the unformed as material for judgment, by allowing us to judge such art nonsynthetically because it is still in process. The "incompatibility of Idea and shape" (77) in the symbolic reflects an overdetermination that makes it necessary to deal with what Fredric Jameson calls "the form of content" and the "content of form." In other words the artwork cannot be approached in straightforwardly expressive terms, but must be understood in terms of what it does not say: through the philosophical assumptions "sedimented" in a form that indicates something different from the content, or through the deformation of content by the structural and syntactic shape it assumes.[31] This deformation does not derive from a lack of technical skill but reflects the "restless fermentation" and "labour" of a consciousness still involved in "producing its content and making it clear to itself" (CJ 438). As a result symbolic representations, though meant to be "expositions of the content remain themselves only enigmas and problems" (438). They are temporary narrativizations of a cultural unconscious that is unreadable but is also the dialectical desire that produces history.

Hegel does not valorize the symbolic but returns to it in the guise of the romantic. His privileging of the romantic has to do with its greater freedom from the ideology of existing shapes. But its "infinite subjectivity" (A 79) is also at odds with his emphasis on the objective, which should attract him not to the withdrawal of meaning from shape but to their "battle" (332). Perhaps the new forms of judgment for which Hegel is a "sign" are to be found in the space *between* the symbolic and the romantic. On the one hand, the romantic artist is superior because he withdraws from the discourses embedded in existing shapes into the clarity of a free resistance, where his symbolic counterpart remains at the mercy of his material, his imagination deformed by what it cannot form. On the other hand, the symbolic artist works on content at the material site of forms. This positivity, which Hegel criticizes, often results in a "bad and untrue determinacy" in which the reflective potential of the dissonance between "Idea and shape" is prematurely foreclosed (76–77).

But though symbolic art is often limited by this bad determinacy, it possesses an indeterminacy that allows for the further development of the Idea. Indeed its premature determinacy is no more than what Jameson calls a "symbolic resolution": a temporary masking of contradictions without which negativity could not be invested in the work of history. As against these positings, the wrenching apart of meaning and shape maintains the negativity of art, by deferring any hypostasis of the Idea through mimesis and beauty. This tension between positivity and negativity makes Hegel's work the pre-text for a uniquely romantic cultural idealism. The possibilities of this idealism *after* Hegel; its relation as an idealism of Subjective spirit to an idealism of Objective spirit that also derives from Hegel and results in what Georg Simmel calls the "tragedy of culture;" and the relation of both idealisms to cultural materialism and cultural studies, are subjects of another essay.[32] Let me only say in conclusion that what emerges beyond Hegel is an "idealism" in two senses: it deals with the material at the level of its form(ation), and it does not approach the history of rationality purely at the level of governmental, technological, and economic structures. Yet it is far from just an idealism in having the material as its object; and it is finally romantic in its disintegration, except at a phantasmatic level, of any "absolute" knowledge or absolute idealism.

Notes

1. Slavoj Žižek, *Tarrying with the Negative: Kant, Hegel, and the Critique of Ideology* (Durham: Duke University Press, 1993), 19–21, 30. Much earlier and quite differently, Karl Rosenkranz had also emphasized the proximity of Immanuel Kant and G. W. F. Hegel in "Introduction to Hegel's *Encyclopedia of the Philosophical Sciences*," trans. Tom Davidson, *Journal of Speculative Philosophy* 5 (1871): 238–43.

2. Kant, *Critique of Judgment*, trans. J. H. Bernard (New York: Hafner, 1974), 5, hereafter cited as CJ.

3. David Carroll, *Paraesthetics: Foucault, Lyotard, Derrida* (New York: Methuen, 1987), 176, hereafter cited as P. See also Jean-François Lyotard, "The Sign of History," in *The Lyotard Reader*, ed. Andrew Benjamin (Oxford: Basil Blackwell, 1989), 396, hereafter cited as S.

4. Lyotard, *Lessons on the Analytic of the Sublime*, trans. Elizabeth Rottenberg (Stanford: Stanford University Press, 1994), 34, 31, hereafter cited as L.

5. Hegel, *Aesthetics: Lectures on Fine Art*, trans. T. M. Knox, 2 vols. (Oxford: Clarendon, 1975), 76–77; hereafter cited as A (pagination is continuous and not by vol.).

6. For more extensive discussion of the structural tensions in the *Aesthetics* see Tilottama Rajan, "Phenomenology and Romantic Theory: Hegel and the Subversion of Aesthetics," in *Questioning Romanticism*, ed. John Beer (Baltimore: Johns Hopkins University Press, 1995), 155–78.

7. Johann Gottfried Herder, *Selected Early Works, 1764–67*, trans. Ernest A. Menze with Michael Palma (University Park: Pennsylvania State University Press, 1992), 67.

8. For instance, in *Peregrinations: Law, Form, Event* (New York: Columbia University Press, 1988), Lyotard locates the sublimity of the French Revolution in its functioning as a *sign* that exceeds its presentation in a form, and in which the "idea of freedom" must be discerned across the monstrosity and "disorders" that disfigure it (41).

9. See Stanley Corngold, *The Fate of the Self: German Writers and French Theory* (New York: Columbia University Press, 1986), 206; Corngold, "Nietzsche's Moods," *Studies in Romanticism* 29:1 (1990): 72.

10. Karl Jaspers, *Kant*, trans. Ralph Manheim (New York: Harcourt, 1957), 46, hereafter cited as K.

11. Michael Inwood, *A Hegel Dictionary* (Oxford: Blackwell, 1992), 60.

12. Lyotard, *The Inhuman*, trans. Geoffrey Bennington and Rachel Bowlby (Stanford: Stanford University Press, 1991), 108–12.

13. Kant, *Critique of Pure Reason*, trans. J. M. D. Meiklejohn (London: Everyman, 1991), 117, hereafter cited as CPR.

14. Kant sees himself as providing a hermeneutic reading of Plato in which he "understand[s] him better than he understood himself" (ibid., 219)—a notion later picked up in the hermeneutics of F. A. Wolf and Friedrich Schleiermacher, as well as by Samuel Taylor Coleridge, who reads Kant as a post-Kantian in *Biographia Literaria* (1817).

15. Rodolphe Gasché, "Foreword: Ideality in Fragmentation," in Friedrich Schlegel, *Philosophical Fragments*, trans. Peter Firchow (Minneapolis: University of Minnesota Press, 1991), xiii.

16. "The Oldest Systematic Program of German Idealism," trans. Diana Behler, in *Philosophy of German Idealism,* ed. Ernst Behler (New York: Continuum, 1987), 161–62.

17. Kant, *Critique of Practical Reason* (1788), trans. Lewis White Beck (New York: Macmillan, 1956), 140–41.

18. Julia Kristeva, *Revolution in Poetic Language*, trans. Margaret Waller (New York: Columbia University Press, 1984), 86.

19. Gilles Deleuze, *Kant's Critical Philosophy* (1963), trans. Hugh Tomlinson and Barbara Habberjam (Minneapolis: University of Minnesota Press, 1984), xi–xii.

20. Friedrich Schiller, *On the Aesthetic Education of Man, In a Series of Letters,* trans. Reginald Snell (New York: Frederick Ungar, 1965), 28.

21. Jacques Derrida, *The Truth in Painting*, trans. Geoff Bennington and Ian McLeod (Chicago: University of Chicago Press, 1987), 42.

22. Corngold, "Error in Paul de Man," in *The Yale Critics: Deconstruction in America*, eds. Jonathan Arac, Wlad Godzich, and Wallace Martin (Minneapolis: University of Minnesota Press, 1987), 92–93.

23. Alois Riegl, *Questions of Style: Foundations for a History of Ornament* (1893), trans. Evelyn Kain (Princeton: Princeton University Press, 1992); Wilhelm Worringer, *Abstraction and Empathy: A Contribution to the Psychology of Style* (1910), trans. Michael Bullock (Cleveland: Meridian, 1967). I borrow the term *critical historians of art* from Michael Podro's book of that title (New Haven: Yale University Press, 1982). Podro sees Riegl as reacting against Hegel's Eurocentrism. On the other hand Margaret Iversen, in discussing the importance of Riegl as a forerunner of cultural criticism, takes a more complex view both of Hegel and his influence on Riegl (Iversen, *Alois Riegl: Art History and Theory* [Cambridge: MIT Press, 1993]).

24. To be sure the other for Hegel is always the signifier of an alterity within the same. But this said, Worringer naturalizes the disruptive elements in cultural otherness by articulating *positively* the reasons why oriental art is as it is. Riegl, who is more sensitive to unresolved elements in non-European art, interprets them teleologically in terms of Western art, even though he does give Eastern art an originary privilege. While this tendency derives from Hegel, Hegel's interest is precisely *in* the disruptive elements that Riegl sidesteps.

25. For elaboration see Tilottama Rajan, "In The Wake of Cultural Studies: Globalization, Theory, and the University," *Diacritics* (forthcoming).

26. Friedrich Creuzer, *Symbolik und Mythologie der altenvolkers, l ésonders die Griechen,* 4 vols. (rpt. Leipzig und Darmstadt: C. W. Leske, 1836–43), 4.530–35, 707).

27. For Hegel's attitude to *Darstellung* see Joseph G. Kronick, "Romance and the Prose of the World: Hegelian Reflections on Hawthorne and America," in *Theorizing American Literature: Hegel, the Sign, and Historys,* ed. Bainard Cowan and Joseph G. Kronick (Baton Rouge: Louisiana State University Press, 1991), 172–73, 176–77. For Hegel's critique of visibility see also Martin Jay, *Downcast Eyes: The Denigration of Vision in Twentieth-Century French Thought* (Berkeley: University of California Press, 1993), 109–10.

28. Martin Donougho, "Hegel & Creuzer: or, Did Hegel Believe in Myth?" in *New Perspectives on Hegel's Philosophy of Religion*, ed. David Kolb (Albany: State University of New York Press, 1992), 65.

29. Johann Wolfgang von Goethe, "Aphorisms on Art and Art History," in *German Aesthetic and Literary Criticism: The Romantic Ironists and Goethe*, ed. Kathleen Wheeler (Cambridge: Cambridge University Press, 1984), 229.

30. Virginia Woolf, "Women and Fiction," in *Collected Essays* (New York: Harcourt, 1950), 2:144.

31. Fredric Jameson, *The Political Unconscious: Narrative as a Socially Symbolic Act* (Ithaca: Cornell University Press, 1981), 242, 99.

32. Georg Simmel, "The Concept and Tragedy of Culture," in *Simmel on Culture*, ed. David Frisby and Mike Featherstone (London: Sage, 1997), 55–75.

Mediality in Hegel:
From Work to Text in the
Phenomenology of Spirit

Jochen Schulte-Sasse

In the "Earliest Program for a System of German Idealism," a two-page manuscript from 1796 that is in G. W. F. Hegel's handwriting but whose authorship is uncertain, the author or authors call(s) for "a new mythology." The manuscript stresses the crucial role that collective narratives—and institutionalized practices of reflecting on such narratives—play in the development of human culture. Myths as fables or legends embodying the convictions of a people require a "reading," a *legein* by a people—which amounts to saying that a mythology is more important than a myth. Thus the author insists that

> this mythology must serve ideas; it must become a mythology of *reason*. Until we make ideas aesthetic, that is, mythological, they are of no interest to the people and, conversely, until mythology is reasonable, the philosopher must be ashamed of it. Thus, in the end, enlightened and unenlightened must shake hands, mythology must become philosophical, and the people reasonable, and philosophy must become mythological in order to make philosophers sensuous.[1]

Metaphorically speaking, collective narratives—and their communal scrutiny—become indispensable in honing the human mind.

Whether or not Hegel authored the manuscript, he never abandoned the notion that texts—or more precisely, textual objectifications of the human spirit—are an indispensable medium for cultural development. The most obvious outcome of this understanding of human history is the series of readings he offers in the *Phenomenology of Spirit* of the works of philosophical predecessors. These serve him to represent the history of the human mind as a sequence of "formations of consciousness" or "formations of the world" that have as their remote purpose or goal "absolute knowing."

What is the status of this "absolute knowing"? I would argue that the projection or positing of such a goal amounts to no more than a problematic construction—a construction that is culturally and historically contingent. Absolute knowing is the necessary, yet never reachable end of a historical process in which humans try to comprehend everything there is to comprehend. Or, as Michael N. Forster put it, "in Hegel's view, the Absolute's essential accomplishment of self-knowledge is identical with the historical process of human subjects progressing toward that knowledge of the nature of the Absolute expressed in Hegelian Science."[2]

Hegel's projection of an inaccessible goal of human development is influenced by Hölderlin's notion of being. For Friedrich Hölderlin, "being" is an existential being, a "feeling" of our existence that *precedes* judgments and therefore cannot be turned into a content of consciousness; it is simply a presupposition that we necessarily have to take for granted if we want to account for the unity of our self-consciousness not only before it divides itself, that is, separates itself into the duality of subject and object, I and Non-I, but also as it makes judgments. Hegel turns Hölderlin's "being" from something that precedes judgments into something that structures them as a *Finalidee*, the "idea of an end." Both Hegel and Hölderlin liked to argue that the homophony, in German, of judgment (*Urteil*) and arch- or primal separation (*Ur-teilung*) has philosophical bearing.[3] As Hegel put it in the Berlin *Encyclopedia*: "The etymological meaning of judgment in our language is richer; it expresses (or reveals) the initial unity of the concept and the latter's differentiation as original/initial separation, which is precisely what judgment is. . . ."[4] Hegel, however, drew different conclusions from this proposition. In reflection, which finds its expression in judgment(s) (*Urteile*) that are the result of arch-separations (*Ur-teilungen*), a request or call for (achieving) unity survives. That is, before its arch-separation "being" cannot be subjected to the thinking of an "I" as Non-I *unless* we turn it into a *Finalidee*. Like "absolute knowing," the unity of our self-consciousness, or identity, is for Hegel an ideal, a *Finalidee* that we only can approach in endless approximations. In other words: for Hegel, as for Hölderlin, we feel or experience a being or prereflexive unity of a self that we lose or leave behind in acts of judgment that are equivalent to an "arch-separation" of the prereflexive unity of ourself. Hegel, however, differs from Hölderlin in one crucial aspect: As an effect of this "arch-separation," the prereflexive unity of ourself turns for Hegel into an ideal which, in reality, is unattainable and unrealizable. "Being" in Hölderlin's sense provides Hegel with the motif, the driving force for an infinite striving, an infinite effort to appropriate or procure the same unity of our being that we previously (prereflexively) experienced in the form of a feeling. Yet the "being" of ourselves that we experience in the form of a *sentiment de l'existence* (Jean-Jacques Rousseau) is simultaneously, from the perspective of knowledge or thought, always and necessarily a missed being.

Is Hegel the antiromantic he is usually taken to be? I would hold that this is, particularly in regard to the similarity of the Hegelian and the romantic projects, inaccurate. The intellectual agendas of both German Idealism and Jena Romanticism were shaped between 1794 and 1796 by the same philosophical debates at the University of Jena where nearly all the Romantics and Idealists were then gathered. Hegel, who did not study at Jena at the time, nonetheless corresponded regularly with several of Jena's students and teachers, above all with Hölderlin.[5] It is, therefore, no coincidence that Novalis's (Friedrich von Hardenberg's) resolution to the problem approximates the one Hegel will eventually reach. Novalis, a very active member of the Jena discussion group, wrote in his "Fichte-Studies" of 1795–96:

> What do I do when I philosophize? I reflect upon a ground. . . . Thus all philosophizing must end at an absolute ground. If such a ground were not given, if this concept contained an impossibility, then the drive to philosophize would be an infinite activity. Thus it would be without end, because there would be an eternal need for an absolute ground, which could only be satisfied to a relative degree and therefore would never cease. Through the voluntary renunciation of the absolute, infinite and free activity arises within us. This activity is the only possible absolute that can be given to us and that we find through our inability to reach and to recognize an absolute. We can only recognize this given absolute negatively, by acting and finding that we cannot reach what we are searching for through any action. . . . This could be called an absolute postulate. Any search for *a single principle* would be like an attempt to find the square of a circle. . . . Reason would be the capability of positing and retaining such an absolute object. Understanding that is stretched by the imagination. . . . The I signifies that negatively recognizable absolute which remains after all abstraction, which can only be recognized through action and which manifests itself through eternal lack.[6]

"Truth," for Hegel, is a fundamentally relative concept, that is, it is relative
to a given "formation of consciousness." In German, he plays with the partial
homophony of *Wahrheit* (truth) and *wahrnehmen* (to perceive). We may perceive only those truths whose recognition is possible in a given episteme.
Hegel, however, clearly believes in the possibility of epistemological progress.
This belief raises a crucial question: If humans share a desire for knowledge
or truth, and if such a desire shapes history, what, then, propels historical
advancements in knowledge? Hegel answers with a complex argument to
which I cannot do justice in a short essay. I would like to emphasize, however, that—according to Hegel—there have been several moments in the history
of humanity where the development of culture might have come to an un-
timely end if things had taken a different turn. For Hegel, there is no *causa
finalis*, no telos, of human culture except those teloi that humans project
themselves. The self-generated ends of culture anchor the latter in a process
of self-formation. Charles Taylor captured this quality thus: "There is something in Hegel's philosophy which is irresistibly reminiscent of Baron
Münchhausen. The baron, it will be remembered, after falling from his horse
in a swamp, extricated himself by seizing his own hair and heaving himself
back on his horse."[7] Taylor says this about "Hegel's God," whom he sees as
"a Münchhausen God." If, as Taylor does, one reads Hegel's God as a cosmic
subject whose vehicle is Man, then the Münchhausen analogy is certainly
illuminating. By positing ends, humans—according to Hegel—pull themselves out of a swamp by their own hair and place themselves back on the
horse, that is, turn themselves—albeit in the unwitting service of a cosmic
subject—into the steeds of history.

We've touched here on an aspect of Hegel's understanding of the human
mind's movement in history that makes his argument baffling to many. Even if
the projection of a state of absolute knowing onto an end of history is no more
than a problematic construct, a *Finalidee* guiding the self-formation of individuals and cultures, this conjecture forces Hegel to posit an "objective Spirit,"
a "cosmic subject" in whose process of self-realization humans serve as means
to a higher end. For Hegel, this is an unavoidable premise, no matter how
"impossible" it is. But is such a premise really that gratuitous?

In trying to articulate the nature of the hermeneutical circle, the literary
critic Paul de Man once wrote that we always have to act as if we already
possess "a certain degree of understanding"—even before we start reading;

> without it, no contact could be established with a foreknowledge that
> it can never reach, but of which it can be more or less lucidly
> aware. . . . The hermeneutic understanding is always, by its very
> nature, lagging behind: to understand something is to realize that
> one had always known it, but, at the same time, to face the mystery

of this hidden knowledge. Understanding can be called complete only when it becomes aware of its own temporal predicament and realizes that the horizon within which the totalization can take place is time itself. The act of understanding is a temporal act that has its own history; but this history forever eludes totalization.[8]

There can be no understanding without a projected or anticipated completion of the process of understanding; and yet this completion or totalization of understanding, as unconditionally atemporal, remains forever outside of time, whereas understanding itself cannot exceed time. Hence, what cannot exceed time remains dependent on something outside time.

Hegel often addressed de Man's temporal predicament as the hermeneutical paradox of purposive action, for instance, in a paragraph that precedes the central passages on the mediality of the artifact (*das Werk*; i.e., "the work produced") by just a few pages:

> an individual cannot know what he [really] is until he has made himself a reality through action. However, this seems to imply that he cannot determine the *End* of his action until he has carried it out; but at the same time, since he is a *conscious* individual, he must have the action in front of him beforehand as *entirely his own*, i.e. as an *End*. The individual who is going to act seems, therefore, to find himself in a circle in which each moment already presupposes the other, and thus he seems unable to find a beginning, because he only gets to know his original nature, which must be his End, from the deed, while, in order to act, he must have that End beforehand. (PS ¶ 401: 240)[9]

The paradox that de Man and Hegel address could be called a necessary surplus or excess both of understanding and purposive action—a surplus or excess which, although eluding understanding, is always involved in—is always part of—any understanding that deserves its name and any purposive action that is guided by a *Finalidee*.

One might better grasp the epistemological nature of this excess or surplus, as well as its relation to Hegel's notion of absolute knowledge, by applying the hermeneutical argument to politics. Totalization in relation to understanding, or the End in relation to human action, corresponds to eternity in relation to politics.[10] As the necessarily timeless exteriority to time, eternity is a political category; that is, the idea of a timeless exteriority to time is productive of historical consciousness, and thus of history. Phenomenologically, "eternity" is the name of the presence of a future in a present that is conceived in terms of a future. Without an idea of time's timeless exteriority, politics would be impossible. Just as the anticipation of a timeless *End* temporalizes historical time, the anticipation of an absolute knowing makes advances in knowledge possible. (This, incidentally, is the point in Hegel's discourse at which the term *desire* becomes indispensable: desire, as defined by the presence of an absence, drives or motivates human action.)

Ultimately, the notion of an "absolute knowing" and its correlated notion of a "world spirit" as an exterior excess or surplus of history allow Hegel to ascertain a notion of human agency as self-originating (thus Hegel's concept of *Bildung* as a concept of self-formation or self-cultivation). His notion of human agency as self-originating, in turn, allows him to establish a notion of the self-formation and self-grounding of human cultures.

If this outline of absolute knowing as a guiding ideal is accurate, that is, if the human mind's movement in history is supposed to find its completion in a process of self-grounding, then Hegel (1) needs a notion of (individual and collective) self, and (2) he needs to consider the possibility of human agency as unconditioned.

The argument Hegel offers in regard to the first point is straightforward, a few aspects of which can lay the ground for a more extensive discussion of the second point. Hegel develops a notion of human agency and, thus, of self, according to which a self-conscious "I" is the point of origin of independent reflection and action. However, he does not equate self-consciousness with identity or self-sameness. For him, the self-consciousness required for selfhood is essentially an activity or process. Hegel's self always distinguishes itself from itself (he takes the term *self-consciousness* literally); as a process, self-consciousness is a reflection into itself that never reaches a point of rest. As Jean Hyppolite put it, "the I of self-consciousness is not, properly speaking, a being. As a being it would fall back into the milieu of subsistence [immediacy]. But it is what for-itself negates itself and for-itself preserves itself in that self-negation."[11] In this sense, Hegel speaks of consciousness as the "absolute dialectical unrest" (PS ¶ 205: 124). Subjectivity accordingly designates an everlasting process of reflecting oneself into oneself and repelling oneself from oneself. It is a process in which the subject, by reflecting on itself as an object, vacillates between being subject and object. When the self-conscious subject reflects itself into itself, it partially severs its links with the world, thus establishing itself as a subject vis-à-vis the world. Self-consciousness is thus characterized by an inner duality; in Hyppolite's words: "this duality of living self-consciousness becomes the splitting and reproduction of self-consciousness within itself."[12]

If the I of self-consciousness is the transitory result of an effort that must be incessantly reinitiated, then human agency is not immediate, that is, it cannot be thought of as unconditioned in and for itself. I shall argue that—according to Hegel—the development of self-forming, self-directed individuals—and thus of self-forming, self-directed cultures—is inherently dependent upon texts as objectifications of the human spirit. In its analysis of the dialectical interaction between human cultures and textual objectifications of the human spirit (*Geist*), the *Phenomenology* may be considered a foundational book of the humanities.

Once a particular stage has been reached in the historical development of "formations of consciousness," their further development comes to depend upon certain means or media. Hegel's argument regarding the significance of mediality begins with his discussion of the notion of work in the famous chapter on the master-slave, or lordship-bondage, dialectic. The slave negates his dependence on, and ties to, the world through his work, objectifying or externalizing himself in his work and, by mirroring himself in his work; this mirroring of himself in his work permits a process of self-discovery. Work initiates the reflection of the self into itself by means of the exteriorization of a "form," "something permanent."

> Through work . . . the bondsman becomes conscious of what he truly is. . . . Work . . . is desire held in check, fleetingness staved off; in other words, work forms and shapes the thing. The negative relation to the object becomes its *form* and something *permanent*, because it is precisely for the worker that the object has independence. . . . It is in this way, therefore, that consciousness, *qua* worker, comes to see in the independent being [of the object] its *own* independence. . . . Through this rediscovery of himself by himself, the bondsman realizes that it is precisely in his work wherein he seemed to have only an alienated existence that he acquires a mind of his own. (PS ¶¶ 195–96: 118f.)

A sense of "selfhood" or identity, the prerequisite for human agency, requires independence: the slave finds (relative) independence by reflecting on, and seeing himself reflected in, the work or artifact he has made. While "work" is *Arbeit* (labor) in German, not the etymologically related *Werk* (the result of labor, as in a "work of art"), it is clear that already in these two paragraphs Hegel displaces the accent from work as procedure to work as object.

From the discussion of lordship and bondage (which starts in PS ¶ 178), to the very last paragraph, (¶ 805), Hegel elaborates his notion of work in numerous paragraphs; and in this process of elaboration, the expanded meaning of "work" increasingly embraces textual characteristics. The most relevant passages on "work" happen to be roughly in the middle of the *Phenomenology* (¶¶ 405–10). Right before the first crucial paragraph on "work" in this segment of the *Phenomenology*, he writes: "He [the individual] can have only the consciousness of the simple transference [*Übersetzung*, literally "translation"] of himself from the night of possibility into the daylight of the present, from the abstract in-itself into the significance of actual being, and can have only the certainty that what happens to him in the latter is nothing else but what lay dormant in the former" (¶ 404: 242). *Übersetzung* alludes to the positing or *Setzen* of a Non-I by an I; Hegel often uses the prefix *über-* to articulate an increasing complexity of an initial, two-dimensional procedure.[13] *Übersetzung* thus conveys the move from a simple positing of an object to a more complex process within which the posited object acts on consciousness and, in turn, a transformed consciousness refines its comprehension of the world—a positing to the nth degree, so to speak. In other words, the positing of a *Finalidee* is an *Übersetzen,* a surplus positing of a guiding principle, which allows us to transform ourselves "from the night of possibility into the daylight of the present"; that is, to actualize ourselves on the basis of projects or projections. However, the subject is never substance in the sense that it is able to act solely on its own. The transformation of consciousness "from the night of possibility into the daylight of the present" requires a medium capable of catalyzing the evolution of consciousness—an enzyme of the cognitive process, so to speak. As Maurice Blanchot put it in reference to this passage of the *Phenomenology,* the writer's "work is alive only if that night—and no other—becomes day, if what is most singular about him and farthest removed from existence as already revealed now reveals itself with shared existence."[14]

The *Phenomenology* embeds this abstract assessment of the exteriorization of the human mind in a theory of modernization. Hegel argues that in early modernity the human subject "discovers the world as *its* new real world, which in its permanence holds an interest for it which previously lay only in its [the world's] transiency; for the *existence* of the world becomes for self-consciousness its own *truth* and *presence*; it is certain of experiencing only itself therein" (PS ¶ 232: 140). According to Hegel, humans in modernity reorient their interest, or gaze, from the vertical (the beyond) to the horizontal (the project of a secular society, of the modern state). In the *Phenomenology,* the transcendent undergoes a more radical transformation into a world-immanent project or objective than in any previous philosophy. The reorientation of the human gaze from the vertical to the horizontal, this positing of a project or objective, is a prerequisite for reason to assume a primary role in human history. For in the object of a this-worldly beyond, an *Entwurf,* "in which it [consciousness] finds that its own action and being, as being that of this *particular* consciousness, are being and action *in themselves*, there has arisen for consciousness the idea of *Reason*, of the certainty that, in its particular individuality, it has being absolutely *in itself*, or is all reality" (¶ 230: 138). Only a subject that at once is reflected into itself and oriented toward a goal or objective is capable of reasonable action. The concerted actions of multiple reasoned subjects lead, in the dimensions of time and space, to the formation of social institutions.

As far as I can see, Blanchot, in his essay "Literature and the Right to Death," is the only reader of the *Phenomenology* thus far to notice the gradual textualization of Hegel's concept of work and to see, moreover, the connection between the subject's reflection of itself into itself and its ability to posit ends that may serve as guiding principles of its action:

> If we see work as the force of history, the force that transforms man while it transforms the world, then a writer's activity must be recognized as the highest form of work. When a man works, what does he do? He produces an object. That object is the realization of a plan which was unreal before then: it is the affirmation of a reality different from the elements which constitute it and it is the future of new objects, to the extent that it becomes a tool capable of creating other objects. . . . These objects, which I have produced by changing the state of things, will in turn change me. . . . Thus is history formed, say Hegel and [Karl] Marx—by work which realizes being in denying it, and reveals it at the end of the negation. . . . But what is a writer doing when he writes? Everything a man does when he works, but to an outstanding degree. . . . this other thing—the book—of which I had only an idea and which I could not possibly have known in advance, is precisely myself become other.[15]

~

I would now like to show in more detail how Hegel's theory of modernization centers on the idea that, for culture to progress and for individuals to gain reflective independence from historically established structures, individual consciousnesses (a) must externalize themselves in "readable" artifacts and (b) must "read" the precipitates of other consciousnesses, namely of human culture.

From ¶ 405 on Hegel shifts the emphasis of his argument more and more from labor (*"Arbeit"*) to the result of labor (*Werk*; the English translation tries to circumvent the ambivalence of "work" by distinguishing the "work produced" from "work"): "The work produced is the reality [*Realität*] which consciousness gives itself; it is that in which the individual is explicitly for himself what he is implicitly or in himself, and in such a manner that the consciousness, for which the individual becomes explicit in his work, is not the particular, but the universal, consciousness" (PS ¶ 405: 242). In everyday German, *Realität* and *Wirklichkeit* have the same meaning. Not so in Hegel. When Hegel uses *Wirklichkeit*, he plays with the etymological and semantic allusion to *wirken* in *Wirklichkeit*; *wirken* means to "have an effect," to "operate." A. V. Miller's English translation usually renders *Wirklichkeit* as "actuality." If Hegel uses reality in the sense of *Realität* here, he obviously does not yet think of the work as a reality that affects the individual. The "work produced is the reality which consciousness gives itself"; that is, it is only *gesetzt* (posited), not yet *übersetzt* (affecting consciousness in return). However, whenever the work instigates a process of reception or reflection in which consciousness becomes for-itself what it is [without the work] in-itself, that is, whenever the work increases consciousness's self-awareness, this work assumes the role of an essential mediator. For Hegel, for-itself (*für sich*) indicates a process of recognition, of becoming reflexively aware of something. The contrast between "for-itself" and "in-itself" is the same as between actuality and potentiality (The translator tried to indicate this by adding "explicitly" to "for himself" and "implicitly" to "in himself"; neither adverb appears in the German text). If the "work produced" helps the individual to turn his or her potentiality into actuality, it takes on an indispensable task in the formation of the individual.

Hegel emphasizes the point that individuality expresses itself in the work produced in such a way that the work mediates a universal, not a particular, consciousness. "In his work, he has placed himself altogether in the element of universality, in the quality-less void of being" (PS ¶ 405: 242f.). In the original, "in the quality-less void of being" reads: *in den bestimmtheitslosen Raum des Seins hinausgestellt*. The translation of *bestimmtheitslos* as "quality-less" is misleading. *Bestimmt* suggests "conditioned" or "determinate" in the sense of being part of a structure whose relations determine the nature of its elements. Hegel was—at least to some extent—a structuralist in the modern sense. He called the elements within a structure "the conditioned" and was convinced that claims to knowledge are possible only if an unconditioned exists. It would thus be more accurate to translate *bestimmtheitslosen Raum des Seins* with "conditionless [or unconditioned] space of being." And indeed, the *Phenomenology* equates "universality" with such a "condition-less space of being." If individuals can acquire a "universal consciousness" in the medium of a work, this means that their interaction with a work permits them to detach themselves from their determinations. Ultimately, a work allows an individual to become absolute, a word that derives, in English or German, "from the Latin *absolutus* ('loosened, detached, complete') the past participle of *absolvere* ('to loosen [from], to detach, to complete'), and thus means: 'not dependent on, [not] conditional on, [not] relative to or restricted by anything else; self-contained, perfect, complete.' "[16]

As previously noted, self-consciousness is a kind of vacillation between a self-sameness it can never fully reach and the splitting of that unity into subject and object. Self-consciousness repels itself from itself by splitting itself into subject and object, only to strive in turn to overcome its own division in an interminable reflection into itself. Heinrich Heine ironized this very double-bind in his inimitable style:

> The ego is supposed to reflect on its intellectual activities while performing them. Thought is supposed to spy upon itself while it thinks, while it gradually becomes warm, then warmer, and is finally cooked to a turn. This operation reminds us of the monkey sitting on the hearth in front of a copper kettle, cooking his own tail. For it was his opinion that true culinary art does not consist merely in the objective act of cooking but also in becoming subjectively aware of the process of cooking.[17]

For Hegel, human understanding would be impossible without such an oscillation between subject as subject and subject as object, for the relative independence a subject may gain vis-à-vis the objective world presupposes precisely such a process. In pondering the possibility of independent thinking, Hegel introduces the term *negativity* into modern thought. He speaks of the "tremendous power of the negative" (PS ¶ 32) in human thinking. Put simply, negation allows us to distinguish among things. As Diana Coole argues "The term negativity gains its most obvious sense from its opposition to the positive," since the positive "refers to those institutions—language, subjectivity, metaphysics, positivist knowledge as well as modes of production, state structures, social stratifications, modern culture—that have become reified, ossified, totalised."[18] If, however, negativity were no more than a capacity to distinguish, we might end up with unchangeable taxonomies or classifications (or the conditioned elements of a structure), which would make historical progress impossible. Once structures or taxonomies or cultural institutions had been accepted by a culture, there would be no way to transgress them. What is at stake, then, in the concept of negativity, is the entirety of the human capacity to rethink and rearrange taxonomies or structural arrangements (including their institutionalizations in the form of state apparatuses). Negativity's objective is not negation but negation squared, so to speak; it finds its destination in its performative activity rather than in the results of such activities, for instance, in something conceptually definable. Hence, to offer a definition of what negativity signifies would "be an enactment of the very stabilising, classifying logic that negativity is invoked to defy and which its practitioners reject."[19]

Negativity makes the infinite approximation of absolute knowing possible. As Coole puts it:

> thought, . . . eternally returning as knowledge, and material existence are endlessly imbricated and moved by an irrepressible negativity. Totalising and disintegration are always replayed, hence the infinity

> of the absolute. . . . Thus unity is "merely one moment of the pro-
> cess of disruption," an abstraction that cancels itself in excluding its
> other. Infinitude is not therefore rest, but the "absolute unrest of pure
> self-movement". . . . Unity is but a moment in the circulation of
> difference. . . . The dialectic is undecidable between identity and
> difference at this vanishing point.[20]

Negativity thus means our ability to make something fluid again, to look at something obliquely; it is a principle of generativity, a concept Hegel needed to be able to think a dynamics of becoming that transgresses closure and systematicity.

Significantly, Hegel conceives of the "tremendous power of the negative" not as an essential and independent quality of the human mind but as a process that involves a dialectic between the human mind and cultural artifacts; for to become operational, negativity requires a catalyst outside the human mind. (This is what, in my estimation, PS ¶¶ 405–10 are all about). The individual places himself in the element of universality by reflecting on his work—*Werk*, not *Arbeit*—and, on the basis of this reflection, reflects himself into himself, that is, into a "condition-less realm of being"; that is, into a being in which he, for a brief and unsustainable moment, frees himself from determinations: "The consciousness which withdraws from its work is, in fact, the universal consciousness in contrast to its work, which is determinate and particular—and it is universal because it is absolute negativity or action in this antithesis [*Gegensatz*]." (This quote and all nonreferenced subsequent quotes ¶ 405: 243.) Consciousness, by reflecting itself into itself, gains interpretative, reflexive, and speculative independence. "It thus goes beyond itself in the work"; that is, it transcends its particularity—or the particular content it has put into the work. Although by reflecting on its work the individual consciousness becomes a "condition-less void that is left unfilled by its work," its relation to the work remains nonetheless essential and indispensable. It steps back (not "withdraws," as the translation suggests) from the work produced while retaining it as the reference point of its reflection.

Hegel's thought concentrates on the apparent contradiction between (a) the work that, *qua existent* (*als seiendes,* that is, "as a work that exists by itself"), is "sublated" (preserved and eliminated) through reflection and (b) the work that "is supposed to *exist,*" so that it may become again and again the occasion, or starting point, for new reflections: "we have to see how in its [the work's] existence the individuality will preserve its universality, and will know how to satisfy itself."

Precisely because the work is the indispensable starting point and catalyst for an individual's movement toward "universality," that is, toward its reflexive independence from structures that otherwise determine it, its "being" becomes "itself an action in which all differences interpenetrate and are dissolved." Hegel describes the interface between the work produced and the reflecting mind in terms quite similar to the double movement of self-consciousness, namely, the mind's simultaneous reflection of itself into itself and repelling itself from itself. In producing its work, self-consciousness repels itself from itself by seeking a concrete expression of itself: "The work is thus expelled into an existence [*Bestehen*, i.e., "consistency"] in which the quality [*Bestimmtheit*, i.e., "determinateness" or "particularity," the opposite of its universality] of the original nature [of the individual] in fact turns against other determinate natures [of individuals], encroaches on them, and gets lost as a vanishing element in this general process." The German original for "encroaches on them" is *in sie eingreift wie diese anderen in sie,* that is, the consciousness that has externalized or objectified itself in a work intervenes (or interferes), qua work, in the specific opinions of other consciousnesses. However, this kind of intervention, of engaging in arguments with others, is possible only if individuals do not remain agonistic, or, in Hegel's terminology, particular [*bestimmt*, i.e., "conditioned by specific structures"], but habitually reflect themselves into themselves and, thus, swap their particularity with their universality. Here, "*within the Notion* of the objectively real individuality [*an und für sich selbst realen Individualität*] all the elements, circumstances, end, means, and realization, have the same value, and the original specific [*bestimmte*] nature has the value of no more than a universal element. . . . " Only "when this element becomes an objective being, its *specific character* [*Bestimmtheit*] as such comes to light in the work done, and obtains its truth in its dissolution" (translation slightly altered). For Hegel, "truth" indicates no more than the role or function performed by a particular thing in a particular context [cf. Hegel's word play with *Wahrnehmen* (perception) and *Wahrheit* (truth), i.e., what is true has to be perceived]. The "truth" of the work lies in its capacity to initiate a process of reflection in which the reader of a work abstracts from the particularity of a work, that is, dissolves its specific nature, and gains a state of universality: "More precisely, the form which this dissolution takes is that, in this specific character [*Bestimmtheit*], the individual, qua this particular individual, has become aware of himself as actual. . . ." The work is real (*real*), the individual in his or her universality actual (*wirklich*). Again, Hegel plays here with the etymology of *wirklich* by associating it with *wirken* (to have an effect).

In sum, it is striking that, from the chapter on Lordship and Bondage to the very last paragraph of the *Phenomenology*, Hegel moves from work as labor more and more to work as artifact, and from the producer of work more and more to the recipient of work (or more precisely: to the reader as a generic category that includes the producer after she has externalized her subjectivity in the form of work). The work becomes "merely an alien reality that is found given" [more precisely, "a found alien reality"]: "The work *is*, that is, it exists for other individualities, and is for them an alien reality, which these individualities must, in turn, replace by their own in order to obtain through *their* action the consciousness of *their* unity with reality; in other words, *their* interest in the work which stems from *their* original nature, is something different from this work's *own* peculiar interest, which is thereby converted into something different." (Translation has been modified slightly.)

Interestingly enough, in all three occurrences of "reality" in this passage Hegel uses *Wirklichkeit* in the original. Yet in his terminology, *Wirklichkeit* does not refer to something that exists objectively, but rather refers consistently, as noted, to something that has an effect. The artifact resulting from a process of externalization or objectification is not on the same level as that of a reality that has become fixed or inflexible; it is *Wirklichkeit* or actuality in the sense that it is the cause, or more precisely: the medium, of progress. Reflection needs a medium, which is provided in human culture by readable "externalizations." The German original for externalization is *Entäußerung.* Here again, Hegel plays with the phonetic materiality of the term in order to bring to light several subtexts of the term. First, *Entäußerung* harbors *Äußerung,* meaning "articulation," "utterance," "expression," or "pronouncement." Second, it suggests *außen* or "external." And finally, it is a synonym for renunciation or disposal. At the heart of the term's various subtexts is the oscillation between *Entäußerung* and *Äußerung,* "exteriorization" and "expression." In the process of cultural history, labor becomes *work*—a term whose German relative *Werk* more strongly suggests artifact. The German *Werk* generates no derivative like the English "worker"; only German *Arbeit* generates the *Arbeiter* (laborer).

Miller's English translation of the *Phenomenology* frequently overlooks the point that the German *Werk* signifies the objectified result of work, not the act of labor. For example the translation reads: "Consciousness, then, in doing its work, is aware of the antithesis of doing and being, which in the earlier shapes [*Gestalten*] of consciousness was at the same time the beginning of action, while here it is only a result" (PS ¶ 406: 244). "In doing its work" is in Hegel *in seinem Werke,* which clearly means "in its work [in the sense of artifact]." Only when we grasp the precise notion of work as objectified subjectivity in Hegel does the centrality of the concept of "work" become apparent. Without "the work" (Hegel often uses the definite article to indicate that he means the *result* of work), cultural progress becomes impossible. The centrality of the concept rests on the mediality of cultural artifacts. Consciousness becomes aware, in its *Werk,* of the opposition of doing and being precisely because of the fact that its "work," once *entäußert,* that is, expressed or articulated, becomes a medium of cultural change. When Hegel says that, in culturally developed formations of consciousness, the opposition of doing and being has become the result of doing, he clearly refers to what I am thus calling the "mediality of artifacts." The new quality of the work produced (*Werk*) in later "formations of consciousness" depends on a culture of reading in which that which can, or indeed must, be read initiates a dialectic between readable objects and reading subjects. This dialectic allows the latter to abstract from determinate and determining structures of the world and, as a result, to reflect freely on the existent. The work becomes, in its mediality, the precondition for nonconditioned reflection or, more generally, for freedom. However, in this process the text or artifact itself can never be transformed, through interpretation, into transparent or fixed meanings. There is always a leftover or surplus, a textual resistance that preserves the work in its mediality. As a catalyst for the movement of consciousness, for consciousness's coming into being, the artifact is like the grain of sand around which the pearl grows: it is an irritant that is never dissolved away. Hegel saw the nature of textuality clearly in a leftover that cannot be obliterated or confined historically except for accidental reasons like the destruction of an archive.

At the end of the *Phenomenology*, in the very last paragraph, Hegel calls history "a conscious, self-mediating process—Spirit emptied out into Time [*der an die Zeit entäußerte Geist*. . . .]" (PS ¶ 808: 492) The term he uses for this emptying-out of Spirit is again *Entäußerung* or "exteriorization" [*der an die Zeit entäußerte Geist*]. "This Becoming presents a slow-moving succession of Spirits, a gallery of images, each of which, endowed with all the riches of Spirit, moves thus slowly just because the Self has to penetrate and digest this entire wealth of its substance." The substance is the precipitate of the Spirit's self-development in the form of historical documents, be they religious or philosophical texts, art, cultural monuments, or social institutions. "As its fulfillment consists in perfectly *knowing* what *it is*, in knowing its substance, this knowing is its *withdrawal into itself* in which it abandons its outer existence and gives its existential shape over to recollection." "Withdrawal into itself" in German is *Insichgehen*, literally "to go into oneself," "to search one's conscience." In such a state, we leave our *Dasein* in the sense of determined existence behind and revive the meaning or Spirit of the archives of history. The documents, the monuments, the texts, in short the precipitates of Spirit in history are like a *Schädelstätte*, a place filled with skulls, or a Golgotha that remains dormant without being "*read*" in the broadest sense of the word. If interpretation revives such precipitates of Spirit, we discover that "The realm of Spirits which is formed in this way in the outer world constitutes a succession in Time in which one Spirit relieved another of its charge and each took over the empire of the world from its predecessor." Hegel's notion of textual externalization is thus not far removed from the romantic notion of a secularized bible or new mythology, a term he himself used in the "Earliest Program for a System of German Idealism."

In the same context, Hegel offers a justification of intellectual history, or intellectual historiography, including art history or the histories of philosophy, literature, religion, and so forth; in which he maintains that

> The *goal*, Absolute Knowing, or Spirit that knows itself as Spirit, has for its path the recollection of the Spirits as they are in themselves and as they accomplish the organization of their realm. Their preservation, regarded from the side of their free existence appearing in the form of contingency, is History; but regarded from the side of their [philosophically] comprehended organization, it is the Science of Knowing in the sphere of appearance." (PS: 493)

That is, it is Hegel's own book, the *Phenomenology of Spirit,* which, in the sphere of appearance, or what I call "textuality," may organize the history of spirit. He clearly was hoping that his very first book would become a mediator of insight, of reflection, of intellectual, ultimately political, progress.

In the end, Hegel hyphenates the German word for "recollection," *Er-innerung,* which the English translation renders as "inwardizing," thus losing Hegel's wordplay. By hyphenating *Er-innerung,* Hegel establishes a balance between the word's literal meaning, recollection, and a meaning teased out of its materiality, internalization. Through cultural recollection and institutionalized reading practices, humans reverse the externalization of the spirit by internalizing. In a different context, Hegel writes: *Er-Innerung als Überholen des An-sich-Seins des Vergangenen* (Memory [or recovery] as a superseding of the Being-in-itself of the past). "Recollection," *Er-Innerung,* is for Hegel a new way of grasping the past as inherent in the present, of comprehending it as something that has shaped the present and has, in turn, been superseded by it. In historical recollection, that is, through the reading of the archives of history, the present *kommt zu sich,* that is, literally translated, "it comes to," or "gains consciousness." The last two lines of the *Phenomenology* (mis)quote Friedrich Schiller's *Die Freundschaft*: "From the chalice of this realm of Spirits/foams forth for Him his own infinitude." What Hegel renders as a realm of Spirits or minds (*Geisterreich*) is in Schiller a realm of souls (*Seelenreich*), and the former's "his own infinitude" is the latter's infinite (*die Unendlichkeit*). Yet both "mistakes" were necessary if the citation was to serve Hegel's purpose. Both "souls" and "the infinite" refer to a transcendent beyond in Schiller and to a practice of meditation representing the opposite of modern reading practices. The terms Schiller uses entail a practice that is, to use Michel Foucault's phrase, geared toward immobilizing consciousness. In "Technologies of the Self," Foucault contrasts practices conceived in the tradition of the patristic-scholastic technology of immobilizing consciousness with modern technologies of verbalization: "From the eighteenth century to the present, the techniques of verbalization have been reinserted in a different context by the so-called human sciences in order to use them without renunciation of the self but to constitute, positively, a new self."[21] For Hegel, as for nobody before him, such techniques of verbalization depend on "textual exteriorizations," on *Ent-äußerungen*. Humans need valuable, even canonical, texts as a medium for reflecting upon their culture and upon themselves. They need textual externalizations of the standards or norms they take as authoritative in order to subject them to critical reflections and, eventually, to modify or adjust them. To be sure, putting Hegel's project into these terms may make it sound like a variation on the Enlightenment project. In fact, Hegel's argument is much bolder than the Enlightenment project in its categorical exclusion of the possibility of "an affirmation or justification or critique of social practices by appeal to anything that would be 'external' to the practices themselves—for example, . . . by appealing to any kind of metaphysical essence that would somehow vouchsafe those practices."[22] Precisely because "modern" communities may justify the standards or norms they take to be authoritative only in a circular way by appealing to traditions, they need textual exteriorizations of these standards and norms. As Terry Pinkard puts it, for Hegel "Philosophy is the reflection on what the community as a whole has come to take as authoritative for its evaluation of [its] practices and its attempts at legitimations of those practices in terms of an appeal to standards of rationality that themselves historically have been developed within the history of that community's accounts of itself."[23] However, one must qualify Pinkard's statement that "Absolute knowledge is *absolute* in that it has no 'object' external to itself that mediates it in the way the natural world mediates the claims of natural science"; this is only partially correct. While clearly the natural world must indeed arbitrate the claims of natural science, absolute knowledge nonetheless needs a *medium* in the strict sense of the word in order to manifest itself; it needs an "object" external to itself that mediates the absoluteness of knowledge. As just noted, knowledge is absolute when, and only when, it frees itself from "conditioned" or "determinate" structures. This liberation requires a medium in the sense of a means or catalyst, in other words texts in the medium of which thought frees itself of that which conditions it in the everyday. If absolute knowing, for its materialization, were not dependent on a medium, it could only be the effect of an essence or agency inherent in the human mind—the effect of a substance different from the human body. And what is this if not the very Cartesian supposition Hegel was determined to overcome?

Notes

1. *Theory as Practice: A Critical Anthology of Early German Romantic Writing*, ed. and trans., Jochen Schulte-Sasse et al. (Minneapolis: University of Minnesota Press, 1997), 73.

2. Michael N. Forster, *Hegel's Idea of a Phenomenology of Spirit* (Chicago and London: University of Chicago Press, 1998), 196.

3. The false etymology of *Urteil* as *Ur-teilung* goes back to Friedrich Hölderlin's and G. W. F. Hegel's teacher Bardili in Tübingen.

4. "Die *etymologische* Bedeutung des Urteils in unserer Sprache ist tiefer und drückt die Einheit des Begriffs als das Erste, und dessen Unterscheidung als die *ursprüngliche* Teilung, was das Urteil in Wahrheit ist." Hegel, *Enzyklopädie der philosophischen Wissenschaften im Grundrisse* (1830), eds. Friedhelm Nicolin and Otto Pöggeler (Hamburg: Meiner, 1969), 155.

5. On the significance of the years 1794–96 at Jena University cf. Manfred Frank, *Unendliche Annäherung* (Frankfurt am Main, Germany: Suhrkamp, 1997).

6. *Theory as Practice*, 107f.

7. Charles Taylor, *Hegel* (Cambridge: Cambridge University Press, 1975), 101.

8. Paul de Man, *Blindness and Insight. Essays in the Rhetoric of Contemporary Criticism*, 2d revised ed. (Minneapolis: University of Minnesota Press, 1983), 31f. For a more detailed discussion of this predicament see Martin Heidegger's *Being and Time* (¶¶ 31–39) trans. Joan Stambaugh (Albany: State University of New York Press, 1996).

9. All Hegel references in the text refer to *Hegel's Phenomenology of Spirit*, trans. A. V. Miller (Oxford: Oxford University Press, 1977), hereafter cited as PS.

10. Cf. Diana Coole, *Negativity and Politics. Dionysus and Dialectics from Kant to Poststructuralism* (London and New York: Routledge, 2000).

11. Jean Hyppolite, *Genesis and Structure of Hegel's Phenomenology of Spirit* (Evanston, IL: Northwestern University Press, 1974), 155.

12. Ibid., 156.

13. Cf. "*übergreifen*" in relation to *greifen* and *begreifen*: "Among other compounds of greifen, Hegel uses *übergreifen*, 'to overlap, encroach on, overreach, outflank': the concept overreaches its other, since, e.g., the concept of what is other than a concept, an object, is itself a concept." Michael Inwood, *A Hegel Dictionary* (Oxford: Blackwell, 1992), 58.

14. Maurice Blanchot, "Literature and the Right to Death," in Blanchot, *The Gaze of Orpheus* (Tarrytown, NY: Station Hill Press, 1981), 27.

15. Ibid., 33f.

16. Inwood, *Hegel Dictionary*, 27.

17. Heinrich Heine, *On the History of Religion and Philosophy in Germany*, in *The Romantic School and Other Essays*, eds. Jost Hermand, and Robert C. Holub (New York: Continuum,1985), 216.

18. Coole, *Negativity and Politics*, 10.

19. Ibid., 1.

20. Ibid., 60.

21. Michel Foucault, *Technologies of the Self*, eds. Luther H. Martin et al. (Amherst: University of Massachusetts Press, 1988), 49. Foucault speaks of a "scrutiny of conscience" that "consists of trying to immobilize consciousness" (46).

22. Terry Pinkard, *Hegel's Phenomenology. The Sociality of Reason* (Cambridge: Cambridge University Press, 1994), 261.
23. Ibid., 262.

Beyond Beginnings:
Schlegel and Romantic Historiography

Gary Handwerk

Gary Handwerk

Zum Andenken an Ernst Behler

> It does not seem possible to ground any conviction about future facts
> upon the designs of providence, for even if the principle: "nature never
> acts without an aim" were set down a priori as a sure guiding thread
> for observation, still only an infinite understanding could determine a
> priori the aim and the means of nature for a particular case.
>
> "Vom Wert des Studiums der Griechen und Römer"

Despite the publication of most of the thirty-five volumes of the *Kritische
Ausgabe* of his works, Friedrich Schlegel remains known to critics almost
exclusively for a small segment of his early writings. As in his own era, his
fame as the theorist of romantic irony and as a guiding force in the Jena
romantic circle has tended to eclipse a range of activity that extended far
beyond these literary and critical projects.[1] If the later Schlegel gets any
attention at all, he is likely simply to be cited as a representative of late,
reactionary romantic Catholicism, a case study of the more general romantic
slide from progressive criticism into political and religious orthodoxy.

To be sure, Schlegel's publications after his 1808 conversion to Catholicism and relocation to Vienna were sporadic, and his general intellectual
influence may well have been in decline. Yet he remained quite active as an

independent scholar, and enough material exists in the form of lectures, journals, and notebooks that we can seriously address the question of what we should make of Schlegel's middle and late career. This was the era when G. W. F. Hegel was emerging as the preeminent German philosopher, and when Schleiermacher was achieving renown in Berlin as a preacher and as the architect of modern hermeneutical theory. Within that postromantic intellectual context, where might we best locate Schlegel? Do the writings of his later periods, that is, constitute an extension, a deflection, or even a betrayal of the early romantic impulses of his work? Pursuing this question is in one sense a biographical project, an attempt to measure the coherence of Schlegel's personal intellectual trajectory. Yet it has considerably broader resonance as well, for Schlegel's self-styled *philosophische Lehrjahre* or philosophical apprenticeship allow us to assess the logic and limits of romantic aesthetic and philosophical theories, and thus to examine the developmental tendencies within romantic thought.

Schlegel's intellectual interests had always been multiple and convergent, broadly cultural in orientation and insistent upon the intersection of theory and history. As Ernst Behler has noted, the idea that "The theory of art is its own history," was a leitmotiv throughout his work.[2] History was for Schlegel an amalgam of social forces, where politics, art, religion, and literature formed constituent parts of a given cultural landscape, no one of them comprehensible without the others. The famous Athenäum fragment 216 is notable, for instance, not just for raising Goethe's *Wilhelm Meister* and Fichte's *Wissenschaftslehre* to equivalent status with the French Revolution as the three dominant tendencies of the age, but just as much for insisting upon the intrinsic relevance of that cataclysmical political event to the cultural productions of the era.

Even more so than that early work, Schlegel's post-Jena writings were ambitiously synthetic in aim and deeply historical in character. The recurrent topics of his concern—philosophy, literature, and language—were all seen by him as comprehensible only within their historical frameworks, and the remarkable scope of his interests gave him an unusually deep appreciation for their historical embeddedness. Yet it would be an exaggeration to contend that Schlegel developed a fully fledged alternative to Hegel's philosophy of history or a clear methodological alternative to the positivist impulse of traditional political and diplomatic historiography.[3] The partialness of Schlegel's projects was at least in part intentional; he remained throughout his life impatient both with theoretical systems and with the detail required for empirical accounts of history. Behler quite rightly described the idea of an historical system as an "ironic metaphor" for Schlegel (KA 20:xxvii), useful for describing an imaginable goal, but intrusive and deceptive if too seriously embraced. Schlegel's position across his career thus remained close to what it had been at the start. As a critic and an intellectual outsider, he was most interested in what he termed the *échappées de vue ins Unendliche* that history could afford us, the ways in which the past could open up our vision, complicating our interpretive understandings rather than closing them off. In distinction to Hegel (or at least to the generally received view of him), Schlegel's work displays a rigorously antisystematic character, refusing to both philosophy and history the closure that Hegel and most heirs of Enlightenment rationality presumed ought (eventually) to be possible. Schlegel's cohesiveness remained local, his syntheses partial or potential. For these reasons, his work offers us glimpses of a possible romantic historiographical project that Schlegel himself never brought to completion, suggesting alternatives outside the totalizing metanarratives that we postmoderns so readily accuse the nineteenth century of having passed down to us.

Relevant Beginnings

History, as Aristotle observed, is inferior to tragedy in an important respect, for it lacks the formal (and thus intellectual) coherence of well-plotted fiction. The plots of history are too often sloppy and unfinished, their lessons uncertain, and as a result their theoretical value is typically less than that which poetry can provide. "Poetry, therefore, is a more philosophical and higher thing than history: for poetry tends to express the universal, history the particular."[4] History can, however, make a good story when it has—or has imposed upon it—a beginning, a middle, and an end, a project most fully realized for the nineteenth century by Hegel's account of world history. This formal completeness renders it what Aristotle terms a *whole*, a unity of action linked by causal coherence from beginning to end. Any meaningful narrative—historical or fictional—must therefore begin with an apt beginning, "that which does not follow anything by causal necessity, but after which something naturally is or comes to be" (ATP 31). A relevant beginning reveals the impetus behind an enchained series of events, none of which is tangential and all of which are essential for the complete understanding of what occurs.

The young Schlegel was quite clearly the heir of the Enlightenment endeavor to render history philosophical, that is, universal in this Aristotelian sense. He shared the Enlightenment fascination with attempting to define the laws that govern historical development, at least within the scope of our transcendental human understanding. "If the conceptions of human beings really are a connected whole—a system," an early essay argues, "then even the reciprocal action of freedom and nature, [i.e.,] history, must be subject to necessary, unalterable laws" (KA 1:631). The goal of this project, as Reinhart Koselleck has noted, was to render history as story, indeed, as a universal story with a single beginning and a single end.[5] It involved a significant departure from the *historia magistra vitae* model of historical inquiry (history as the teacher of life) which had been dominant in European historiography well into the eighteenth century. There, one looked to the past for parallels, treating history as a compendium of examples whose usefulness in guiding present activities was not determined by their particular place within the chronology of the past—that is, all examples were presumed to be equally available and potentially relevant to one's present situation. Rather than seeing history as marked by such (possible) repetitions, Enlightenment historiography pursued an alternate structure of anticipation and fulfillment that both hearkened back to the Bible and forward to Hegel's dialectical account of history. Its notion of progress implied a teleological structure for history, one that could be charted and known.

Although Schlegel shared this Enlightenment faith in the existence of discoverable laws for human history, his studies in classical culture quickly led him to a methodological impasse. While the classical and modern eras were clearly parts of a shared European history, the classical past was so different from modernity that it appeared impossible to subsume them under common laws or patterns. Both could, of course, be characterized as similar efforts at "human cultivation" or *Bildung*, yet they remained fundamentally different because the impetus to that effort came in each case from a quite different source. "Either freedom or nature must give the first, decisive impetus to human cultivation, and thereby determine the direction of the path, the law of its progression, and the final goal of the whole process" (KA 1:230).[6] Schlegel's early literary historical works, from his *Über das Studium der Griechen and Römer* (1795, publ. 1797; KA 1:217–367) and "Vom Wert des Studiums der Griechen und Römer" (1795–96; KA 1:621–42) through his *Geschichte der Poesie der Griechen und Römer* (1798; KA 1:395–568), struggled to resolve this antinomy and to define the bearing that the past might have or be made to have upon the present.

In these essays, Schlegel argues that both past (i.e., classical) and present history are developmental in an organic sense; they follow the path common to all animate entities of "gradual growth" into ever-more highly formed stages (KA 1:435). Yet the differing impetus of classicism and modernity means that they follow different historical laws, the past subject to a cyclic dynamic that the progressive path of modernity promises to escape. We should therefore concede that "a twofold form of cultivation, and thus of history, might be possible" (1:631), with only the totality of history able to encompass the divergent historical dynamics of both eras. If classical antiquity marks the relevant beginning for modernity, it cannot do so in any causal, Aristotelian sense. Indeed, the antithetical nature of each age is manifested in their wholly contrastive aesthetic ideals, the objective beauty of classical art set against the subjective (or "interested" in Schlegel's vocabulary), yet therefore infinitely perfectible, beauty of modern art.[7]

Yet Schlegel insists that, despite its irreconcilable difference from modernity, Greek aesthetics (and culture generally) remains a touchstone for the present. Its highest manifestations have a potentially catalytic force for all times and places, so that the historical study of their genesis and forms ought to be, as Klaus Behrens has argued, fundamentally *Gegenwartsbezogen*, "attentive to how the past bears upon the present."[8] The spirit of Greek culture "contains at least traces of a perfected ideal that is a valid law and a general *Urbild* for all times and peoples" (KA 1:284). As this quote suggests, Schlegel's model of historical continuity here is not a linear, genetic one; it does not restrict the lines of historical affiliation within national or cultural boundaries, nor does it require temporal contiguity as a basis for possible influence. He does at moments invoke a teleological pattern, as when he contends that "ancient history is indispensable for the explanation of the present, in that every later age is contained in embryo (*Keim*) in the earlier one, as if in a series of boxes, and so reason is not allowed to stand still at any one link of the infinite chain as long as it is still possible to grasp a higher one" (1:626). Yet despite this historicist sensibility, his deeper allegiance is in a certain sense with pre-Enlightenment thought, his spirit more akin to the *historia magistra vitae* model of history.

At the same time, Schlegel significantly transforms that model, explicitly rejecting the sort of mimesis that had been advocated by neoclassical aesthetics. The classical past does not really provide us, in his eyes, with a permanently available repertoire of examples (in either aesthetic or ethical terms), from which we could freely pick and choose appropriate models for the present. Its availability is more narrowly circumscribed and more uncertain. The relevance of Greek culture for modernity depends both upon its diachronic depth (it serves as an absolute point of origin for European cultural history) and its synchronic breadth (it constitutes an integral whole, not a set of detachable models). Yet its relation to the present remains open and potential, its assimilation into the present not guaranteed by the automatic functioning of any dialectical process.

In these early essays, we can see Schlegel working to articulate his own distinctive model of historical imitation, a mechanism by which the past could be assimilated to the present and the value of that past for the present harnessed. To characterize the exemplary character embodied in the highest instances of Greek art or civic culture, Schlegel adopts the term *Urbild*, "archetype," or more literally, "originary image." By the late 1700s, this term had already acquired a considerable history of use within the German philosophical tradition, having been used from the seventeenth century on as an equivalent for the Greek ιδέα by figures such as Herder, Jacobi, and Goethe. Schlegel doubtless encountered the term in Kant, whose *Foundations of the Metaphysics of Morals* uses it in a discussion of Plato that critiques the value of any all-too-tangible models for our ethical decision making. Kant refuses to concede that exemplars can have any usefulness whatsoever as embodiments of moral principles, concluding that "Imitation has no place in moral matters, and examples only serve for encouragement . . . examples can never justify us in setting aside their true original, which lies in reason, and letting ourselves be guided by them."[9]

But the figural force of the *Urbilder* that Kant so rigorously resists is precisely what attracts Schlegel. His *Studium* essay invokes *Urbilder* at the key point of its argument, as it attempts to explore the relation that abstract maxims can have upon aesthetic practice (Schlegel blends, even blurs the moral and aesthetic aspects of this issue). He insists upon the necessary role of art as an incitement to the moral and cultural development encompassed in the idea of *Bildung*. "The law must become *inclination*. . . . The pure law is empty. In order for it to be *filled out* and for its real application to become possible, it requires an intuition in which it could appear, as if visible in uniform completeness—a highest *aesthetic Urbild*" (KA 1:274). We aspire to higher versions of ourselves—the sort of civic selves represented by the highest instances of Greek culture—only through our identification with and imitation of such *Urbilder*, which link us to the human species as a whole. "Human beings are connected to their species by an inclination completely independent of the drive or the goal of comprehensive knowledge or one's own ethical improvement, whose object is the immediate pleasure in humanity," an inclination that Schlegel asserts contemporary culture can only imperfectly arouse (1:637). By contrast, "The *Urbild* of humanity at the peak of ancient *Bildung* provides so great a pleasure that every other one could seem prosaic by contrast, and, in order not to become dangerous, it dare not remain idle" (1:637). *Urbilder* drawn from history thus perform the cultural work of translating pleasure into ethical and social energy, sparking a pleasure so intense that it demands an outlet in self-cultivation.

The ideal mimesis evoked by the presence of Greek *Urbilder* is figured by Schlegel in an image of magnetic attraction that he adopts from Plato's *Ion*, while transforming it to serve his own model of aesthetic experience. "I am speaking," he says, "of that *communication of the beautiful* through which the connoisseur touches the artist and the artist touches divinity, as the magnet does not simply attract iron, but through its touch also communicates to it the magnetic power" (KA 1:274–75). Plato had used this image to insist upon the *derivative* and passive nature of the rhapsode's (and implicitly, the poet's and the audience's) aesthetic activity and, in consequence, the severely limited degree of his wisdom. But Schlegel instead imagines the magnetic power itself passing without diminution from source to recipient, so that the receiver becomes in turn an active creator, in a certain sense, divine—with Greek culture providing his ideal example of how this worked in the past and could continue to work in the present. One might term this an affective idealism, akin to (and quite possibly derived from) the model of incitement to philosophy that Plato outlined in the *Phaedrus*.

"Does divinity get transformed into earthly form?" Schlegel asks. "Are there mortal works in which the law of eternity becomes visible?" (KA 1:275). The answer, of course, is yes, and the site of such aesthetic ideals is ancient Greece. "The *Urbild* of humanity at the highest step of antique *Bildung* is the sole possible *foundation* for all modern *Bildung*: a visible law which, insofar as it is infinitely determined, contains more than the empty law, yet insofar as it remains always limited and single, contains less than the pure law. Imitating means appropriating to oneself this determination without those constraints" (1:638).[10] A simple enough rule for us to find and to follow, it would seem, and one which, up to this point, seems largely consistent with neoclassical aesthetics. Yet Schlegel complicates his theory of the *Urbilder* by insisting that they can be found nowhere in particular in Greek culture. One cannot simply copy Homer or Sophocles or Plato, for all such models are marked by their own local defects, their partial assimilation of the ideal. Schlegel's *Urbilder* therefore hover between collective and individual embodiment and thereby acquire a broadly historical character. Apprehending them correctly (which is essential for any valid imitation) requires a deep understanding for *all* of Greek history.[11] "We cannot imitate Greek poetry correctly, so long as we *do not* really *understand* it. We will learn to explain it philosophically and value it aesthetically only when we study it *en masse:* for it is such an inwardly connected whole that it is impossible to grasp and to judge correctly even the smallest part of it isolated from its connection" (KA 1:347). Examples cannot be detached from their context. Hence the modern critic or artist must not display a preference for this or that predecessor, but instead be driven by a love "for the *Urbildlichen* itself, for the whole of antiquity" (1:398). One imitates in one's person or one's art an ideal object that exists nowhere in surviving Greek literature or art. That mimetic target must instead be triangulated from among the array of artifacts that we do possess. Precisely because it adopts no singular object, this sort of higher imitation allows us to go beyond the Greeks, beyond a merely reiterative reconstruction of the beginnings of European culture.

As an historical model, Schlegel's theory of the *Urbild* offers a version of temporality that is discontinuous in two distinct ways. First, since assimilation of the past depends upon the right sort of imitation, there is no guarantee that the past will be in connection with the present at any given moment. But second, when a connection with the past does occur, that circuit provokes a leap beyond the present that creates a further break in historical continuity. As Behrens and Behler have both noted, Schlegel's early historical perspective is marked by a mentality of crisis that can be traced to the impact upon him of the traumatic upheavals of the French Revolution. Seeing, as he always did, clear lines of affiliation between political and cultural events, Schlegel articulated in his early essays a strategy for transforming the cultural and psychological landscape of modernity through a revolutionary recourse to the past, an aesthetic revolution (KA 1:269) whose consequences would touch all spheres of modern existence.

Beyond Mimesis

In the years after the breakup of the Jena romantic circle, Schlegel produced a series of lectures whose historical scope was significantly wider than his early philological studies. His 1803–4 Paris lectures on the history of European literature (KA 11:1–188), his 1804–5 Cologne lectures on the development of philosophy (KA 12:107–480; 13:1–175), his 1805–6 lectures on universal history (KA 14: whole volume), his 1808 study *On the Wisdom and Language of the Indians* (KA 8:105–433), and his 1812 lectures on ancient and modern literature (KA 16: whole volume) all indicate his continuing desire to deal with history in an ever more comprehensive fashion. This encompassing ambition also led him to fundamentally rethink his understanding of how the past bears upon the present and his views of the value of historical inquiry. The events of his own life during this period also played a large role in reshaping Schlegel's sense of relevant beginnings. His residence in Paris, his study of Sanskrit and Persian, his conversion to Catholicism and study of the Middle Ages, and his move to Vienna all contributed to widening his vision of European history and eroding his sense of its self-contained nature.[12] The status of classical Greece as an exemplary object of historical study, uniquely valuable because of its unparalleled cultural integrity, became less certain to him. The ready dualism of his "grécophilic" youth gave way to a more expansive vision that sought to take account of what lay both between and beyond the polar opposition of classicism and modernity. And thus the status of mimesis itself as an ideal mode of historical recuperation and cultural provocation came into question as it became increasingly unclear what the appropriate models for such mimesis would be.

One can find traces of Schlegel's commitment to a more open-ended view of history even in his earliest works. In his 1794 review of Condorcet's *Esquisse d'un tableau historique des progrès de l'esprit humain,* for instance, Schlegel questioned the premise that the unity (and thus also the probable direction) of history could be discovered.[13] The stress of the French *philosophes* upon the perfectibility of humanity became, from Schlegel's incipiently romantic perspective, a stress upon the *infinite* perfectibility of our capacities. Under the influence of Fichte, Schlegel was already conceiving of historical *Bildung* as an open-ended process whose totality would not be subsumable under any rational concept. Likewise, his 1798 essay "Vom Wert der Geschichte" reveals a deeply skeptical awareness of the difficulty of fully comprehending history. The quote that serves as an epigraph to this essay summarizes Schlegel's conclusions. It acknowledges that the idea of universal history may well make sense, while asserting that we are never likely to know enough to be sure, nor ever be in a position to reliably predict the future. In the works of the middle period, Schlegel turns this insight in the opposite direction as well, translating this vision of future progress into a perspective upon the past. The fruit of Schlegel's ironic sense of history proves to be a radical skepticism about ever determining with any certainty an ideal Aristotelian beginning.

The Paris lectures exhibit most clearly the tension between Schlegel's aspiration to an Enlightenment version of totality and his commitment to a more open-ended, romantic version of change. They claim for European literature what the Cologne lectures claim for European philosophy, that it constitutes an indivisible whole, and that its significance and value are contained within (or perhaps better, evoked out of) this totality. We should therefore not "want to restrict ourselves to the literature of one specific time or nation, because one [literature] always leads back to another and all literature forms a single great whole, [its parts] inwardly connected not only before and after one another, but also beside one another" (KA 11:11). In creating order from this massive body of material, Schlegel says, we could proceed theoretically or philosophically, dividing literature into its genres and kinds and classifying texts by their mode. But the historical method leads us further, he insists, because "It gives us a living, visible image of the whole according to its origin and development." "The historical method can encompass within itself the philosophical one," provided it adopts an appropriately "critical and characterizing" mode of analysis (11:12). The most complete concept of literature, Schlegel asserts, is its history (11:6), a claim the Cologne lectures likewise echo with regard to philosophy.

Where, though, does the core of historical understanding lie? What exactly is the historian's task? Schlegel describes the goal here as reading literature to disclose the fundamental character or tendency of each culture and era. Literature may be the deepest expression of the spirit of a particular culture, but it is attuned to all the other expressions of that culture as well, its politics, its religion, and its art, which it both reflects and reveals. Literature is in that sense deeply allegorical and cannot be rightly understood in isolation from those other realms of culture. As a category, it includes philosophy and historiography as well. The Paris lectures, for instance, present philosophy as the dominant literary genre in the third era of

Greek cultural development, the critical age that succeeds the epic and lyric/dramatic ages.

As the totality of cultural history becomes the appropriate object for historical study, however, the mimetic aesthetic that Schlegel had earlier used to describe the ideal relation of past to present begins to lose its force. As his sense of the past expands, its ready accessibility and its exemplary relevance for the present become more problematic; the image of Greece as *Urbild* undergoes a dramatic change. What Schlegel now sees in construing the monuments of Greek culture is their decidedly local, historically limited character. "Now this mixture of what is generally valid and what is special and local in all the forms and genres of Greek poetry and prose is the reason why wholly literal imitations can never be sanctioned" (KA 11:59). This ban upon mimesis holds across all genres, from the Platonic dialogue or the Thucydidean history to the Pindaric ode (11:58, 71). Regardless of where one looks into the literature of the past, the products of imitation "do not deliver *Urbilder* to us in a pure way, but only with the dross of locality" (11:59). Under these circumstances, the attempt to mold one's art upon the attainments of the past would not only be futile, but inhibiting. "In imitating the ancients, all freedom, power, liveliness, and naturalness would be lost and nothing but a forced and frigid thing would result" (11:71).

The Paris lectures thus set the stage for a reconceptualization of Schlegel's understanding of historical continuity; the aesthetically determined model of mimesis no longer seems to him capable of taking sufficient account of historical particularities. The role of the historical study of literature is no longer that of making models available in either a specific or a generalized sense, but the more general one of "arousing and keeping in motion that infinite capacity for development and training that is grounded in the organism of humanity itself" (KA 11:3). *Urbilder* incite, without serving in any precise sense as guides. And while a range of such incitements might seem desirable, as a way of training the capacity for aesthetic judgment,[14] the comprehensive historical understanding required by Schlegel's earlier notion of the *Urbild* no longer seems to be required.

From the start, Schlegel's Cologne lectures of 1804–5 adopt a different methodical tack, primarily because he does not see in the history of philosophy developmental cycles comparable to those in literature. He insists, to be sure, upon the importance of historical understanding, "because one philosophical system supports itself upon the other, [so that] understanding any one of them requires knowledge of the preceding one, and philosophies form a connected chain where knowledge of one link is always necessary for knowledge of another" (KA 12:111). Despite this broadly historical claim, however, Schlegel's perspective in these essays is synoptic, not developmental. One needs a broad knowledge of the history of philosophy not to understand how it unfolds in any necessary way over time, but in order to have a sufficient basis for critiquing the partial truths of different philosophical systems. Only by knowing history can one "discover the reason for the failure of all previous attempts and thoroughly illuminate the errors, weaknesses, imperfections of the various systems" (12:166).

Revision is fundamental to the philosophical enterprise that Schlegel depicts. Philosophy is itself a process, forever incomplete. "Now if the object of philosophy is positive *knowledge* of an infinite reality, it is easy to perceive that this task can never be completed. . . . [Philosophy] is really more of a *searching*, a *striving* for science than itself a science (KA 12:166). Like literary archetypes, the philosophies of others can have an inciting role. "Nothing will more powerfully and effectively incite and maintain *thinking for oneself* than an acquaintance with foreign opinions and thoughts" (12:168), but the specifically historical nature of this acquaintance seems relatively unimportant.

Thus Schlegel's approach in what he explicitly entitles the "development" (or "unfolding," *Entwicklung*) of European philosophy is classificatory rather than genetic. This introductory historical survey constitutes the largest section by far of Schlegel's lectures and provides what he sees as the essential framework for discussion of any specific field of philosophy. It begins not with the earliest European philosophers, but by discriminating analytically among five possible kinds of philosophy. This "characteristic" of philosophical modes breaks all philosophies into five classes: empiricism, materialism, skepticism, pantheism, and idealism.[15] These kinds cannot be mapped onto a linear historical grid, nor, although Schlegel has a clear preference for idealism, can one really see an absolute superiority of any single one or any progressive evolution from one kind of philosophy to another.

Following the introduction, Schlegel does devote the remainder of this chapter to a historical characteristic of philosophy in its successive unfolding. He traces the predominance of particular genres across time in the work of individual philosophers ranging from the pre-Socratics to Kant and Fichte. For each thinker, he takes as his task the determination of how the different strands of philosophy are combined within his philosophical system. At this microhistorical level, that is, within the texture of an individual philosopher's work, one can see developmental patterns of a kind that are missing at the macrohistorical level, patterns that are in fact the key to a correct understanding of whatever system may result. "The philosophy of a human being is the history of a spirit, the gradual arising, shaping, advancing of his ideas. . . . Only in the definite, methodical advance of his philosophical investigations, not, however, in a finished proposition and result produced at the end, do we find the large-scale unity that characterizes the form of his philosophy" (KA 12:209). As Schlegel asserted about his own career, it is the record of the "philosophical apprenticeship," the *Lehrjahre*, which gives the essence and measure of a thinker, not the fixed system that arises at whatever point—inevitably a somewhat arbitrary point—where his thinking ultimately comes to a standstill.

In an important way, then, history in these lectures comes to be internalized within the figure of the individual philosopher, visible only as biography and only in the moments before his thoughts congeal. In accordance with this principle (and as in the Paris lectures), the centerpiece of the Cologne lectures is a lengthy "Characteristic" devoted to Plato. The emphasis is a logical one, since Plato "maintains the first rank among self-thinkers of all times and nations; he is at once source and *Urbild* for us" of all that philosophy should be (KA 12:225). But Plato serves here as an *Urbild* in a radically new sense, less the distillation or apex of Greek thought than a reminder of its insufficiency. Plato is, to be sure, a particularly capacious philosopher. The biographical unfolding of his philosophical project is exemplary for the history and practice of philosophy because it replicates within itself the entire developmental history of Greek philosophy as a whole. His struggle with various problems and ideas condenses within itself the larger history within which it is located.

Already in the Paris lectures, Schlegel had developed one justification for the importance of Plato, whose deeply intuitive understanding of the nature and purposes of philosophy was perfectly manifested in the form and style he gave to his works. Plato was the first European philosopher to apprehend what for Schlegel was the essential truth that philosophy is an activity and a process, not a set of doctrines or truths. "He was never finished with his thinking, and he attempted to represent artistically in his dialogues the trajectory of his spirit, striving ever onward toward perfect knowledge and understanding of the highest things, this eternal becoming, shaping, and unfolding of his ideas. This is what is most characteristic of Platonic philosophy" (KA 11:120). Plato understood and, more importantly, strove to embody within his written works the ironic insufficiency of all philosophy. The realization that "The thinking and knowing of the highest things can never be adequately represented," is what Schlegel terms the "principle of the relative unrepresentability of the highest things" (11:124).[16] Plato's choice of the dialogue form, with its question-answer format and its progressive, partial unfolding of philosophical questions, is for Schlegel the perfect stylistic embodiment of this important philosophical insight.

The Cologne lectures reiterate this praise for the Platonic method and form, but they add to it something that is, in the course of Schlegel's work, fundamentally new and enormously significant. In these lectures, Schlegel develops what will prove to be for him a new angle of historical vision. Plato remains exemplary, to be sure, in that he "had only a philosophy, but not a system" (KA 12:209). But what Schlegel's more careful study of his philosophical trajectory here uncovers is an important insight about the whole history of Greek philosophy. As Schlegel explores Plato's dialogues and doctrines, he increasingly recognizes the crucial importance of foreign elements to the fabric of Plato's thought. It is the nonintegrity of Greek culture that comes to the surface when one studies the works of Plato, through which one can perceive that its ideal excellence derives from its assimilative openness to a wide range of foreign influences. The historical force that Schlegel discerns in Plato's philosophical trajectory undoes the image of the cultural self-sufficiency of Greece that Schlegel's own early works had emphasized. Plato proves to be of such great importance to the history of philosophy not because of what he was or did, but because of all that passed through him. One finds in his works, playing a central rather than incidental role, traces of those many cultures prior to and outside of the Greek tradition.

From one perspective, Platonic philosophy can indeed look like a project wholly within the frame of Greek intellectual history, an attempt to reconcile the divergent metaphysical conceptions of Heracleitus and Parmenides. On this view, Plato's theory of the ideas can be seen as an effort to bridge the span between changelessness and change, creating a model of mimesis and dissemination that Schlegel adapted and historicized in his own early theory of the *Urbild*. But for Schlegel, the theory of ideas was also the point at which Plato's philosophy got stuck, the point at which its own commitment to process and progress got undermined. "In this influence of Eleatic pantheism lies the primary reason why his philosophy did not advance toward completion" (KA 12:218). The concept of persistence or subsistence (*Beharrlichkeit*) intrinsic to his doctrine of the ideas, that is, prevented Plato from construing divinity in the fully idealist sense as active energy and force.

Yet the Platonic ideas open his philosophy out in other, even more important ways. In trying to explain how it is that we can have these sorts of ideas, Plato requires two additional premises that were borrowed from Indian philosophy, the doctrines of recollection and transmigration of souls.

> Plato's teaching of the *ideas*, which the human spirit did not derive from the world of the senses, but which sprang instead from the recollection of a former intuition, was always an arbitrary presupposition: in order to establish it, *recollection* must be assumed in an equally arbitrary way, to which the *transmigration of souls* then gets attached, yet these doctrines do not necessarily go together with the foundational principle of his philosophy, as is the case in Indian [philosophy]. (KA 12:223)

Precisely because of their anomalous character within Platonic philosophy, these two doctrines reveal their foreign origin. Their partial assimilation and obscure origins are signaled by their presentation in the dialogues in mythical rather than logical form. They are, Schlegel contends, more consequentially developed and more consistently part of the Indian philosophical tradition (12:220–21) than they are as parts of Platonic metaphysics. That tradition conceives of the divine creative impulse more fully as active energy, neither animalistic (in the manner of the earliest Greek philosophers), nor purely rational, as Plato tended to do.

In a crucially important way, then, the historical understanding of Plato's philosophy that the Cologne lectures attempt to provide, breaches the self-sufficient totality of the Greek philosophical and cultural tradition. Its originality is called into question; its exemplarity proves conditional. Schlegel adopts here what we might call a "regressive genetic method," an unraveling of origins that ultimately shatters the foundational premises of his own early work. It uncovers and insists upon the unacknowledged debts of the Greek philosophical tradition to Indian philosophy, and to other preceding traditions in Egypt and the Middle East as well. The infinity of history now opens out to the past as insistently as it opens out into the future. The process, indeed, is endless.

> In this difficult undertaking, the philosophical researcher will pursue the track of philosophy through all the stages of its development and formation to its first source, insofar as this permits itself to be discovered in history; he will find nowhere a resting place; he will pass through the whole chain of opinions and ideas, which engender one another and reciprocally determine one another, up to its first link, and only stand still at the point where all historical data forsake him and the historical beginning of philosophy loses itself in impenetrable darkness." (KA 12:167–68)

The same holds true for literature, and presumably for all other modes of cultural representation as well. European literature recedes in a similar way back beyond the Greeks and toward an unreachable vanishing point, born amid developmental dark spots that we will never fully elucidate . . . but that signal inexorably the derivative and dependent status of our cultural exempla. "Concerning the origin of the Greek nation and its composition and mixture, history leaves us pretty much in the dark" (11:19) Beyond the beginning, another beginning always looms.

Historical Humility

Between 1813 and 1827, Schlegel published relatively little, devoting himself first to political activities (serving as a delegate of Metternich at the Frankfurt Congress) and working later on the journal *Concordia*. During the last three years of his life, however, he did deliver and prepare for publication three series of lectures on the philosophy of life, the philosophy of literature, and the philosophy of language. These late works, along with his essay "Signatur des Zeitalters" (1820–23) reflect both his intervening political engagement and an increasing religious mysticism that continued through the end of his life. In political and intellectual terms, the impact of these texts was relatively insignificant. They did not broaden Schlegel's audience or influence; the lectures were very sparsely attended, the publications often unsympathetically reviewed. Schlegel's vision of a federative, corporatively structured, religiously oriented Europe was not embraced by either the peoples or the politicians of the era with the ardor that Schlegel might have wished. Even a putative ally such as Metternich found the visionary qualities of Schlegel's projects hard to accept, complaining at one point (according to Adam Müller) that the Austrian romantic writers such as Schlegel were "losing themselves on eccentric detours" and, instead of producing "effective writings," were offering only "fantastic recommendations" (KA 7:cxlix). Yet the late works do mark a further transition in Schlegel's historiographical work; they adopt a more aggressively polemical tone and draw out, from Schlegel's Catholic perspective, specific ideological consequences that follow from his decentering of European history.

These works did spark vehement reaction in a certain segment of Schlegel's audience, the liberal, Protestant intellectual circle that his brother, August Wilhelm, continued to represent. August Wilhelm broke off relations with his brother after the "Signatur" essay, and later responded indignantly to charges that he had himself become "half-Catholic." He described himself as "far removed from wanting to separate himself from the community of my father, of my older brother, and of so many relatives who were not simply adherents of the evangelical [Protestant] faith, but for more than two hundred years its preachers as well, or to damn them as pernicious heretics, and to toss their bones out of Christian burial sites" (KA 7:cxlvii). For August Wilhelm, this debate was clearly not just a matter of true and false beliefs, but a contest about the meaning of the personal and collective lineage he shared with his brother. It was, on a larger scale, a debate about the narrative of the European past that was then being given shape. Schlegel, at the intellectual margins as he was by the 1820s, had little influence upon how that narrative came to be written. But his marginal position gave him an advantageous vantage point upon the emerging liberal philosophical and political orthodoxy.

Schlegel's 1828 lectures on the philosophy of history do not so much mark a new direction as articulate in a more polemical fashion the implications of displacing Greece from its originating status within the Western tradition. He devotes considerable space in these lectures to non-European cultures; four of the nine chapters on antiquity deal with China, India, Egypt, Persia, and other world cultures, stressing their seminal impact upon European culture. In his assessment of these cultures, he asserts a cultural relativism much like Herder's. "For even heathen antiquity . . . has a foundation of truth," so that "we must take and judge every age for itself, according to its own concepts, because only in this way do we put ourselves in a position to understand it correctly and assess it rightly" (KA 9:301). In terms that echo "Vom Wert der Geschichte," this cultural openness puts the very notion of universal history into question. The historian "must not want to explain everything. . . . It is always very risky to explain everything immediately and entirely and to immediately want to complete what seems to have gaps or to add what is lacking" (9:14). The reason for such interpretive hesitancy, from Schlegel's Catholic perspective, is that we would "bring a too quickly completed system of divine intentions, measured by human insights and views, into the still incomplete drama of world history," whose scope and mystery far exceed the small measure of what human beings can know or judge with certainty (9:226).

Schlegel's critique of the modern era is particularly sharp, a striking reversal of his early romantic efforts to recuperate contemporary culture and help it not simply regain, but surpass, the heights of antiquity. In these lectures, the modern era is most clearly defined by the predominance of an *Eroberungssucht*, an "imperalist drive for domination that arises out of what he terms its 'religion of reason.' " The origins of this impulse lie in the East; Persia is for Schlegel the first nation to manifest this aim. Yet it was the cultures of the West, Alexander's Hellenistic empire, and the Roman Empire, which he sees as refining and universalizing this drive. Nor is liberalism an antidote to this impulse, the defender of national liberation movements that it would portray itself as being. It represents instead the culmination of ancient Persian aspirations, its expansionist mentality as deeply rooted in classical democracies and modern republics as in autocratic monarchical systems, its ideology of national self-sufficiency and national self-aggrandizement antithetical to a more truly cosmopolitan vision of the world. Schlegel's analysis of recent European history, for instance, describes the movement from Louis XIV to the French Revolution to Napoleon and the Bourbon Restoration as a logical progression rather than a series of reversals in direction. In a gesture complimentary to neither, he argues that secular, rational Enlightenment philosophy, "if it had only been sufficiently candid and consistent, ought to have had the courage to acknowledge and to publicly honor Mohammed, if not as a prophet, at least as the true reformer of humanity . . . and the real founder of the resonant religion of reason" (9:275). What they share in his eyes is a common imperialist impulse that only a different, more truly Catholic religion can moderate.

As historical criticism, it is again Schlegel's attempt to erase the presumed origins of Western culture in Greece that has the most far-reaching implications for what we should study, what we should read, and how we should imagine the past. While acknowledging and praising the achievement of Greek civilization, he reiterates even more strongly the fundamental point of the Cologne lectures—the fecundity of that culture was the consequence of its assimilative openness to external culture influences. Greece was the sum of all that flowed into it and fell into cultural decline when the impact of those influences diminished. "The oldest inhabitants of Greece were quite crude in their concepts and harsh in their customs," he points out, "until, along with that more noble line of Deucalion, the sons of Prometheus from the Caucasus, the other starting points of a higher culture, the Phoenecian, the Egyptian, and others of Asian origin, also became active and gradually gave even the land itself a new shape" (KA 9:182). Schlegel's short formula for the genius of Greek culture therefore consists of three names: Cadmus the Phoenecian, with his gift of written languages; Kekrops the Egyptian, with his gift of political order to Athens; and Orpheus the Thracian, with his gift of the mystery of religions.

Indian culture is again the standard against which classical Greece gets measured, and against which it is frequently found wanting. Greek mythology lacks the richness and philosophical depth of Indian literature, Schlegel asserts, and Greek philosophy reaches its highest point only when it most fully assimilates the wisdom of Hindu teachers. There is, in short, no bottom to Greek history, no absolute historical beginning to be found for "Western" culture. To be sure, one should not claim too much here about the anti-Eurocentric thrust of Schlegel's thought. Foreign cultures remain more appealing to him the more they recede into the past; more contemporary cultural and political presences, such as Islam, are still felt as threats, and his overall understanding of them is both partial and romanticized. Yet his appeal to the value of those cultures, a value both intrinsic to themselves and seminal for the emergence of Western culture, provides substantial buttressing for his critique of European imperialism. Furthermore, Schlegel's attempt to adopt a vantage point outside of the European tradition makes visible for him the deep ideological affinities among imperialism, Enlightenment rationality, Protestant views of the self, and the faith in the inevitable forward progress of history.

There is—even for us, even now—an essential opening outward that results from examining Schlegel's attempts to define a history without beginnings, a sense of possibility that would eventually disappear from European historiography in the age of metanarratives. What Schlegel offers as an alternative remains determinedly vague, rooted in a sense of originary religious revelations that are destined to remain irrecoverable for us, present only in the already distorted traces of their wisdom that we find in places like India. Fragmentary though they are, those traces shatter the smug self-sufficiency of

European culture, and it is in insisting upon their presence that these late lectures find their value and their limit. What they open out to remains—programmatically or not—unclear.[17] A history that would be neither mimetic, repeating the past, nor teleological, dialectically consuming its traces, remains infinitely alluring, and yet impossible for Schlegel to envision in coherent intellectual terms. What he did, however, was to continue to resist the temptation to seek refuge from metanarratives in the chaos of merely local histories. To the end, he continued to believe in both the value and the possibility of deeper and more meaningful immersion in the particularities and the affinities of a truly world culture.

Notes

1. As evidence, one might point to the available translations of Friedrich Schlegel's work into English, which remain confined to multiple collections of his Lyceum and Athenäum fragments and to occasional essays from the same romantic period.

2. See, for instance, Schlegel, *Kritische Ausgabe seiner Werke* (2:290). Subsequent citations to the *Kritische Ausgabe*, ed. Ernst Behler (Paderborn, Germany: F. Schöningh, 1958–) will be given by volume and page number, hereafter cited as KA. On this topic, see Ernst Behler, " 'The Theory of Art Is Its Own History': Herder and the Schlegel Brothers," in *Herder Today*, ed. Kurt Mueller-Vollmer (Berlin: de Gruyter, 1990), 246–67; and Behler, "Concepts of History in the Comparative Literary Histories by the Schlegel Brothers," *Comparative Literary History as Discourse*, eds. A. Owen Aldridge, Daniel Javitch, and Mario Valdés (New York: Peter Lang, 1992), 23–40.

3. Behler's characterization of Schlegel's achievement in this regard thus seems to me generous, but overstated. "Schlegel's political philosophy is perhaps the most logically thought through alternative to the Prussian philosophy of history, which was for its part most consistently worked out by Hegel." See Behler, "Concepts of History," 7:xviii.

4. *Aristotle's Theory of Poetry and Fine Art*, trans. S. H. Butcher (New York: Dover, 1951), 35, hereafter cited as ATP. By "universal" Aristotle says he means in accordance with the law of probability or necessity.

5. Reinhart Koselleck, *Futures Past: On the Semantics of Historical Time*, trans. Keith Tribe (Cambridge: MIT Press, 1985).

6. As various critics have noted and Schlegel himself conceded, this contrastive structure clearly echoes Friedrich Schiller's essay on the naive and sentimental. Both were written at nearly the same time, but the delay in publication of Schlegel's essay forced him to take distance explicitly from Schiller's categories (and possible influence) in the introduction to his own essay. For contrasting views on the relative modernity of Schlegel's and Schiller's historical models, see Richard Brinkmann, "Romantische Dichtungstheorie in Friedrich Schlegels Frühschriften und Schillers Begriffe des Naiven und Sentimentalischen," *DVLG* 32 (1958): 344–71, and Hans Robert Jauss, "Schlegels und Schillers Replik auf die 'Querelle des Anciens und des Modernes,' " *Literaturgeschichte als Provokation* (Frankfurt am Main, Germany: Suhrkamp, 1970), 67–106.

7. For an analysis of Schlegel's deployment of the idea of infinite perfectibility within the context of Enlightenment thought, see Behler, "The Idea of Infinite Perfectibility and its Impact upon the Concept of Literature in European Romanticism," in *Sensus Communis: Contemporary Trends in Comparative Literature*, eds. Peter Boerner, János Riesz, and Bernhard Scholz (Tübingen, Germany: Günter Narr, 1986), 295–304.

8. Klaus Behrens, *Friedrich Schlegels Geschichtsphilosophie (1794–1808)* (Tübingen, Germany: Niemeyer, 1984). See, for instance 16–17. Although it deals only with the period up until 1808, Behrens's study remains the most thorough and perceptive account of Schlegel's historiographical work.

9. Immanuel Kant, *Foundations of the Metaphysics of Morals*, trans. Lewis White Beck (New York: Macmillan, 1990), 408–9. I have discussed Kant's stance toward such *Urbilder* in Gary Handwerk, "The Aesthetics of History: Friedrich Schlegel's *Urbilder*," in *The Scope of Words* (New York: Peter Lang, 1991), 399–417.

10. Schlegel notes elsewhere that this "*Urbild* of the purely human provides intuitions that are in agreement with the laws and concepts of pure reason." See Schlegel, *Kritische Ausgabe,* 1:489.

11. Schlegel's development of *Urbilder* as collective singulars may well derive, at least in part, from his thorough study of F. A. Wolf's revisionist interpretation of the Homeric texts as accretive and collective works, rather than being the products of any single artist. Athenäum Fragment 55, for instance, describes nations and eras as "historical individuals," arguing that their characteristic vision (their monadic essence, in a Leibnizian sense) lies in the classificatory systems they use to describe the world.

12. On the influence of Schlegel's Sanskrit studies, see Handwerk, "Envisioning India: Friedrich Schlegel's Sanskrit Studies and the Emergence of Romantic Historiography," *European Romantic Review* 9 (spring 1998): 231–42.

13. This review is in Schlegel, *Kritische Ausgabe* (7:3–10). On Schlegel's reading of Condorcet, see Behler's introduction to volume 20 of the *Kritische Ausgabe*, especially xv–xix.

14. As, say, in Hume's aesthetics.

15. Schlegel coined the term *Characteristic* to describe a genre of his own critical essays, ones that—by contrast with occasional essays on individual works—sought to examine in a more ambitious way the intersection of authorial intent, formal and thematic content, historical context and reception that defined the essence of a given author's entire work. He published with his brother a collection of their essays under the title *Charakteristiken und Kritiken* (1801), including four essays from 1797 to 1798 on Jacobi's *Woldemar*, Georg Forster, Lessing, and Goethe's *Wilhelm Meisters Lehrjahre* (KA 2:87–146). As the essay on Jacobi states, the goal of the Characteristic is to identify the biographical-intellectual essence of particular works, their "genuine character," their "highest intent" and their "result," by contextualizing them within a larger authorial project. On Schlegel's development and use of this form, see Behler's introduction to *Kritische Ausgabe* (2:xvii–xxxv).

16. In accordance with his rejection of *Urbilder* and mimesis, however, Schlegel also underscores the local limits of Plato's philosophy, its excessive rationality, and its extreme separation of the real and the ideal. See Schlegel, *Kritische Ausgabe* 11: 122–24.

17. The key aspect of this topic that remains to be plumbed is the nature of Schlegel's intellectual affiliation to, and expectations for, the religious mysticism, to which he devoted considerable time in the later period of his life, but about which he published virtually nothing and wrote, even in his notebooks, only in deeply coded ways.

Curvatures: Hegel and the Baroque

~

Arkady Plotnitsky

The Idealist, the Materialist, and the Mathematical Hegel

The problem of Hegel has been given many names, idealism and the absolute arguably most prominent (and most often misleadingly applied) among these names. The very name Hegel may be best seen as the name of a problem. The question is whether such a problem, as it is posed each time, places G. W. F. Hegel and his work further out of reach or even makes him a kind of thing-in-itself, or, conversely, (re)defines the problem as the way toward or even *as* a solution, in a process that Gilles Deleuze envisions, or whether it would make our, perhaps unavoidable, oscillations between these two poles more productive for our understanding of Hegel and for our thought and culture.[1] Could one think, for example, of a materialist or even "materialist-mathematical" Hegel, such as that invoked by Fredric Jameson?[2] And how materialist could mathematics, perhaps the most refined form of ideality, if not idealism, be?

Jameson may, first of all, be thinking of a Hegel whose genealogy extends from the philosophical and scientific materialism of the Enlightenment, rather than only from post-Kantian philosophical idealism. That scientific materialism develops from that of the natural, mathematical sciences, in particular physics, to that of Adam Smith's political economy, crucial to the development of Hegel's thought and then to Karl Marx and Marxism, in relation to which Jameson places his mathematical-materialist Hegel. This Hegel "comes *after* the *Grundrisse*; quite unlike the idealist conservative Hegel who *preceded* the writing of Marx's first great work, the unpublished commentary of the *Philosophy of Right*" (LM 241).

113

On the other hand, rather than only a philosophy of matter or philosophy grounded in materiality, materialism is for Jameson also a particular philosophical and political anti-idealist strategy or set of strategies—something which, while a product of human, material history, and politics, is not simply (physically) material, although it is not merely phenomenal or merely social either. It would be difficult to find anything ever simply phenomenal in any significant Idealism, in particular that of Immanuel Kant or that of Hegel, as Paul de Man argues.[3] In considering de Man's work, Jacques Derrida speaks of "materiality *without* matter," thus also suggesting (differently from Jameson) a certain strategy of intervening in and undermining metaphysical idealism, which could also take the form of a metaphysical materialism, an idealism of matter.[4] From this viewpoint, a materialist Hegel is hardly out of place, whether as a precursor of Marx or otherwise.

There is, however, plenty of matter and materiality *with* matter in Hegel. Earlier, in *Positions*, Derrida speaks of his work as "materialist." There is a crucial proviso, according to which "matter" is now inscribed, in a certain general economy (in Georges Bataille's sense), through the radical alterity of *différance*.[5] At the same time, it is still a question of a displacement of Hegel and of the system of the *Aufhebung* and speculative dialectic, the displacement that is both infinitesimal and radical (P 43–44). Thus, the question of inscription (subject to a material regime of its own) and a conceptuality displacing, infinitesimally and radically, that system is crucial to any rigorous materiality, anyhow impossible without its relationships with phenomenality and conceptuality. It may, thus, be necessary to place the question of materialism in a Hegelian "idealist" regime. Reciprocally, this placement makes materiality, with or (if this is ever possible) without matter, an equally necessary part of this regime. The materialist and the idealist Hegel are ultimately indissociable and must be engaged interactively. This is an argument I shall pursue here.

I shall also argue that, in view of this reciprocity of the two Hegels, materialist and idealist, a certain mathematical—reciprocally both, materialist-mathematical and idealist-mathematical—Hegel emerges as well, or there emerges something mathematical or *mathematical*-materialist in Hegel's philosophy. This mathematical or, one might say, "quasi-mathematical" element may be seen as a form of mathematical materialism, a particular strategy of intervention, which also allows us to emancipate the mathematical in Hegel and in mathematics itself from its idealist appurtenances. One here confronts a conceptuality that works against mathematical idealism and that, while not in itself mathematical, is irreducible in mathematics and ultimately makes it possible. (Accordingly, it may indeed be more accurate to speak of this conceptuality as "quasi-mathematical.") This is the problematic that Edmund Husserl addressed in *The Origin Geometry*, the subject of Derrida's first published book, where much of the groundwork for Derrida's key ideas and strategies was laid.[6] My trajectory will be different from that leading from Hegel to Derrida (via Marx and others) or that extending from Husserl's questioning of mathematics and Derrida's reading of Husserl. Both are potentially viable approaches to the mathematical-materialist, or materialist-mathematical, Hegel. Here, however, I shall approach the problem of Hegel from the perspective of the Baroque, via Leibniz and Deleuze, specifically, on the Baroque, *The Fold: Leibniz and the Baroque*, and on philosophy and the concept, in (with Felix Guattari) *What Is Philosophy?*[7]

On the side of the Baroque, differential calculus, a Baroque invention par excellence, was as crucial to Hegel's thought as it was to that of Deleuze. Ultimately more significant for Hegel were the more fundamentally philosophical aspects of Leibniz's thought that underlie the ideas of differential calculus. Leibniz was one of the very few thinkers in whose thought mathematics and philosophy were working together, even more so than in Descartes and Pascal, two other (near contemporary) cases of equal achievements in mathematics and philosophy. These reciprocal workings of the mathematical and the philosophical in Leibniz were crucial to Hegel's thought, as, and correlatively, were the concept and the practice of the fold, especially as the inter*fold* of matter and spirit, joining "the pleats of matter" and "the fold in the soul" (F 29).

On the side of conceptuality, "Hegel" is perhaps the greatest name of the problem of concept. In *What Is Philosophy?* Deleuze and Guattari define philosophy as the creation of new concepts, indeed concepts that are forever new, thus also making it, in Friedrich Nietzsche's phrase, always the philosophy of the future. This understanding may be argued to be Hegelian, and is seen by Deleuze and Guattari as perhaps uniquely anticipated by Hegel (*What Is Philosophy?* 11–12). The term *concept* itself must be used in the specific sense given to it by Deleuze and Guattari rather than in any common sense of it, in particular that of an entity established by a generalization from particulars or from "any general or abstract idea" (11–12, 24). A philosophical concept has a complex multilayered structure and is, above all, always a multiplicity and a combination, as "there are not simple concepts" (16). It is a multicomponent conglomerate of concepts in their conventional sense, figures, metaphors, particular elements, and so forth.

This concept of concept is, however, in turn reciprocal with the Baroque, to which Deleuze gives a conceptual, rather than only historical sense, thus extending the Baroque to our own time (F 33–34). Hegel makes only a single but a singularly important appearance in *The Fold*, which is, equally importantly, a joint appearance with Joseph Louis Lagrange and his conception (in either sense) of differential calculus. I shall speak of the Hegelian Baroque and the Hegelian fold. Leibniz and the Baroque give Hegel the fold and the richness of the fold, including in its quasi-mathematical dimensions. Hegel (now also helped by Galileo's and Isaac Newton's physics, or, again, Lagrange, who gave Newton's mechanics its modern form), gives the Baroque fold a fundamental temporality and dynamics, and through them history. There would be no modern science without dynamics, that is, the processes (in time) through which particular phenomena emerge. Charles Darwin's move from Linnaeus's classification of species ("phenomena" of animal biology) to the evolution (dynamics) of species may be the most dramatic illustration of this argument, and, as Nietzsche observes, there would never be Darwin without Hegel.[8] It is true that, in contrast to physics, most mathematics does not depend on dynamics. Yet throughout the history of modern mathematics—from differential calculus to the theory of dynamic systems, culminating in chaos and complexity theories—mathematical theories dealing with dynamics have played major roles in mathematics and physics, and in all natural science. Some of these theories owe their debt, however indirect, to Hegel. Reciprocally, Hegel's debt to mathematics and physics is crucial in shaping the materialist and antiabsolutist force of his "idealism."[9]

The Spaces of the Baroque (with Leibniz, Riemann, and Deleuze)

The conceptual architecture of the Baroque or, at least, the architecture of Deleuze's concept of the Baroque is shaped by its reciprocity with the actual, material architecture of the Baroque (which architecture is of course also conceptual and conceptually Baroque). The Baroque's concept of the interior and Deleuze's "allegory" *of* the Baroque house are defined by "common rooms with 'several small openings': the five senses," juxtaposed to a "closed private room, decorated with a 'drapery diversified by folds' " (F 5). This architecture enacts a complex reciprocal interplay—interfold—of materiality and conceptuality, or phenomenality. The term *interior* in Deleuze's discussion of the Baroque (following Leibniz's monadology) must be understood in the sense of phenomenality. Deleuze invokes El Greco's and Tintoretto's "two-floor" visions as exemplary of the Baroque:

> [The] Baroque contribution par excellence is a world with only two floors, separated by a fold that echoes itself, arching from two sides [matter and spirit] according to a different order. It expresses . . . the transformation of the [Platonist] cosmos into a [Baroque] "mundus."
>
> Among the apparently Baroque painters, Tintoretto and El Greco shine, and are incomparable. And yet they have in common this same Baroque trait. [El Greco's] *The Burial of Count Orgaz* is, for instance, divided in two by a horizontal line. On the bottom bodies are presented leaning against each other, while above a soul rises,

along a thin fold, attended by saintly monads, each with its own spontaneity. In Tintoretto the lower level shows bodies tormented by their own weight, their souls stumbling, bending and falling into the meanders of matter; the upper half acts like a powerful magnet that attracts them, makes them ride astride the yellow folds of light, folds of fire bringing their bodies alive, dizzying them, but with a "dizziness from on high": thus are two halves of the *Last Judgment*. . . .

God does not determine the total quantity of progress either beforehand or arfterwards, but eternally, in the calculus of the infinite series that moves through all increased magnitudes of consciousness and all the subtraction of the damned. (F 30, 75)

This argument is amplified by a description of monads that is nearly quantum-mechanical, albeit shaped by the Baroque (rather than quantum) wave and particle optics, which is contrasted to the optics of Descartes, "who remained a man of the [more Platonist] Renaissance, from the point of view of a physics of light and a logic of ideas," or Newton (92). Deleuze writes:

The Baroque is inseparable from a new regime of light and color. To begin with, we can consider light and shadow as 1 and 0, as the two levels in the world separated by a thin line of waters: the Happy and the Damned. An opposition is no longer in question. If we move to the upper level, in a room with neither door nor window, we observe that it is already very dark, in fact almost decorated in black, "fuscum subnigrum." . . . Yet this is not in opposition to light; to the contrary, it is by virtue of the new regime of light. Leibniz makes the point in *Profession de foi du philosophie*: "It slides as if through a slit in the middle of shadow." Should we be given to understand that it comes from a vent, from a thin opening, angled or folded, by intermediary mirrors, the white consisting "in a great number of small reflecting mirrors"? . . . Since monads have no openings, a light that has been "sealed" is lit in each one when it is raised to the level of reason . . . through all the tiny inner mirrors. It makes whiteness, but shadow too: . . . Chiaroscuro fills monads. (31–32)

Both passages are crucial in defining the Baroque materiality, and short of the reciprocity with this materiality, the mathematical or mathematical-philosophical phenomenality and ideality of the Baroque will be taken over by the absolute. Conversely, short of a certain quasi-mathematical or perhaps even a certain mathematical ideality (without absolutes), the materialist idealism, the idealism of matter and its absolutes, would take over in turn. The space (topos) or protospace, or, in the language of Plato's *Timaeus*, the *khora*, where the Baroque could emerge, is defined abstractly but as *permitting* the Baroque, in the manner in which Bernhard Riemman's general mathematical definition of space could in principle permits both Euclidean or/as Cartesian geometry and non-Euclidean geometry. The actual space (topos) itself of the Baroque is then defined by the two-floor structure and materiality within it, just as an actual physical space is defined, as Euclidean or non-Euclidean, by matter, in accordance with Riemann's and then Albert Einstein's view.[10] Much of the geometry of the Baroque may be seen in parallel with the non-Euclidean geometry (which obtains in a curved space of Einstein's general relativity, his non-Newtonian theory of gravity).

Of course in this situation, especially in speaking, as does *What Is Philosophy?*, of spatiality and configurations of concepts, geometry and to-pology, or spatiality itself, can only be used as broad metaphors or, as in Deleuze, as philosophical, rather than mathematical, conceptual conglomer-ates (leaving aside for the moment that certain quasi-mathematical machinery is also operative in mathematics itself). The deployment of geometric and topological formations becomes part of the philosophical production of con-cepts, as defined in *What Is Philosophy?*, whose topo-ontology of concepts is a great example of Deleuzean philosophical topology, which is also Leibnizean, Baroque. The concept of the Baroque interior announces the multifarious richness of shapes, variations, and mirrors or reflections (in ei-ther sense) of the Baroque fold, arising from the Baroque topos, or, in Plato's terms, *khora*. The Baroque is inconceivable without the vision and practice, and freedom, of variations, especially variations of curves and curvatures, and on the theme of "curve" and "curvature," found in Bernini's and Borromini's architecture; Tintoretto's, El Greco's, and Caravaggio's paintings; or in Ba-roque music. (Baroque literature appears to be defined more fundamentally by allegory.) Borromini's curves in his San Carlino Church in Rome not only have different curvatures; each also has a varying (rather than permanent) curvature. This mathematical architecture helps Borromini to define a particu-larly striking case of the Baroque mundus, material, and conceptual, which, as we contemplate it, our imagination continuously expands and indeed cre-ates, to begin with, by adding new curves and varying their curvatures.

The two tropes, "geometry" and "topology," are distinguished by their mathematical provenances. Geometry fundamentally involves measurement, while topology disregards measurement, and deals only with the structure of space qua space and with the essential shapes of figures. Insofar as one deforms a given figure continuously (i.e., does not separate points previously connected and, conversely, does not connect points previously separated) the resulting figure is considered equivalent. Leibniz's ideas concerning topology or "analysis situs," as he called it, were among his greatest contributions to mathematics, developed into modern topology in the nineteenth century by Karl F. Gauss, Bernhard Riemann, Henri Poincaré, and others.[11]

Both geometry and topology come together in the concept of manifold (many-*fold*), especially important for Deleuze (*Thousand Plateaus*, 485). The idea of manifold may, again, be traced to Leibniz. The (mathematical) concept itself is, however, due to Riemann, another major inspiration for Deleuze. A manifold is a kind of patchwork of (local) spaces, each of which can be mapped by a (flat) Euclidean-Cartesian coordinate map, without allowing for a global Euclidean structure or a single coordinate system for the whole, except in the limited case of the Euclidean space itself. That is, every point has a small neighborhood that can be treated as Euclidean, but the overall manifold cannot be. Manifolds are, thus, locally flat but are, in general, globally curved. The concept of manifold is essential to the idea of non-Euclidean geometry, one of which, the geometry of positive curvature, was discovered by Riemann. (His teacher, Gauss, was a codiscoverer of the geometry of negative curvature.) Crucially, it is not a matter of curves in a flat space but of the curvature of the space itself. The idea may be illustrated by considering Paul Klee's painting *The New Harmony,* the title alluding to Leibniz, while the same title of the last chapter of Deleuze's *Fold* alludes, along with Leibniz, to Klee (121). The painting deforms a Cartesian space by giving it curvature and a complex color scheme, thus allegorizing a curved, non-Euclidean space. Deleuze sees Klee's work as one of the primary examples of the Baroque in his extended sense, to which Riemann's ideas would conform as well.

The flows of fabric in the draperies of Baroque interiors or garments of Baroque paintings are also allegories of the Baroque fold. But consider a helicoid, a geometric object introduced during the Baroque (around 1690s), a kind of ribbon-like spiral surface, extending the idea of the spiral (the Greek word *helicoeidés* means "something having a spiral form"), which could be generated by a straight line moving so as to touch a fixed spiral. Helicoids are manifolds in the mathematical sense explained earlier: locally (infinitesimally) flat but globally curved. The Tower of Babel as painted by Peter Breughel or Frank Lloyd Wright's Guggenheim Museum gives one an idea of such an object. In these cases the line generating the surface would be cut to a finite interval. If the line were not cut (it would have to be in any material object), visualizing such an object would be quite a bit more difficult, indeed impossible. A spiral topology of that type can be used to represent or to stand for, as a symbol or (to distinguish them along de Man's lines) allegory, a more or less complex or vertiginous movement.[12] It may be a movement up (more often diagonally than vertically), say, toward the divine—God or Geist—as in Plato, Leibniz, or Hegel. This verticality, may, thus, need to be treated as a key signifier and often as a transcendental, governing, signifier (sometimes related to a "vertical," transcendental signified, such as God). Or it can be a movement, in the absence of any transcendental support, toward bottomless abysses as in famed deconstructive vertigoes. It is difficult to say whether these vertigoes result from moving or looking up or down, although in these cases one indeed finds more vertical, up/down, lifts and falls, and ruptures. Friedrich Hölderlin's "abysses above" may well be the best way to see them. A different—irreducibly ruptured—allegorical form of verticality or "vertiginality," beyond even the Kantian sublime, is at stake, and I shall comment on this crucial (almost crucifixional) discontinuity later. These vertigoes extend the philosophical, between reason and madness, vertigoes of Hegel's dialectical reflection, although, while aimed upward, it is hardly less than bottomless. In Deleuze, rather than moving up, such a "surface" may be thought of as extending—folding, unfolding, interfolding—horizontally, rhizomatically.

An equally defining feature of the Baroque is the multiplicity of varying and curved—convex and concave—mirrors, such as that of Parmigianino's self-portrait in a convex mirror. Baroque houses are full of mirrors, and seem to need mirrors more than windows. As we have seen, Leibniz's monads have no windows, but they are full of mirrors inside and are themselves mirrors, reflecting the curvatures and variations of the world, and them into the world. Leibniz's world of monads is a universe of mirrors, modeled on, or serving as a model, for the Baroque palace. In the picture just sketched, one can imagine the curved surfaces as mirrored and reflecting in each other, and changing their forms in the process.

One should also add Derridean chandeliers (*lustres*) reflecting in all these mirrored surfaces so that one cannot unequivocally distinguish sources of light from their reflections, or indeed claim the possibility of an absolutely original source of light, which, however, would shift the register of the image into that of phenomenal allegory. Unlike real chandeliers, Derrida's allegorize the circumstances that disallow one to unequivocally distinguish sources of light from their reflections or what mirrors from what is mirrored, or to claim the possibility of an absolutely original source or set of sources of light. The play of reflections cannot be reduced to an unequivocal discrimination between sources and images, which is not to say that nothing materially exists. What Derrida calls "dissemination," or *différance*/dissemination ("chandelier" is part of his, itself disseminating, matrix of names) *reflects* this irreducible play and plurality.[13] It does not, however, reflect or map the ultimate efficacity of such effects, that is, an agency capable of producing such effects but to which one cannot ascribe causality, or any conceivable attribute or name, "agency" included. Such an efficacity or (they are always as plural as their effects, and both are unique each time) efficacities can be "reflected upon" philosophically and inferred through their effects, but they cannot be *illuminated*—accessed or conceived—by any means. Derrida's dissemination of light is arrived at in part via his reading of Stéphane Mallarmé, and, for Deleuze, too, "the fold is probably Mallarmé's most important notion, and not only a notion but the operative act that makes him a great Baroque poet" (F 30). While Deleuze pairs Mallarmé with Leibniz, Derrida links Mallarmé's differentiating-disseminating fold to Hegel (and a deconstruction of a certain Hegel), and both Derrida and Deleuze link Mallarmé's fold to Martin Heidegger's *Zweifalt*. For the moment, the features just outlined combined suggest an initial image of the Baroque as a space of mirrored and mutually reflecting surfaces, curves and curvatures, folds and unfolding, and sources of light without absolute origin or center, or an absolute reality, or, it follows, an absolute mirror.

To give this picture yet further, more properly Baroque, complexity and structure, I shall now introduce a new concept, "superfold," which reflects the fourth defining feature of the Deleuzean Baroque—the multiplicity and architecture or architectonics of variations, and variations upon variations, folds upon folds. While also due to Riemann, this concept is indebted to more recent developments, extending to some of the most arcane areas of modern mathematics. One may describe the philosophical content of the concept as follows. In analyzing certain objects, such as geometric curves or surfaces, one considers jointly all—or a large enough number of—variations or deformations of the structure that defines such an object, itself seen as a varied, such as Riemannian, space. Then one combines such space into a new, higher-level structure or space, other points of which would be (the second-level) variations of the initial (already varied) space. This enables one to see this combined structure as a single object or space and each object/space as a "point" of this new space, and yet also to see this space in terms of its more standard topology, whose points are regular dimensionless points. Since, however, it is not effective and in practice impossible, to consider all such variations, one must determine which variations are sufficiently equivalent to be subsumed within a single variation, which should be discarded, and how some among such variations can be organized. Why construct such objects? First of all, the structure of such objects provides new information, perhaps otherwise unobtainable, about the original object. Second, the process leads to a construction of new "spaces," which are useful in approaching the initial configuration or are in their own terms. Third, superfold structures also helps us to understand that which exceeds all possible formalization or conceptuality, or indeed all phenomenality. Superfold structures, even the mathematical ones, are ultimately inaccessible to visualization. Yet, while themselves inaccessible, they also serve as allegories of other inaccessible objects. They refer to that which, while irreducibly involving or producing, as effects, both materiality and phenomenality, is itself neither material nor phenomenal in any given sense we can give to these terms. I shall return to this epistemology later.

From this perspective, Klee's space in *The New Harmony* (one might also think of variations of light and color) may be seen an *element*—a point— of a higher-level space, other points of which are variations of this manifold space. In a certain sense, as we look at the painting, we "see" such a multiplicity. Another great Baroque work, Johann Sebastian Bach's *Goldberg Variations*, may give us the best model. One can see each variation as a musical space, and then combine them in the whole thirty-two-piece work, suggesting a potentially infinite varying multiplication of this space. While the work itself is (finitely) closed by Bach, the potential number of variations is, in principle, infinite, although a superfold structure, suggested by Bach's variations, would form a certain (infinite) subset.

The Baroque is thus defined by organized variations of already varied spaces, folds upon folds, and folds of folds, invoked by Deleuze, via Mallarmé and Boulez (F 33–34).[14] According to Deleuze,

> the ideal fold is the *Zweifalt*, a fold that differentiates and is differentiated. When Heidegger calls upon the *Zweifalt* to be the differentiator of difference, he means above all that differentiation does not refer to a pregiven undifferentiated, but to a Difference that endlessly unfolds and folds over each of its two sides, and that unfolds the one only while refolding the other, in a coextensive unveiling and veiling of Being, of presence and of withdrawal of presence. (30)

It is thus also a matter-spirit interfold, defined by two heterogeneous and yet interactive folds (147 n.8). In contrast to the fold of the historical Baroque, such as that of Tintoretto's work, this *Zweifalt* need not be seen in these *vertical* terms, while it is defined by the same (Baroque) geometric and topological structure. *Our* Baroque, that of Klee, Heidegger, Mallarmé, Boulez, Stockhausen, Dubuffet, or of Deleuze is defined by suspending the *vertical* movement of the fold, toward God, for example, and moving to the new *horizontal* and divergent harmonies. It moves from monadology and its vertical space (singular) to nomadology and its smooth space*s* (plural), with which Deleuze closes *The Fold* (F 137). I would further add that the "points" of the "surface" of Difference invoked by Deleuze are differentiations of a differentiated fold, thus converting the *Zweifalt* into a superfold defined by variations of a given fold. The Baroque conceptual architecture, codefined by the matter-spirit interfold and the superfold topology is one of the great legacies of Leibniz's philosophy to Hegel. Hegel gives the concept of history a Baroque shape and gives history to the Baroque, joining both in the Hegelian Baroque. This is Hegel's legacy to our Baroque.

The Hegelian Baroque 1: The Continuity of the Fold

Hegel makes "history" a defining part of his concept of philosophy or, more accurately, he makes both history and philosophy reciprocal parts of the same conceptual architecture, and thus makes his perhaps most decisive philosophical discovery, as Alexandre Kojève argued. This reciprocity thus makes history, as the history of the Spirit, Geist, the history of philosophy, and philosophy a historical concept, as is, concomitantly, Hegel's concept of concept. As Hegel is well aware, this view is only a particular human perspective on the World, assuming that the very terms *philosophy*, or *history* or *process*, or *world*, could apply. Crucially, however, Hegelian history is defined by the complex interactions, in the course of this history, between Geist and humanity. These interactions are given both the "formal" quasi-mathematical topology and geometry of the fold as superfold and the Baroque architecture of two floors, two folds of matter and spirit, and of their interfold, to which Hegel gives the temporality and historicity of movement, without which the Baroque could not be the determinant of our culture. I shall discuss first some the key features of the Hegelian Baroque, in particular, the reciprocity of materiality and phenomenality (the interfolded reciprocity of the folds of matter and spirit); the superfold character on the Hegelian fold; and the historical topology of the unfolding of concepts. Hegel sees history as the history of concepts, close to Deleuze and Guattati's sense, and specifically as the history of the Concept (*Begriff*), a complex conceptual architecture of unity and multiplicity, which relationship follows Leibniz. Ultimately, this architecture entails, even if against Hegel's own grain, an uncontainable (rather than synthesizable) plurality of conceptual mappings, on the joint model of Derrida's dissemination and Deleuze and Guattari's multiple ("Riemannian") mapping. This concept of concept opens itself up to a new form of ideality, free of absolutes or idealism, idealist or materialist.

Hence, certain materialist dimensions are essential to Hegel's "idealist" philosophy. It is materialist both in the sense of the materiality of nature—the irreducible relationships between Spirit and Nature (or matter)—and in the sense of the materiality of history—an irreducible linking of Spirit and humanity, thus fully anticipating and in some respect superceding Marx. In the language of *The Fold*, "the pleats of matter" and "the folds in the soul" continuously interact with, interfold, and pass into each other, and mix their curvatures, shaping a critical force of Hegel's "idealism." This force, however, is equally and reciprocally due to the topology of all Hegelian folds, crucial in mitigating the effects of metaphysical materialism. That is, the multifarious and specifically superfold, Baroque character of Hegel's conceptual topology is defined by the reciprocal interfolding of materiality and phenomenality within Hegel's

Baroque fold. If there is a "spiral" of history in Hegel, it designates the gradient, toward Absolute Knowledge, of this grandiose unfolding, with many complex loops and returns ("circles of circles"), rather than a reduction of its richness to a linear progression. The closure of the greater *Logic* or that of the *Phenomenology of Spirit* reveals precisely this topology.[15]

The process may be seen in terms of a particular, let's call it "diagonal," economy of enrichment. The question is how to give or associate with a given structurally impoverished object a kind of structural richness comparable to that associated with an analogously defined object that is structurally rich, or how to transfer such structural richness onto the initial objects. Geist's spiritual endowment is rich, indeed infinitely rich, whereas that of humanity is poor, and no spiritual, upward movement for humanity is possible without traversing the available portion of Geist's spirituality. The task of philosophy and human practice is to maximally enrich the spiritual endowment of humanity on the model of, and approximating that of, Geist through a certain upward or "diagonal" movement. That Geist's endowment is already constructed or, in Derrida's terms, supplemented upon human models (mathematical or other), however enriched (this human enrichment is the point here), is often forgotten by theology or even by philosophy. On the other hand, supplementarity allows one to suspend the theological or ontotheological determination of the situation, while keeping the possibilities of enrichment in place. In "the strange structure of the supplement," Derrida argues, "by delayed reaction, a possibility produces that which it is said to be added on."[16] If so, however, the diagonal enrichment, even if in the name of the divine, is precisely what is thus opened to human productions and invention. Naturally, in this case, the reverse "descent" to the lower level to be thus enriched must proceed from some other human, rather than divine, conception or field, which must be invented on whatever (human) basis. This, however, is hardly an impediment, rather a resource. Nietzsche's concept of the Overman (*Übermensch*) may be the best example of this process of the ideal, but not divine or otherwise idealist, enrichment, insofar as our understanding of the human itself is concerned. There are equally spectacular examples elsewhere, including in mathematics and science. We are continuously discovering new ways of enriching our knowledge, and by so doing we also learn how to emancipate idealism or ideality from its theological and ontotheological absolutes.

While ultimately supplementary, Hegel's economy of enrichment is enabled by a joint and interactive historical progression of Geist and humanity, with Geist (claimed) always ahead of human development. This interactive reciprocity and the very development (in either sense) of Geist are accomplished through the development of concepts within a conceptual architecture or economy defined by Hegel in terms of the Absolute Concept, or the Idea in his later works. Hegel, thus, anticipates Deleuze and Guattari's concept of concepts and their concept of philosophy as the creation of concepts, and they see Hegel's concept of concept as his arguably greatest contribution to philosophy:

> Hegel powerfully defines concept by the Figures of its creation and the Moments of its self-positing. The figures become parts of the concept because they constitute the aspects through which the concept is created by and in consciousness, through successive minds; whereas the Moments form the other aspect according to which the concept posits itself and unites minds in the absolute of the Self. In this way Hegel showed that the concept has nothing whatever to do with the general or abstract idea anymore that with an uncreated Wisdom that does not depend on philosophy itself. (*What Is Philosophy?* 11–12)

Hegel's concept of concept cannot, however, be fully appreciated without taking into account his superfold topology of concepts and its historical character. Hegel converts history into a grand conglomerate of Baroque folds and superfolds in their historical movements, with a vertiginous spiral movement built into it, defined by its irreducibly conceptual nature. On the other hand, once this movement is coupled to a certain Kantian or (de-Manian) allegorical, irreducibly discontinuous rupture, this fold-like topology could only be seen as an allegorical diagram relating to that which is irreducibly inaccessible by means of any diagram and ultimately by any means. It is that which exceeds any theology, even negative theology, or any ontotheology.[17] This conceptuality and epistemology are more radical both in their (differential) continuity, that of the Baroque fold, and in their insurmountable allegorical discontinuity.

Hegel says in the *Phenomenology*: "The movement of carrying forward the form of [Spirit's] self-knowledge is the labor which Spirit accomplishes as actual History [*wirkliche Geschichte*]," which can, accordingly, be also seen as material history (PS 488). However, he also realized and pursued the enormous complexity of this process, resulting from the Baroque interfold of matter ("the pleats of matter") and spirit ("the folds in the soul") within it, as both interact with, and pass into, each other, and mix their curvatures. The process can be understood by spirit (specifically through conceptual work and through interacting with nature and history)—whether "spirit" refers to the divine spirituality of the Hegelian Spirit, Geist, or to human spirituality and in particular philosophy, such as Hegel's. According to Hegel, it is only to Geist that the process and its nature can be accessible in full measure. The complete comprehension of this nature by Geist, via the Concept or later the Idea, is what Hegel calls "Absolute Knowledge." In the end of the *Phenomenology* Hegel *unfolds* this economy via his concept of sacrifice, which transforms many a Judeo-Christian spiritual economy, but accomplishes much more than that, in view of the concept of discontinuity it entails, on which I shall comment presently. This economy, including as concerns the interplay of continuity and rupture, was further radicalized by Bataille, a key link between Hegel and Derrida and Deleuze, among others. Many a Greek "theogram," from Plato on, is also refigured in the process. The whole history of Judeo-Greek theoculture is *converted* into an immense historical fold.

This manifold process is what Hegel's "spirals" or "helicoids" allegorize. The Hegelian spiral-diagonal enrichment, never straightforward or unidirectional, from the human to the divine can only be accomplished, first, by way of a radical rethinking of both the human and the divine through an irreducible interaction between them, and, second, through an equally irreducible interaction between spirituality, human and divine, and materiality, as nature and as history. An extraordinary vision, one of the greatest philosophical visions ever, is suggested in the three monumental paragraphs closing—or unclosing—Hegel's *Phenomenology*. The movement, Baroque in its conceptual topology, of these paragraphs would require a separate analysis.[18] My point here is that Hegel's vision is made possible by a philosophical "alchemy" that both mixes and separates exteriority and interiority, spirituality and materiality, philosophy and history, contingency and necessity, and so forth—perhaps all conceivable conceptual oppositions and multiple clusters that one might form. This multiplicity is irreducible and is played out throughout Hegel's work, involving the invention or construction of concepts themselves. It is this construction (envisioned in terms of a historical fold-economy) that Hegel calls the "Concept."

Hegel conceived history as an immense conglomerate of, interactively, concepts of history and historico-political practices, with multiple economies, continuous and discontinuous, organizing both theory and practice, and the interactions between them. Hegel considers *ensembles* or *families*—superfolds—of conceptual and social-political formations and, and in, the interactions between them, rather than merely such formations themselves. His philosophy is that of conglomerates or aggregates, folds and superfolds, of material and spiritual structures, theoretical conceptualities and historico-political practices, continuities and discontinuities, multiple economies of necessity and chance, and so forth, and of the interactions between such (apparent) oppositions and junctures. The question of the structure and economy of the grand whole, and of the very possibility of assigning any wholeness to this interplay, defines the Hegelian problem of history. What Hegel sees in the *Phenomenology*, as "the slow-moving progression of Spirits," whose "ultimate goal is the revelation of the depth of Spirit [*Geist*], which is *the absolute Concept*," entails all variations of the conceptual and historical structures that it considers—perception, consciousness and self-consciousness, and spirit; or ethics, religion, art, philosophy, and history (PS 492; translation has been modified slightly). These structures and hence the structure of "the absolute Concept" itself are conceived of as irreducibly varied and manifold (also in Deleuze and Guattari's Riemannian sense of the multitudes of maps). Hegel combines these structures into a new, higher-level super fold-like structure or, again, a manifold of structures and of the interactions between them. In Hegel such multiplicities can often be best described in terms of one another. Each may serve as a descriptive quasi–mathematics ("calculus," "algebra," "geometry," "topology," or "analysis") or allegorical translation of the other, even though all of them are also placed in the service of what they or anything else cannot access. History is a calculus or an allegory of philosophy; philosophy is that of history; matter of mind, mind of matter, consciousness of the unconscious, unconscious of consciousness, and so forth. Hegel gives all cognition both fundamentally multifold and fundamentally historical dimensions, along with and *as* the Hegelian continuity, versus the "Kantian" discontinuous exteriority. As will be seen, however, this exteriority subsists, indeed nearly expressly, in the allegorical economy accompanying Hegel's superfolds.

Since, as I said, it is not effective and is in practice impossible to consider all such variations, it is important to understand how some of them are organized, or how these variations unfold and how some of them can be folded together or fold upon themselves. Hegel offers a variety of historical sequences and stages (and other classifications) in his works. These, however, are only various modes of organization or folding of multiple historical trajectories. These mappings reflect folds and superfolds of configurations found at any point of history and still more complex formations resulting from linking them within longer historical intervals (to the extent that one may even speak of *points* of history in this superfold topology).

This is why, while Hegel's spiral, if there is any, does indicate an upward movement of Spirit and humanity, even if still grafting the diagonal verticality of theos onto its unfolding, this spiral could only be seen as a diagram, indeed a diagram within a diagram. Even the more complex images, such as those of the Baroque mirrored folds with Derridean disseminating chandeliers, are only allegorical diagrams for Hegel's historical-conceptual (khoral) topology, even if one suspends allegorical ruptures in the Hegelian process. Ultimately this allegorization may be interminable, infinite, thus also defining the ultimate nature of the Hegelian infinite, for example, as that of the infinitude of Spirit emerging, via a (mis)quotation from Friedrich Schiller's *Die Freundschaft, ad fin* in the end of *Phenomenology*, still figured through the irreducible rupture of death and sacrifice. For the moment, one might envision Hegel's spiral as circling along an immense Baroque fold. Each cross section along this spiral is an immense superfold of structures and connections, which cannot be reduced to an unequivocal, unitary, or punctual simplicity, or be seen outside the Baroque "two-floor" interfold of the material and the phenomenal. Hegel, it is true, could be, and has been read along the lines of, the Platonist and Neoplatonist tradition, as described by Deleuze, in contradistinction to the two floors or two folds of the Baroque. In Platonism, "the world was thought to have an infinite number of floors, with a stairway that descends and ascends, with each step being lost in the upper order of the One and disintegrated in the ocean of the multiple" (F 29). Hegel retains and enriches certain topological aspects of this process. But he follows Leibniz and the Baroque in making his world the two-floor, two-fold matter-spirit world, separated and yet joined by "a fold that echoes itself, arching from the two sides according to a different order," matter on one side and spirit on the other (29). It is this trifold world, and not the Platonist one, that Hegel's circles of circles fold and unfold in a historical-dialectical movement, more contrapuntal and closer to Bach (if not quite as horizontal as in Boulez) than is Leibniz's monadology, but no less Baroque.

The Hegelian Baroque 2: The Discontinuity of Allegory

Crucially, however, the Hegelian process entails discontinuities and ruptures, such as death and sacrifice. One might, accordingly, also see the Hegelian dialectic as an allegory of discontinuity, as de Man does, or as interminable oscillations, bordering on madness, of continuity and discontinuity, which de Man approaches in terms of irony.[19] Tragic ruptures become effects of Hegel's negativity or of a still more radical negativity, which emerges in Hölderlin's work and the power of which Hegel tries to contain, while inevitably reinscribing it in his text, as he climbs or builds simultaneously both the Mountain of Purgatorio and the Tower of Babel, and translates each allegory into each other. Given the Baroque as a background, the appeal to allegory may well be inevitable. Allegory is a major Baroque concept, and in invoking it I refer especially to de Man's work but also to that of Walter Benjamin, invoked by Deleuze in the way pertinent here (F 127). I shall now address the allegorical character of the Baroque fold, its irreducibly allegorical character in de Man's sense of allegory. It may be helpful, first, to retrace my quasi-mathematical Baroque topoi as allegories, rather than as objects or simply images.

The families of (mirrored) helicoids, my first geometric/topological allegory, were introduced only as reasonably visualizable models (to the degree that one can visualize even these "pictures") of more complex mathematical objects. Insofar, however, as these more complex objects are used in order to approach the philosophical topologies here considered, they give the first, helicoid allegory of these topologies a more complex quasi-mathematical structure, which may itself not be visualizable or even conceivable. An analogous (if suitably adjusted) argument could be made with regard to the mathematical concepts from which these quasi-mathematical structures derive. The most crucial epistemological point here, however, is that the philosophical topologies in question are themselves allegorical insofar as they serve to approach yet something else. In other words, we deal, at least, with a triple allegorization, which de Man sees as history and that Hegel's economy of history both involves and resists (AI 132). The first allegory is defined by a certain visualizable geometry or topology that allegorizes nonvisualizable objects or concepts. These—this is the second allegory—in turn allegorize (and sometimes participate in) the conceptual "topology" (the use of this term is already an allegory) of certain philosophical concepts here considered. This last topology, however, further allegorized yet something else; and one needs to consider the concept or, in turn, allegory of allegory itself in order to ask it what that may be. In view of the epistemology that ensues, it may be rigorously impossible to answer this question. Indeed this inaccessibility has its effects at the lower levels of the allegorization in question: the (helicoid) objects of the first allegory are already ultimately inaccessible.[20]

Although nearly all of de Man's work on allegory is relevant here, his view of allegory as expressed in "Pascal's Allegory of Persuasion" is especially fitting: "the difficulty of allegory is rather that this emphatic clarity of representation does not stand in the service of something that can be represented" (AI 51). Indeed it may be said to stand in the service of that which cannot be represented by any means, is intolerant of attribution of any properties, and is ultimately beyond any conception or phenomenalization. De Man's conception of materiality, with and without matter, and of matter itself is related to this irreducibly inconceivable, ultimately inconceivable even as inconceivable. This "matter" is something into which the Baroque trifold of matter and spirit and of their interfold ultimately dissolves, but that also makes all these folds possible. There are certain manifest material effects and phenomenal effects of representation, some of which possess an "emphatic clarity" of individual definition and collective organization, and some of these manifest configurations that may, as it were, "defer" or eclipse the unrepresentable, or make us "blind" to it. Indeed, how could we rigorously infer the unrepresentable, rather than simply imagine it, short of such effects?

Now, what kind of effects are these? Their character is defined by a particular relation between the individual and collective character of these effects. In the regime of de Man's allegory, there is always a certain level at which a particular form of "organization" of certain individual elements/ effects (linguistic, conceptual, or other) is bound to emerge. This "organization," however, is not organic but "allegorical" (and hence also discontinuous), and as such may be juxtaposed to the "organicism" (and continuity) of symbol and the aesthetic ideology based on it, to which it is so tempting to reduce Hegel's topology in view of its, in turn, irreducible, continuous aspects. The particulars involved are organized in the sense that we may meaningfully consider certain configurations of these particulars. This organization, however, does not govern (as symbolic wholeness would) these particulars in their particularity: it offers no synthesis of them. At the limit, this type of organization would make each particular unique or singular in its emergence and would make it impossible to access or conceive of its efficacity. At the level of concepts, this view would be in accord with Deleuze and Guattari's concept of concept as defined by the organization of particulars. However, it also takes the conceptual architecture involved to an allegorical limit, at which conceptual particulars begin to diverge—de-cohere—to the point of complete independence from the collective order in which they partake and indeed to form. In order to "see" such an organization, we must inevitably displace, be "blind" to, the nature and history of its constitutive elements, to which no coherence of any kind could be assigned. This may be the ultimate difference between symbol and allegory in de Man.

This argument is not paradoxical, although the price we pay for avoiding a paradox is that the ultimate "nature" and "history," the efficacity of such elements and hence of their organization, is irreducibly inconceivable. This efficacity produces, as effects, each element and "organizes" their collectivity, but the character of this efficacity is not derivable from the nature of this collectivity, and is unavailable to any derivation from anything, any analysis, conception, and so forth. It is, thus, irreducibly mysterious in the sense of being beyond any knowledge or conception, but, it follows, not mystical insofar as it prohibits assuming any given, especially causal, form of agency behind such effects, such as the God of theology, positive or negative. The efficacity in question is irreducibly inaccessible or inconceivable by any means available to us or by any means that will ever be available to us, is inaccessible even as inaccessible or as "that." Accordingly, it cannot be seen in terms of independent properties, relations, or laws, which, while still unavailable to us, would define a single entity that would exist in itself and by itself while, in certain circumstances, giving rise to certain individual or collective effects. Instead, it must be seen as reciprocal with, and indeed indivisible from, its effects in the sense that it can never be, in practice and in principle, conceived as isolated from them and ever conceived as being "by itself" or "in itself." Nor, however, can it be seen as "continuous" with any of its effects. It also follows that, while always inaccessible, each such efficacity is each time unique, as unique as and reciprocally with, each effect. This radical discontinuity is also fundamentally linked to chance (Hegel appeals to contingency [*Zufälligkeit*] in closing the *Phenomenology*).[21]

As I have indicated, the inaccessibility in question can appear already at the level of a given allegorical representation (or a signifier, rather than only a signified or a referent). For such a representation may already be rigorously inaccessible in the same sense and can only be related to allegorically by means of other concepts, metaphors, or signifiers. We deal with certain ultimately, but only ultimately, inaccessible *objects* (this term is ultimately inapplicable as well) representing or (one cannot speak of representation either) relating to equally inaccessible *objects*. This would, among other things, problematize any standard (or naively reversed) hierarchy, such as that between signifier/signified or form/meaning, or any fixed borders between such concepts. Such relational chains of the ultimately inaccessible strata could be extended interminably, which extension is close to de Man's "irony," as a trope of temporality, especially in Hölderlin and Hegel. It is also fundamentally linked in de Man or Derrida (as in *différance*) to a certain inaccessible materiality (*with* and without matter), which is in turn linked (as inaccessible) to the Deleuzean Baroque trifold, which now appears at the level of manifest material and phenomenal effects, and of their relationships.

Nor, accordingly, does this epistemology suggest that nothing exists which, in circumstances of allegorical representation, gives rise to the effects in question, but, again, only that the efficacities in question are inconceivable in any terms that are or perhaps will ever be, available to us. Naturally, "existence" or "nonexistence" (or "matter" and "materiality") are among these terms, along with the possibility or impossibility of "conceiving" of it, or "possibility," or "impossibility," or, "it" and "is." At this ultimate level, no knowledge, even that of the impossibility of knowledge, is possible, but only at this level, for, at other levels knowledge, even an abundance of knowledge, is possible. Indeed some knowledge is only possible as an effect of such efficacities and by virtue of taking them into account, thus relating the knowable and the unknowable and maximizing both. We may be dealing with relating something ultimately inaccessible to something else equally ultimately inaccessible, or interminable chains of such relations. But we need many accessible effects of these relations, including for ascertaining the inaccessibility in question. It follows that phenomenality, ideality, and conceptuality are equally irreducible and necessary, but that deploying them no longer allows for idealism or absolutes.

Hegel's quasi–mathematics is irreducibly allegorical, even if sometimes against his own grain. It is always an allegory insofar as the continuity of any fold or folds involved or, conversely, any discontinuous assemblage, ordered or random, of events, is an after-the-fact (*nachträglich*) or supplementary architecture ("monumentalization," de Man would say) allowed by certain material or phenomenal effects. The efficacity of their occurrence is irreducibly inaccessible and irreducibly irreversible (AI 132). This irreducibly inaccessible and irreversible efficacity may enter at any level, thus disrupting any apparently sufficient representation, continuous (fold), or discontinuous. The allegorical nature of this economy is made all the more radical by the temporality of the Hegelian fold. More accurately, this economy is manifest in this temporality, which is ultimately defined by the irreversibility of the efficacious dynamics just invoked. It also reveals the irreducible temporality of the trope of allegory (or irony), at least once the latter is taken to its de Manian limit, although Benjamin already goes quite far on that road. This fold-allegorical economy is Hegel's and indeed, jointly, Kant's and Hegel's, great legacy to modern history, as it is also in part the result of their thinking through Leibniz's philosophy, the philosophy of the continuous, or so it appears.

Conclusion: New Harmonies

This fold-allegorical economy of the new Baroque is not the end but a new starting point of an immense philosophical and historical analysis, and of cultural practice, of new ways of folding and unfolding everything. I close, accordingly, with Deleuze's conclusion in *The Fold*, which gives this idea the dimension and the harmony, the divergent harmony, of the new Baroque:

> To the degree that the world is now made up of divergent series (the chaosmos), or that crapshooting replaces the game of Plenitude, the monad is now unable to contain the entire world as if in a closed circle that can be modified by projection. It now opens on a trajectory or a spiral in expansion that moves further and further away from a center. A vertical harmonic can no longer be distinguished from a horizontal harmonic, just like the private condition of a dominant monad that produces its own accords in itself, and the public condition of monads in a crowd that follows the lines of melody. The two begin to fuse on a sort of diagonal, where the monads penetrate each other, and modified, inseparable from the groups of prehension that carry them along and make up as many transitory captures.
>
> The question always entails living in the world, but Stockhausen's musical habitat or Dubuffet's plastic habitat do not allow the difference of inside and outside, of public and private, to survive. They identify variation and trajectory, and overtake monadology with a "nomadology." Music has stayed at home: what has changed now is the organization of the home and its nature. We are all still Leibnizian, although accords no longer convey our world or our text. We are discovering new ways of folding, akin to new envelopments, but we all remain Leibnizian because what always matters is folding, unfolding, refolding. (F 137)

These divergent spirals, however, also tell us that we may be even more Hegelian than Leibnizean, which also means Kantian, as these names—Leibniz,

Kant, and Hegel—designate the problems that inhabit each other in Baroque spaces and folds. Their contrapuntal fabric (*textum*) has so many topoi of matter and spirit, and of materialism and idealism, with and without absolutes. No absolute, however, materialist or idealist, positive or negative, is capacious enough to contain these folds—the pleats of matter and the folds in the soul in their irreducible reciprocity, and, least of all, that which lies beyond them, but without being absolutely beyond them, and, thus, is also that which is "beyond" the beyond.

Notes

1. See Gilles Deleuze, *Difference and Repetition*, trans. Paul Patton (New York: Columbia University Press, 1993), 179–80; and Deleuze and Felix Guattari, *A Thousand Plateaus*, trans. Brian Massumi (Minneapolis: University of Minnesota Press, 1987), 351–79ff.

2. Fredric Jameson, *Late Marxism: Adorno, or the Persistence of the Dialectic* (London: Verso: 1990), hereafter cited as LM.

3. See Paul de Man, "Phenomenality and Materiality in Kant" and "Sign and Symbol in Hegel's *Aesthetics*," in de Man, *Aesthetic Ideology* (Minneapolis: University of Minnesota Press, 1996) and related essays in the book, hereafter cited as AI. See also Arkady Plotnitsky, "Algebra and Allegory: Nonclassical Epistemology, Quantum Theory, and the Work of Paul de Man," in *Material Events: Paul de Man and the Afterlife of Theory*, eds. Barbara Cohen et al. (Minneapolis: University of Minnesota Press, 2000), 49–92.

4. Jacques Derrida, "Typewriter Ribbon: Limited Ink (2) ("within such limits"), in Cohen et al, *Material Events* (277–360). This problematic is crucial to Derrida's *Specters of Marx: The State of the Debt, the Work of Mourning, and the New International*, trans. Peggy Kamuf (New York: Routledge, 1994).

5. Derrida, *Positions*, trans. Alan Bass (Chicago: University of Chicago Press, 1981), 64. See Arkady Plotnitsky, *In the Shadow of Hegel: Complementarity, History, and the Unconscious* (Gainesville: University Presses of Florida, 1993); and Plotnitsky, "Points and Counterpoints: Between Hegel and Derrida," in *Questioning Derrida*, ed. Michel Meyer (Hampshire, Great Britain: Ashgate, 2000).

6. Derrida, *Edmund Husserl's Origin of Geometry*, trans. John P. Leavy Jr. (Stony Brook, NY: Nicolas Hays, 1978).

7. Deleuze, *The Fold: Leibniz and the Baroque*, trans. Tom Conley (Minneapolis: University of Minnesota Press, 1993), hereafter cited as F; Deleuze and Guattari, *What Is Philosophy?* trans. Hugh Tomlinson and Graham Burchell (New York: Columbia University Press, 1993).

8. Friedrich Nietzsche, *The Gay Science*, trans. Walter Kaufmann (New York: Vintage, 1974), 305–6.

9. G. W. F. Hegel, *Science of Logic*, trans. A. V. Miller (Atlantic Highlands, NJ: Humanities Press International, 1990), 259–314.

10. Cf., for example, Hermann Weyl's classic, *Space-Time-Matter*, trans. Henry L. Brose (New York: Dover, 1952), 101–2.

11. These mathematical themes are discussed in Plotnitsky, "Topo-philoso-phies: Plato's Diagonals, Hegel's Spirals and Irigaray's Multifolds," in *Histories of Theory*, eds. Tilottama Rajan and Michael O'Driscoll (Toronto: University of Toronto Press, 2002).

12. See de Man, "The Rhetoric of Temporality," in *Blindness and Insight: Essays in the Rhetoric of Contemporary Criticism* (Minneapolis: University of Minnesota Press, 1983).

13. See "The Double Session," in *Dissemination*, trans. Barbara Johnson (Chicago: University of Chicago Press, 1980).

14. Deleuze invokes Mallarmé and Boulez's "Fold after Fold," inspired by Mallarmé, and brings together Mallarmé and Leibniz almost along Derridean lines of textuality.

15. Hegel, *Phenomenology of Spirit*, trans. A. V. Miller (Oxford: Oxford University Press, 1977), hereafter cited as PS.

16. Derrida, *Speech and Phenomena and Other Essay on Husserl Theory of Sign*, trans. David B. Allison (Evanston, IL: Northwestern University Press, 1973), 89.

17. Cf. Derrida, "Différance," in *Margins of Philosophy*, trans. Alan Bass (Chicago: University of Chicago Press, 1982), 6; and Derrida, "How to Avoid Speaking: Denials," in *Derrida and Negative Theology*, eds. Harold Coward and Toby Foshay (Albany: State University of New York Press, 1992).

18. These elaborations are considered in Plotnitsky, *In the Shadow of Hegel* (198–205).

19. Both the closure of Hegel's *Phenomenology* (491–93) and the famous elaboration in the preface on "tarrying with the negative" (18–19) are relevant here, and are discussed in Plotnitsky, *In the Shadow of Hegel* (228–30, 270–74).

20. These questions are considered in Plotnitsky, *The Knowable and the Unknowable: Modern Science, Nonclassical Thought, and the "Two Cultures"* (Ann Arbor: University of Michigan Press, 2002).

21. The question of chance is discussed in Plotnitsky, "Algebra and Allegory" (72–74).

Three Ends of the Absolute:
Schelling, Hölderlin, Novalis

~

David Farrell Krell

> The worst of criticizing Hegel is that the very arguments we use
> against him give forth strange and hollow sounds that make them
> seem almost as fantastic as the errors to which they are addressed.
> The sense of a universal mirage, of a ghostly unreality, steals over
> us, which is the very moonlit atmosphere of Hegelism itself. What
> wonder then if, instead of converting, our words do but rejoice and
> delight those already baptized in the faith of confusion? To their
> charmed senses we all seem children of Hegel together, only some
> of us have not the wit to know our own father.
>
> —William James, *The Will to Believe*

Even if one is not writing *about* G. W. F. Hegel, one is writing *of* and *from*
Hegel, certainly insofar as one is invoking "the Absolute." Such is the gist of
James's perceptive—and rather jaded, or at least weary—remark. James is
weary and wary when it comes to "Hegelism" *and* the self-styled refutations
of "Hegelism." He would surely affirm the tendency of many twentieth-century readings of Hegel, however, which arise from the need to respect and pay
heed to the larger legacy of German Idealism and Romanticism while at the
same time eschewing all appeals to the absolute. *Dialectic* is only one of the
words that captures something of this legacy. Indeed, German Iealism and
Romanticism embrace a great deal more than dialectic. The present essay

135

reads three thinkers who never wished to be dialecticians, and who had grave problems with every discourse of the absolute. The three in question are Novalis (Friedrich von Hardenberg, 1772–1801), Friedrich Hölderlin (1770–1843), and F. W. J. von Schelling (1775–1854). I will pursue three ends of the absolute in these thinkers, focusing on their ideas of absolute inhibition, absolute separation, and absolute density.

Allow me an introductory remark on what might well be readers' initial skepticism with regard to the entire project. First of all, absolute inhibition, separation, and density appear to repeat and thus to reinstate the gestures of absolute knowing and absolute spirit, not to bring them to an end. By now we are familiar with conundrums of the "ends of metaphysics," "the end(s) of man," and so on. One might try to steer clear of these conundrums by insisting that with Novalis, Hölderlin, and Schelling a certain *materiality* and *elementality* come into play, something perhaps beyond or beneath (i.e., subtending) the Heideggerian and even deconstructionist emphasis on history and historicity. Yet the skepticism will not be so readily quashed. To be sure, one can easily think of a number of *twentieth*-century adventures in idealism, from Whitehead to Merleau-Ponty, which have a highly developed relation to materiality and elementality. One might think, for example, of Luce Irigaray, who in books like *Forgetting the Air* takes Gaston Bachelard's elemental thought in her own Empedoclean direction, or of Jacques Derrida's *Glas,* his remarkable response to Hegel's absolute knowing as absolute phantasm.[1] Yet is it truly conceivable that the thinkers and poets of German Idealism and Romanticism who I am invoking here—Schelling, Hölderlin, and Novalis—could have been engaged in such an adventure? Did they not rather anticipate, or in some way participate in, the elevation of the absolute (as the absolute knowing of an absolute spirit) in Hegel's philosophy? *Ends* of the absolute in Schelling, Hölderlin, and Novalis? At first blush, nothing seems less likely.

Consider, for example, the case of Novalis, who confesses to A. W. F. Schlegel on February 24, 1798, that with his study of chemistry the danger of getting lost in the details is greater than it is with his study of mathematics. "However," he continues, "my old inclination toward the absolute is once again rescuing me from the imbroglio of the empirical, and I am now and perhaps for ever hovering in loftier and altogether singular spheres *[ich schwebe jezt und vielleicht auf immer in lichtern, eigenthümlichern Sfären]* " (WTB 1:661). Many of Novalis's philosophical-scientific notes appear to confirm this self-description: his predilection for the absolute defines his own tendency to absolutization, which is his own definition of the Romantic as such. Referring to Johann Wolfgang von Goethe's *Wilhelm Meister* and *Fairy Tale,* Novalis writes under the heading "romanticism": "Absolutizing—universalizing—classification of the individual moment, of the individual situation, etc., is the proper essence of *romanticizing*" (2:488).

Well, then, *absolutizing*—and not the *end* of the absolute, not idealism *without* absolutes. In the third and last part of my essay, I will take up Novalis's penchant for absolutization, and argue that this very penchant spells the end of the absolute. First, however, a word about Schelling and Hölderlin— about whom virtually the same objection could be raised, and in whom one will always find *traces* of a devotion to the absolute—before turning to my main subject, Novalis.

Absolute Inhibition: Schelling

In *Contagion* I argued that the philosophy of organic nature from Goethe and Immanuel Kant onward provides something like a theater in which we observe the failure of the absolute, and precisely in the imbrication of the phenomena of human sexuality, disease, and death. In the present essay I will refer to several places in that book where the absolute is discussed, although I do not want to belabor the points made there. Allow me to begin with Schelling, and with what I am calling "absolute inhibition." I will be referring principally to Schelling's major work in the philosophy of organic nature, his *First Projection of a System of Nature Philosophy* (1799), although the matters developed there continue to reverberate throughout the later stages of Schelling's career of thought, especially in his seminal *Treatise on Human Freedom* (1809) and his monumental *Ages of the World* (1811–15).[2]

Many of the fundamental concepts and presuppositions of Schelling's philosophy of nature doubtless stem from Fichte, so that it is difficult if not impossible to begin without reference to Schelling's, Hölderlin's, and Novalis's great mentor. Yet Fichte's *Wissenschaftslehre* is its own bottomless pit. Let me therefore evade it, and with the guilty conscience of the skulker begin with the *First Projection* itself.

Schelling recognizes that the realms of freedom and nature are opposed to one another as being is opposed to becoming and as spirit is opposed to matter. Freedom, being, and spirit are "infinite activity," that is, they are characterized by the absolutely active and unconditioned deed; nature, becoming, and matter, by contrast, are characterized by conditioned, compelled, necessitous activity. Yet Schelling will try to exhibit "the concealed trace of freedom" in nature (EE 13). He will argue that the "formative drive" in nature is itself a path to freedom. Yet Schelling—at least at first—is clear about the limits of free activity in nature: "The essence of all organism is that it is not absolute activity. . . . For the subsistence of the organism is not a *being* [Seyn] but a perpetual *becoming reproduced* [*ein beständiges* Reproduciertwerden]" (222). The bedeviling problem for Schelling—as for the entire generation of thinkers after Kant—is how infinite activity could ever have submitted to compulsion or to a condition or determination of any kind—above all, to the compulsion of inhibition *(Hemmung),* which inheres in infinite activity as such and is therefore a particularly crippling condition, indeed a condition that neutralizes any and every sense of an unconditioned absolute.

Schelling would love to promote a monistic system of infinite activity as the sole possible system of reason, and yet he is compelled over and over again to posit a dualism. It is not a dualism of the traditional sort, nature versus freedom, matter versus spirit, becoming versus being. For Schelling adopts the Fichtean notion of inhibition as a principle internal to, and inherent in, infinite activity. Schelling's difficulty is that he identifies both an "original dualism" in nature and an "infinite activity" in it. Absolute or infinite activity will therefore have to be inhibited absolutely or infinitely, in such a way that the distinction between free activity and necessitous inhibition becomes extremely tenuous. Schelling himself *emphasizes* the following words: *"If nature is absolute activity, such activity must appear as inhibited into infinity. (The original ground of this inhibition must, however, be sought **in nature itself** alone, inasmuch as nature is active **without qualification**)"* (EE 16). Nature as becoming—not *being* but a perpetual becoming reproduced—and yet as *absolute* activity? And again, absolute activity, active without reservation or qualification—yet also inhibited into infinity? Schelling is perfectly aware that he is here confronting "an insoluble difficulty" (17; cf. 151 n. 169, 219). For *inhibition* in the present instance means the presence in nature of "infinite negations" (20). Schelling's system of nature philosophy is in effect tormented by the necessity of absolute inhibition, and one might designate his entire system of idealism as *tormented* idealism.

Whence this notion of *Hemmung*? How did it make its way into Fichte's *Wissenschaftslehre,* and from thence into Schelling's philosophy of nature? We know how important the concept of inhibition will be for psychoanalytic discourse, as well as for various twentieth-century philosophies of biology. We know that Fichte and Schelling alike use it, and we know that it plays a role in Kant's third *Critique, The Critique of Judgment,* indeed precisely in the Analytic of the Sublime, where, arguably, aesthetic and teleological forms of judgment meet—in "the feeling of a momentary inhibition of life forces."[3] Does it play a role in Kant's physiological and anthropological texts? Does it appear in Leibniz's account of *vis*? Can it be traced back through the grand systems and summae of medieval philosophy, or in various abstruse compendiums in the history of medicine? Does it have its origin in Aristotle's βιά, violent motion? I know the answer to none of these questions, and this is frustrating to me, because I sense that something like a *history of inhibition* is called for, very much in the sense of Martin Heidegger's *history of being.* For it may well be that what Heidegger calls the mystery *(das Geheimnis)* of self-occluding, self-withdrawing being in the destiny or sending of being *(Geschick des Seins)* lies in an as yet untold *Hemmungsgeschichte.*

But to return to Schelling's *First Projection*. The problem of the dualism in nature, which is the product of an infinitely inhibited infinite activity, is stated in the boldest possible terms in the following passage:

> **Thus a common cause of universal and organic duplicity is postulated.** The most universal problem, the one that encompasses all nature, and therefore the *supreme* problem, without whose solution all we have said explains nothing, is this:
>
> **What is the universal source of activity in nature? What cause has brought about the first dynamic exteriority [*Außereinander*],** with respect to which mechanical exteriority is a mere consequence? **Or what cause first tossed the seed of motion into the universal repose of nature, duplicity into universal identity, the first sparks of heterogeneity into the universal homogeneity of nature?**[4]

Schelling is never able to answer these questions, each of which circles about the problem he calls "insoluble." What he learns repeatedly is that heterogeneity can never be merely "introduced" into homogeneity. In order for heterogeneity and duality to advene they must always already have been there—as disposition and latency, as dormant yet potent—from the outset. One example of the problem of motion is intussusception, the intake of liquid nourishment by a living entity by what used to be called "infection," today "osmosis." Schelling writes:

> Inasmuch as an intussusception between heterogeneous bodies is possible only insofar as the homogeneous is itself split *in itself,* no homogeneous state can be *absolute;* rather, it can only be a *state of indifference.* In order to explain this, we must suppose that there is in the universe a universal effect that replicates itself from product to product by means of (magnetic) distribution, which would be the universal determinant of all quality (and of all magnetism as universal). (EE 260).

Although the role of magnetism will diminish in Schelling's later philosophy, the "state of indifference" to which he has only now referred will be a mainstay: it is the crucial moment of the *Treatise on Human Freedom,* though no longer of the *Ages of the World.* What we may say, making a very long and complex story short, is that Schelling discovers that the absolute is heterogeneous even before anything is "thrown" at it. He writes: "But to *bring* heterogeneity *forth [hervorbringen]* means to create duplicity in identity. . . . Thus identity must in turn proceed *[hervorgehen]* from duplicity" (EE 250).

Schelling must, then, conceive of an "original duplicity," a *dyas,* in which infinite activity and infinite inhibition work together to produce the natural world. What rises to disturb his account of their interaction is the happenstance that the very site of inhibition is *sexual opposition,* and that sexual opposition shares many traits with *illness.* Sexuality and illness alike tend toward the universal and the infinite. It is as though infinite activity itself, the absolute as such, were both sexually active and subject to ultimate passivity and even to an inevitable infection or malignancy. It becomes difficult, if not impossible, for Schelling to locate the duplicitous source of life without colliding against the ultimate source of illness and demise—Hegel's notorious "seed of death."

True, there are places in the treatise where Schelling dreams of an "absolute organization," one that would dispense with duality and sexual opposition while also accounting for their eventual emergence on the scene. One such place is the following, where he conjures an *Urbild* or "proto-image" of a seamless or at least wholly annealed nature:

> This proto-image would be the absolute, it would be *sexless,* and would no longer be either individual or species; rather, it would be *both at the same time;* in it, therefore, individual and species are conflated. For that reason, the absolute organization could not be depicted by an individual product, but only through an infinity of particular products, which taken *individually* deviate into infinity from the ideal, but which when taken together as a *whole* are congruent with it. Thus the fact that nature expresses such an absolute original by means of all its organizations taken together is something that could be demonstrated simply by showing that all variation in the organizations is only a variation in the approximation of each to an absolute. We would then experience this absolute as though these organizations were nothing other than different developments of one and the same organization. (EE 64)

Schelling's dream of a sexless absolute, while a *necessary* dream in and for every inheritor of the ontotheological tradition, turns into a nightmare in which the absolute is an undeveloped simplex, a monotonous simpleton that has not yet developed in those opposite or counterposed directions *(die entgegengesetzte Richtungen)* that Schelling himself constantly invokes as the essential directions of the path of freedom. The one-and-the-same organization of all organizations in the graduated sequence of stages in nature would therefore have to be as complex as its most complex stage, and if its complex stages are always and everywhere stages for *duplex* states, a simplex god looks a little silly. No, not merely silly. For what is the unexpected force of

Schelling's suggestion that the various organizations of infinite organization "deviate into infinity from the ideal"? The word *deviation* turns out to be the key word for Schelling's account of *illness*. Furthermore, deviation *of* infinity *into* infinity sounds a little bit like an infinite regress, or an infinite regression, or a regression *of* the infinite *(genitivus subiectivus et obiectivus)*. The god of infinite organization should not be simpler than a sponge or polyp; he or she ought to be at least as complex and duplex as, let us say, naming one set of living creatures among others, women and men. However necessary and inevitable the dream of a sexless absolute may be, the dream of a common origin for all the deviations and gradations to come, the compelling *necessity* of those deviations, variations, and organic exfoliations rouses the deviant dreamer from his dogmatic slumber.

It is of course far too early to speak of the demise of the absolute in the Schelling of the 1799 *Erster Entwurf.* Yet the absolutely inhibited absolute will slip henceforth into an ever more remote past, a past that never was present and that never will entertain a future—and that is a little bit like death, and very much like an end of the absolute. No doubt the two most important texts in this regard are the 1809 *Treatise* and the *Ages of the World,* begun soon after the *Treatise* but never completed. One might be justified in saying that in the *Treatise* and in the *Ages of the World* Schelling encounters something like a traumatic experience early in the life of the absolute. The trauma has to do with sexuality and mortality—those two shadows of a philosophy of nature—and no amount of either inhibition or dialectic will relieve it. Indeed, one might rather say that absolute inhibition is another name for the trauma of the absolute, and that the trauma turns out to have lethal effects.[5]

Absolute Separation: Hölderlin

The separation I am thinking of here—although in Hölderlin's view, at least early on in his career of thought, it could never be called "absolute"—is discussed in those famous lines of Hölderlin's "Seyn, Urtheil, Modalität" concerning division *(Theilung)* and separation *(Trennung).*[6] Long before Schelling formulates his "identity philosophy" in the early 1800s, Hölderlin indicates his skepticism about the very notion of identity. Separation is essential to conscious identity, indeed, to consciousness of any kind. "Thus identity is not some sort of unification of object and subject that takes place in a straightforward manner, and thus identity does not = absolute being" (SW 2:50). *Urtheil* Hölderlin takes to be *Ur-theilung,* the primeval sundering or dividing of consciousness and its object that he hopes an intellectual intuition will heal. To be sure, there is no thought here that the separation could possibly be absolute: that intimation comes later, in Frankfurt and in Bad Homburg, with the work on *The Death of Empedocles* (1797–1800) and *The*

Tragedies of Sophocles, and it will come as a thought about *love,* if not sexual opposition as such.

One should of course trace the role of *intellectuale Anschauung* in Hölderlin's theoretical writings very carefully, from its appearance in "Being, Judgment, Modality" to later references in the poetological essays. Whereas, according to the first-named essay, subject and object are "most intensely united" in intellectual intuition (SW 2:50), the later poetological essay, *"Wenn der Dichter einmal des Geistes mächtig,"* struggles to find that unity in "elongated" points, which nonetheless are points of "scission," *Scheidepunkte* (2:86–87). The *living* unity Hölderlin seeks, which he also calls "the larger nexus of life," will not be found in mere reflection; it will be "the hyperbole of all hyperboles, the boldest and ultimate effort of the poetic spirit" (2:88). If intellectual intuition is no more than the harmony of subject and object, a subject-object whole that is doubtless "mythical" and "rich in images," the kind of intense unity of life that Hölderlin envisages surpasses all intuition. Nevertheless, such unity does remain a matter of intuition in the Kantian sense, insofar as it is bound up with sensibility and receptivity: Hölderlin writes of an *Empfindung* that is *"beautiful, holy, divine"* (2:94–95).

According to another of the poetological essays, the proper bearer or "metaphor" of intellectual intuition is "the tragic poem," which is "ideational in its significance" (SW 2:102). Hölderlin defines the intellectual intuition that undergirds tragic poetry as "that unity with everything that lives," a unity that arises from "the impossibility of an absolute separation and individuation" (2:104). Yet the very impossibility of *absolute* separation seems to be what tragedy—and what Hölderlin calls "actual separation" and "tragic dissolution"—is all about:

> The unity that is at hand in intellectual intuition becomes sensuous *[versinnlichet sich]* to the precise extent that it goes out of itself and its parts are separated from one another, the parts separating only because they feel excessively unified *[zu einig]* whenever they are closer to the midpoint of the whole, or because they do not feel unified enough, with a view to completeness, whenever they are merely ancillary parts, lying farther removed from the midpoint, or, with a view to vitality, when they are neither ancillary nor essential parts in the designated senses, because they are rather merely divisible parts, parts that have not yet come to be. And here, in spirit's excess of unity, and in its striving for materiality, in the striving of the divisible for the more infinite, more aorgic, in which everything that is more organic must be contained, inasmuch as everything determinate and necessarily existent makes something less determinate and more contingent necessary, in this striving of the divisible

infinite for separation, a striving that communicates itself in the condition of the supreme unity of everything organic to the parts contained in it, in this necessary, arbitrary act of Zeus lies the genuine, ideal beginning of the actual separation. (SW 2:106)

Hölderlin sees the arbitrary act of Zeus—the act of separation, caught up in a striving for the more infinite, the more untamed, and in search of the materiality and elementality of nature, an act having more to do with the ancillary parts of the whole than with the self-concentrating midpoint—at work in a particularly striking way in Sophocles' *Oedipus the King*. He does not elaborate on the matter at this point, yet one is reminded of the way in which the later *Anmerkungen* to his translation of *Antigone* will speak of both Zeus and the entire process of nature as being more decisively turned back to the Earth.[7] While Hölderlin does not advance to a clear "doctrine" of the end of the absolute, there is something telling about the way in which the divine unity of intellectual intuition is brought to tragic separation and dissolution.[8] A late fragment on tragedy, apparently intended for an introduction to his translations of Sophocles' tragedies, does not declare the end of the absolute, but does identify the "original," which is surely related to what has traditionally been called the "absolute," as suffering from some sort of weakness or "debility":

The significance of the tragedies is most readily grasped on the basis of paradox. For, inasmuch as all abundance is justly and equally apportioned, no original appears as actual in its original strength; rather, it genuinely appears in its debility alone, so that quite properly the light of life and the appearance of debility pertain to every whole.[9] Now, in the tragic, the sign is meaningless in itself, without effect; yet the original comes directly to the fore. For the original can appear in a genuine way only in its debility. Yet insofar as the sign in itself is meaningless and thus = 0, the original too, the concealed ground of every nature, can present itself. If nature presents itself genuinely in its weakest gift, then the sign that is given when it presents itself in its strongest gift = 0. (SW 2:114)

It is far from clear what the relation of original and sign in Hölderlin's reflections may be, yet the very proximity of debility to strength in the self-presentation of nature and the original bodes ill for the absolute, as does the meaning that equals zero. Precisely what sort of ill becomes clearer when we examine in greater detail Hölderlin's lifelong preoccupation with tragedy.

In a secondary school essay, "History of the Fine Arts among the Greeks up to the End of the Age of Pericles" (SW 2:11–27), young Hölderlin notes that the Greeks invented for their gods bodies of great beauty, inasmuch as beauty was one of the "national traits" of the Greeks; moreover, the Greeks implanted in their gods "a receptivity for the beautiful," and "caused them to descend to the Earth for the sake of beauty" (2:12). Decades later, in his notes on Sophocles' *Antigone,* Hölderlin emphasizes the chorus' account of descent of Zeus to the cell of the beautiful Danaë, who is celebrated in the fifth choral ode of the play (lines 981ff.). Hölderlin interprets the famous golden shower by which Zeus visits Danaë as the golden hours that the father of Earth and Time spends with her. They are hours that she counts or ticks off—as though Zeus were learning from her nothing less than the time of his mortality. In that early school essay, Hölderlin also notes that the Greeks were particularly "receptive to tragedy" (2:23); he draws attention to Aeschylus' *Prometheus Bound,* the play in which the demise of Zeus is foretold. For even if, as he later writes in the "Fragment of Philosophical Letters," love and beauty are "happy to uncover tenderly," what they yearn for is solace in the face of the "profound feeling of mortality, mutability, one's temporal limitations" (2:60).

Françoise Dastur argues convincingly that *time* is the consistent theme of Greek tragedy as Hölderlin conceives of it.[10] From early on, Hölderlin thinks of tragedy in terms of that ticking of the clock for immortals, a ticking that seems to begin when the immortals are drawn by desire to the earthbound mortals. As in Empedocles' account of the wandering δαιμονες who abandon the reign of Φιλια (Love) for the reign of Νεῖκος (Strife), surrendering their blessed abode for the blood-drenched plain of Ατη, Hölderlin sees the immortal gods drawn out of their (impossible) absolute separation into a fatal commingling with mortality. Like mortals, immortals eventually come to experience the passage of time as pain and suffering. Perhaps the most durable theme of Hölderlin's mature work is therefore that of time and temporality. Hölderlin already hears the ticking of the clock in his *Hyperion,* written and published between the years 1792 and 1798; in that novel he appeals to the figure of Empedocles, inasmuch as he is already beginning to sketch out *The Death of Empedocles*; Empedocles, like the namesake of Sophocles' *Antigone,* which tragedy Hölderlin is translating between the years 1800 and 1803, hears the ticking of the clock—precisely as Zeus heard it in Danaë's cell. Looking ahead to *Antigone* and to *The Death of Empedocles,* Hölderlin writes in *Hyperion*:

> And now tell me, is there any refuge left?—Yesterday I was up on Etna. I recalled the great Sicilian of old who, when he'd had enough of *ticking off the hours,* having become intimate with the soul of the world, in his bold lust for life plunged into the terrific flames. It was because—a mocker afterwards said of him—the frigid poet had to warm himself at the fire.

O how gladly I would precipitate such mockery over me! but one must think more highly of oneself than I do to fly unbidden to nature's heart—put it any way you like, for, truly, as I am now, I have no name for these things, and all is uncertain *[es ist mir alles ungewiß].*[11]

Hölderlin's *Hyperion* is also the text to which I want to refer all the ideas discussed so far about unity and separation, strength and debility, and the god's striving for raw materiality and elementality through sexuality and mortality. For in *Hyperion* and in the preliminary drafts of that novel the themes of unification, love, and beauty are brought into the greatest possible proximity with debility, dissolution, and death—including, I would argue, the death of all originals and all absolutes. Perhaps the greatest single advance in the conception and characterization of mortal love occurs in the metrical version of *Hyperion* (along with its draft in prose). Here Hyperion realizes that the "school of destiny and of the sages" has caused him to underestimate and even to scorn the world of the senses and the realm of nature, which is inevitably bound up with mortal love. The wizened sage, the stranger who now communicates the doctrine of Plato's Socrates in *Symposium* (for Diotima is not yet invoked by name), speaks with a more human voice—a more mortal voice—than the alternating angelic and strident voices one hears in the earlier drafts of the novel:

> Allow me to speak in a human way. When our originally infinite essence first came to suffer something, and when the free and full force encountered its first barriers, when Poverty mated with Superfluity, Love came to be. Do you ask when that was? Plato says it was on the day when Aphrodite was born. At the moment, therefore, when the world of beauty commenced for us, when we became conscious, we became finite. Now we profoundly feel the confinement of our essence, and inhibited force [shades of Schelling!] strains impatiently against its fetters. Yet there is something in us that gladly preserves the fetters—for if the divine in us were bound to no resistance, we would know nothing outside ourselves and therefore nothing about ourselves either. And to know nothing of oneself, not to feel that we are in being, and to be annihilated—these are one and the same. (1:513)

Perhaps it is not too much to say that the absolute—here called "infinite essence" and "free and full force"—faces a singular alternative: either it becomes conscious and thus finite, that is, bound for *eventual* annihilation, or it remains in absolute separation, catatonic isolation, and absolute autism, which is the equivalent of *immediate* annihilation. In effect, there is no alternative for conscious life—no alternative to living out the temporal unfolding of one's life as Danaë ticks off the golden hours. Consciousness and finitude are reciprocally related, and not merely at the level of epistemology. The reciprocity of consciousness and finitude derives from the genealogy of ἔρως, born of Resource and Poverty, Πόρος and Πενία. "Absolute separation," the *solus ipse* of an absolute spirit, is impossible—unless spirit is either unconscious or dead.

Later on, from 1798 to 1800 in Bad Homburg, Hölderlin is working intensely on the first version of his tragic drama, *The Death of Empedocles*. (The first volume of *Hyperion* has already been published, and work on the second volume has already been completed.) During these days of reflection on the life and death of the great Greek thinker of Love and Strife, which are also the days in which he meets fleetingly with Susette Gontard in order to exchange letters and a few stolen touches,[12] Hölderlin's thinking advances as far as that of anyone in the era of German idealism and romanticism—including that of his teacher Fichte and his erstwhile friends Hegel and Schelling. At the farthest advance of his thought, Hölderlin envisages something like the end of the absolute—in the figure of an impossible "absolute monarchy." In a letter to Isaak von Sinclair, dated December 24, 1798, Hölderlin writes:

> The transience and mutability of human thoughts and systems strike me as well-nigh more tragic than the destinies one usually calls the only real destinies. And I believe this is natural, for if a human being in his or her ownmost and freest activity—in autonomous thought itself—depends on foreign influences, if even in such thought he or she is modified in some way by circumstance and climate, which has been shown irrefutably to be the case, where then does the human being rule supreme? It is also a good thing— indeed, it is the first condition of all life and all organization—that in heaven and on earth no force rules monarchically. Absolute monarchy cancels itself out everywhere, for it is without object; strictly speaking, there never was such a monarchy. Everything that is interpenetrates as soon as it becomes active. . . . Of course, *from every finite point of view some one of the autonomous forces must be the ruling force,* yet it must be observed to prevail only temporarily and only to a certain degree. (2:723)

Himself caught up in the daily, weekly, and monthly interpenetrations of Φιλία and Νεῖκος, Πόρος, and Πενία, Hölderlin sees that every dream of solitary rule, every phantasm of the absolute, thus every monism, is bound to dissolve. Friedrich Nietzsche will experience the evanescence of the dream in his own way, and will become famous for that experience; Heidegger will occupy that finite point of view in which time and the temporal announce themselves as the horizon of the only sense of being that gives itself to mortals. Yet Hölderlin arrives on that scene a century or more before them. Absolute separation, whether in intellectual intuition or in the violent, ephemeral pairing of gods and mortals—mortals from a small number of houses in a universe of tragedy—is itself the end of the absolute.[13]

Absolute Density: Novalis

I cannot offer here a detailed account of Novalis's "magical idealism," or what I prefer to call his "thaumaturgic idealism," preferring thaumaturgy both in order to retain the reference to philosophy as beginning in wonder (θαυμάζειν) and to suggest the shamanistic role that Novalis expects the philosopher to play. Nor can I offer an account of his exponential and logarithmic methods or his own brand of logic, quite beyond any familiar sense of dialectic, which he calls *Fantastik*. Nor, finally, do I want to repeat very much of his extraordinary accounts of medicine and physiology, accounts with which my book *Contagion* is preoccupied. Yet the problem of the density of the absolute, an issue raised at the end of Novalis's notes toward *Das allgemeine Brouillon* (The Universal Sketchbook), is a problem posed in *Contagion*, and so I will begin by restating the problem developed there as succinctly as I can.[14]

Here are the laconic lines—each constituting its own paragraph, each standing there stonily and silently in the late notes of Novalis—that I most want to understand in the present undertaking:

> God is of infinitely compact metal *[von unendlich gediegenen Metall]*—the most corporeal and the heaviest of all beings.
>
> Oxidation comes from the devil.
>
> Life is a sickness of spirit, an activity born to undergo *passio* [literally, "a passionate deed," *ein leidenschaftliches Thun*].
>
> Annihilation of air establishes the Kingdom of God. (WTB 2:820)

What is this strange idolatry, this God of solid gold, this compact, corporeal, massive, dense, unbreathing, rust-free divinity? Of what suffocating heaven is Novalis (who died at age twenty-nine of tuberculosis) dreaming? Does it not seem as though he had read Milan Kundera on the lightness of being and wanted to make reply, or that he had perused Hegel's mocking and cruel account of tuberculosis?

Allow me to track the absolute through Novalis's brief career and astounding production. His early "Fichte-Studien" appear to make trouble for Fichte's positings concerning any and every sense of an absolute ego or subject. Whether it is the theme of feeling within intellectual intuition or of the hieroglyphic sign, of chaos, drives, or life itself, Novalis seems destined to resist Fichte's and his own predilection for the absolute, which we cited at the outset: "Has not Fichte too arbitrarily deposited everything into the ego? With what legitimacy?" (WTB 2:12). And, several pages later, "Thus ego and not-ego, without absolute ego!" (2:15). Novalis continues to wrestle with the Fichtean hypothesis of an absolute ego (2:28–29), yet his way of resisting the absolute ego is to dilate and expand that notion exponentially. Alongside "systematics" in Novalis's notes stand "encyclopedics" and "prophetics," and the tendency of these last two is expansionist. Furthermore, Novalis insists on the primacy of practice: "The practical is a longing *[Sehnen]* " (2:57), even if "praxis proper simply cannot be grasped conceptually" (2:57). Early on, it seems, Novalis is clear about the goal of his studies: "Spinoza ascended to the point of nature, Fichte to the ego or the person, I to the thesis of God" (2:63).

Novalis's God, however, turns out to be exceedingly strange, absolutely dense. If at the outset of Novalis's theoretical work his God appears to be the usual spiritual Creator, by the end of it creativity and spirituality are less comprehensible than they ever were. Early on, Novalis writes, "Matter and spirit correspond to one another quite precisely—one is like the other. Each has its pure causality in the other alone" (WTB 2:77). Yet as he continues with his encyclopedic studies, it is the causality at the heart of matter that comes to dominate his thought. If the grounding of God and world, spirit and matter, is a "mutual grounding," as Novalis emphasizes, the traditional ways of understanding God and matter will have to change. "If only we could come to know the matter of spirit, and the spirit of matter" (2:167). Such a coming to know would have implications especially for human beings, whom Kant pictured as hovering somewhere between the angelic and the bestial. By contrast, Novalis writes: "The sensuous must be presented spiritually, the spiritual must be presented sensuously" (2:194). At first these opposites seem to stand quite remote from one another and to resist one another absolutely. Yet they must commingle. Novalis can write, without apparent discomfort, "Devil and God are the extremes from which the human being originates" (2:198). However, these very oppositions will soon (1) reverse their position in the hierarchy of values, and (2) thoroughly contaminate one another, so that (3) the contamination will prove fatal to any straightforward opposition as such.

A growing respect for the mysteries of what the tradition has scorned as "passivity" characterizes Novalis's thought, passivity, and receptivity— once again, shades of Kantian *Empfindung.* A growing respect for mixture and even fatal contamination baffles the "pure," which may be one of the most familiar attributes of the absolute: "Pure—that which is not related, not relatable. . . . The concept *pure* is thus an empty concept. . . . —Everything pure is therefore a deception produced by our imagination—a *necessary* fiction"

(WTB 2:87). Among the mixtures, that of activity and inhibition—once again, shades of Fichte and Schelling—holds a special place in the third group of handwritten "Fichte-Studies" (2:118, 124, 127). As we have seen, the strange dialectic of absolute activity, that is, the activity of positing by an absolute ego and of absolute inhibition by that same ego, dominates the young Schelling's philosophy of nature. Novalis states it in the form of a paradox, tautology, or riddle: "Inhibited activity can be inhibited only by activity" (2:124, cf. 204). No doubt related to the theme of inhibition is what Novalis calls *Renitenz*, a kind of adversity or resistance that stands opposed to action (2:130). Such adversity is essential to creativity. Novalis pictures a flutist: "Certain inhibitions may be compared to the fingerings of a Baroque recorder player who, in order to tease this or that tone from his instrument closes of this or that opening; to all appearances he makes the most arbitrary connections between the sounding and the mute openings" (2:217). In words quite reminiscent of Hölderlin's notes on "Being, Judgment, Modality," Novalis writes: "Being *[Seyn]* does not express any absolute characteristic, but rather only a relation of the essence to a property in general—a capacity to be determined. It is an absolute relation. Nothing in the world *is merely*; being does not express identity" (2:156). If the vaunted absolute by definition "stands alone," *solus ipse,* without relation to anything else, "absolute relation" is the oxymoron that explodes all discourse on the absolute. *"Nichts in der Welt* ist blos."* Nothing is merely, nakedly, what it is; everything stands always in relation to another, not accidentally but essentially. Yet that means that nothing stands as absolute, on its own, except the inflated and bemused human cogitator of the absolute. Novalis cites without comment a "derivation" of (the concept of) God from the German word for genus or species—or, understood as a verb, the word for mating: *Gott = Gattung* (2:145). Even if he later identifies the genus with the sphere, hence with a kind of monism, it is clear that the *monas* is a complete mystery: "We simply do not know what the genus consists of, what sort of a one" (2:161). Novalis is instead the thinker of the manifold. We may paraphrase his *Apprentices at Saïs* as saying, *Mannigfache Wege gehet der Gott,* "the absolute walks manifold paths." And it may well be that every one of those paths, as Schelling believed, culminates in sexual, mortal embodiment.[15]

The upshot of all this is that Novalis's thaumaturgic idealism is condemned to a kind of *hovering* between extremes. Sometimes such hovering or oscillating seems to him a weakness: "I am too much on the superficies— not the tranquil inner life—not the kernel—working its effects from the inside out, from a midpoint—but rather on the surface—by way of zigzag—horizontally—without steadiness of character—play—accident—not lawful effect— the trace of autonomy—the externalizing of *one* essence" (WTB 2:167). And the despairing self-indictment, "Why must I always pursue things with painful insistence—nothing calm—leisurely—with releasement" (2:169). At its best, hovering *(Schweben)* promises a kind of harmony and integration of extremes; at its worst, it seems a form of self-deceptive vacillation suffered by a hyperactive imagination (2:177). Yet hovering is assuredly the best way to describe the thinking that produces the "genuine philosophical system," whose primary characteristic is "systemlessness": Novalis's directive to all who seek a monistic system is that "we must seek out the dichotomy everywhere" (2:200–201). In effect, this means the surrender of the philosophical search for ultimate or absolute grounds.[16]

And so we arrive at one of the most telling of Novalis's notes on the absolute: "By means of a voluntary renunciation of the absolute, an infinitely free activity originates in us—the sole possible absolute that can be granted us and that we can find only by means of our incapacity to achieve and recognize an absolute. This absolute, the one granted to us, can be known only negatively, by our acting, and by our discovering that no action ever achieves what we were searching for" (WTB 2:180–81). The absolute is our absolute inability to think or act in conformity with an absolute. Whence, then, our drive to think and act on the horizon of such impossible absolutes?

Perhaps the most detailed observation by Novalis concerning the drive to universals and absolutes comes in the first group of handwritten notes for The Universal Sketchbook. Allow me to quote it at length:

> ENCYCLOPEDICS. Every science has its God, which is at the same time its goal. Thus mechanics actually thrives on the *perpetuum mobile*— and at the same time it seeks to construct a *perpetuum mobile,* which is its supreme problem. Thus chemistry thrives on the *menstruum universale*—and on *spiritual* matter, or the Philosophers' Stone. Philosophy seeks its first and its sole principle. The mathematician seeks the squaring of the circle and a principal equation *[eine Principalgleichung].* The *human being—God.* The physician seeks an elixir of life—a rejuvenating tonic, a complete feeling about the body, and a complete method of dealing with it *[Gefühl und Handhabung].* The politician seeks a perfect republic—eternal peace—a free state. (WTB 2:530)

Novalis now inserts a parenthetical remark, centering it on the page, as he so often does in his notebooks, apparently for emphasis: "(Every disappointed expectation and every renewed expectation, over and over again, gestures toward a chapter in the lore of the future. See my first fragment in *Blüthenstaub.*)" The familiar first fragment of *Pollen* reads: *Wir suchen überall das Unbedingte, und finden immer nur Dinge* (We seek the unconditioned in every nook and cranny, and all we ever find are [conditioned] things) (WTB

2:227). In *The Universal Sketchbook,* Novalis formulates what he himself calls his "principle of approximation," his asymptotic principle. It is as though he were declaring himself a disciple of Heraclitus, whose one-word fragment ἀγχιβασιη suggests unending approach: "On the obstacles that block the accomplishment of every one of these tasks. (The principle of approximation. Belonging to it is also the *absolute ego.*)" I interrupt to note that, if there is an absolute obstacle to the absolute ego, neither the obstacle nor the ego appear to be absolute—although, granted the cruel nature of paradox, it may well be that the only true absolute is precisely the absolute obstacle, absolute ἀπορία (and if ἀπορία is not Πόρος," it must be absolute Πενία), which is to say, *Ausweglosigkeit, huit clos,* poverty, resourcelessness, impenetrability—absolute density. Yet we approach the tantalizing and tantalized character of Novalis's thought as we complete our reading of his observations on asymptotic approximation:

> That these tasks are not successfully completed lies solely in the flawed nature of the objects of these tasks, in the imperfect relations of the chosen constructive *elements* of these objects. (Elements are *accidents.*) The tasks are theoretically true and are identity propositions, pleonastic statements, as, for example, *perpetuum mobile, eternal life—measured circle.* The philosophy of these tasks. (WTB 2:530)

It seems as though Novalis is engaging himself to the impossible task of the absolute (his old familiar predilection), to be carried out through infinite approximation, in the hope that if the elements of construction are more wisely chosen a lifetime spent in the search for a pleonasm might be a life well lived. Such a life would contribute, as we have already heard, to the lore of the future: "LORE OF THE FUTURE OF HUMANITY. (THEOLOGY.) Everything that is predicated of God contains the human lore of the future. Every machine that now thrives on the grand *perpetuum mobile* is itself to become the *perpetuum mobile*—every human being that now thrives on God, through God, is himself or herself to become God" (WTB 2:531). A cheerful prospect: the lore and lure of the future in the lives of mortals is the promise or dream that they will become God—waiting only for Jean-Paul Sartre to remark on the human quest as *une passion inutile.*[17] Yet Novalis does not have to wait for Sartre. In a note under the misleading rubric "psychology" Novalis writes:

> All passions come to an end, as does a mourning-play. Everything that is one-sided comes to an end in death—thus the philosophy of sensation—the philosophy of fantasy—the philosophy of the thought. All life comes to an end in old age and death. All poesy manifests a tragic trait. (Real pain underlies seriousness. The tragic impact of

> farce, of puppet theater—of the most motley life—of the common,
> of the trivial.) (WTB 2:541)

There is something tragic too about the philosopher's search for a system. Under the rubric "philosophy," Novalis notes, somewhat laconically, "1. Supposition: there is a philosophical system—2. *Description* of this ideal—of this phantasm. . . ." (WTB 2:611). Novalis's Copernican Revolution is therefore quite different from Kant's and Fichte's: *"Die Philosophie macht alles* los." "Philosophy sets everything in *motion*—relativizes the universe. Like the Copernican system, it cancels all *fixed* points—and makes of everything at rest something hovering [*ein Schwebendes*]" (2:616). Setting in motion, oscillating, vacillating, hovering, and finally, "crooked rules": "At the basis of every ideal lies a deviation from the common rule, or a *higher rule* (a crooked rule)" (2:653). Among these crooked rules at the foundation of every ideal is of course the moral law, which claims to propound maxims for praxis (2:653).

If we think back to the discussion in *Contagion* of Novalis's "theory of voluptuosity," which hovers at the core of his thaumaturgic idealism, we can say that in accord with his theory of approximation Novalis's theories of love and illness arrive at nothing more than an approximation to the absolute, to the "well-nigh" absolute:

Theory of Voluptuosity

> It is *Amor* that presses us together. The basis of all the functions
> mentioned above [i.e., dancing, eating, speaking, communal experi-
> ence and work, companionship, as well as hearing, seeing, and feel-
> ing oneself] is voluptuosity *(sympathy)*. The genuinely voluptuous
> function is the one that is most mystical—well-nigh absolute—or
> the one that compels us toward the *totality* of unification (mixture)—
> the *chemical*. (2:666)

If one insists on pursuing such a theory of voluptuosity into the neighborhood of chemistry, a chemistry that once seemed an imbroglio from which only an absolute could rescue Novalis, one runs the risk of absolute contagion. Novalis accepts the inevitably ambiguous diagnosis of the absolute drive to perfection and completeness. He writes:

> An absolute drive to perfection and completeness is illness as soon
> as it exhibits its destructive attitude, its disinclination with respect to
> the *imperfect*, the incomplete.
>
> If one wants to act in such a way as to achieve something in
> particular, one must stake out boundaries that are determinate, even if

provisional. Whoever cannot bring himself to do this is the perfection-
ist, one who refuses to swim until he knows precisely how to do so.—
    He is a magical idealist, just as there are magical realists. The
former seek a miraculous motion, a miraculous subject; the latter
seek a miraculous object, a miraculous configuration. Both are caught
up in *logical illnesses,* forms of delusion, in which, to be sure, the
ideal reveals or mirrors itself in a twofold way—[both are] holy—
[both are] isolated creatures—that refract the higher light miracu-
lously—true prophets. . . . (WTB 2:623, cf. 481–82, 499, 624)

The line in Novalis's *Fantastik* between true prophetics and logical
illness is, at best, a crooked line, and Novalis never knows what side of that
line he is standing on. Novalis straddles. Novalis hovers. Not because he
lacks resolve, but because he is not a charlatan. Ambiguity concerning the
illness or well-being of the magical idealist extends to the very limits of life
itself. Novalis argues that life is "phlogistic process," that is, the process of
oxidation and combustion. All illness, accordingly, is "antiphlogistical" process, that is, anything that inhibits oxidation (WTB 2:818–19). Yet there is
something about combustion itself that is destructive. Oxidation is corrosive.
Moreover, the corrosion is *of spirit,* not of material nature. "Transience,
vulnerability is the character of a nature that is bound up with spirit. It
testifies to the activity, the universality, and the sublime personality of spirit"
(2:818–19). Not to flee a transient world and a vulnerable corporeality to a
disembodied spirit, but to recognize that transience and vulnerability are the
very earmarks of spirit, as it were: that is Novalis's insight, the insight that
condemns him to a kind of underground—a limbo at the heart of the Western
tradition in which he must hover.
    Novalis pushes that insight. On the same page of his notebooks he
indicates (1) that "all dead matter is *phlogiston,*" and (2) "*Phlogiston* = spirit,"
leading himself and his readers to the conclusion that (3) spirit is dead matter.
At all events, a kind of stasis and inertia, or heaviness *(Schwere),* is attributed
to divinity, and the following propositions (toward which we have been heading all along) ensue, one after the other, isolated and terrible in their impact
and import:

God is of infinitely compact metal *[von unendlich gediegenen
Metall]*—the most corporeal and the heaviest of all beings.
    Oxidation comes from the devil.
    Life is a sickness of spirit, an activity born to undergo *passio
[ein leidenschaftliches Thun].*
    Annihilation of air establishes the Kingdom of God. (WTB
2:820)

Whither such a breathless thought? Novalis is heading toward that bizarre conception of divinity projected by Georg Simmel early in the twentieth century, projected, it is true, in remembrance of Schelling rather than Novalis. Simmel recognized that the only way to escape from the consequences of the death of God was to think, in a cogent and coherent way, the fact that God always was dead, that the attribution of life and breath to the divine was the original error and the original sin. Simmel calls the assumption that God lives a "vulgar stupidity," *eine Borniertheit.* He urges his readers to return to Schelling's metaphysics of "indifference," to Spinoza's radically ungraspable "infinite attributes," and, above all, to medieval German mysticism, which is "freer and deeper than all earlier or later dogmatics and philosophies of religion."[18]

Whether Meister Eckhart or Richard of Saint-Victor or Spinoza or Schelling ever conceived of their pantheisms as a festival of death, however, is a question that should give us pause. Perhaps now we can understand why the "religious task," in Novalis's view, is "to show compassion toward divinity": *Mitleid* mit der *Gottheit zu haben* (WTB 2:759). Compassion for the dead is possible, at least as mourning, but compassion for what was never alive? That the absolute should end as absolutely dead—as having never, absolutely never, been alive—is a thought to which we may still be entirely unaccustomed. Novalis was clearly on his way to it.

IV. Coda

Remarkably, the first reference to the absolute in the book *Contagion* is not to absolute knowing or absolute spirit but to absolute death.[19] It is a reference to the way Goethe resists the possibility of absolute death, a resistance expressed in his concept of "relative death." Only the individual dies, not the species, so that any given death is always "relative." Yet what about the mortal individual, who, "in each case," is at least under the illusion that her death is her "own"? Is there not something absolutely cruel about relative death? An early aphoristic work on nature, copied into a notebook by Goethe (*Die Natur,* ca. 1780), expresses in its antiphonal form—in the intense, unresolved, unrelieved dialectic of its every assertion and counterassertion—the ambivalence Goethe feels toward nature:

> Nature! We are surrounded and embraced by her—without being able to exit from her or to enter into her more deeply. Unasked and unwarned, we are taken up into the circuitry of her dance; she has her way with us, until we grow weary and sink from her arms. . . .
>
> We live in the midst of her and are foreign to her. She speaks to us ceaselessly and does not betray her secret to us. We work our endless effects on her, yet have no dominion over her.

> She seems to have invested all her hopes in individuality, and she
> cares nothing for the individuals. Always she builds, always she
> destroys, and we have no access to her workshop.
>
> She lives in a profusion of children, and their mother, where is
> she?—
>
> She squirts her creatures out of nothingness, and does not tell
> them where they came from and where they are going. Their task is
> to run; *hers* is to know the orbit.[20]

In an essay from the year 1824, Goethe has much to say about "relative
death," and the absolute absence of "absolute death" in nature (1:424). Yet it
is the constant hovering of this dire relative of relative death—absolute demise—that shadows and haunts Goethe's otherwise inspiring and inspired
philosophy and science of nature. For is not death always *absolute* for the
individual that undergoes it in each case, whether wildflower or human being? Are not all of nature's hopes invested in the individuals she invariably
consigns to demise? And is not absolute death somehow coiled at the very
heart of life and love, whether in a rose or in a rose by any other name? "She
seems to have invested all her hopes in individuality, and she cares nothing
for the individuals." "And their mother—where is she?"

She appears to have a heart of stone? Well, then, let us go all the way
with such a mother. Let us adore compact metal.

Now we know why Hegel rejected the individual and went for the
genus—the *Gattung* that is God. He found it in logic, however, rather than in
unruly crowds of the living. And we also understand the courage of Schelling,
Hölderlin, and Novalis, who never let their logics distract them from the
weak-voiced plea of the dying individual, for whom even a relative death is
absolutely absolute.

Yet there may well be a fitting time for this thought of relative death—
if it be a time before absolute death advenes. Novalis takes up the notion in
what he calls "inoculation with death"—*nota bene,* not inoculation *against*
death, but *with* it. "Death is the romanticizing principle of our life" (2:756),
even if death is "minus," and life "plus." Negativity invigorates life: "Life is
strengthened by means of death" (2:756).

Well, then, *life*—and not absolute density. A life of oxidation and combustion, a life in the mix of air, even if oxygen is of the devil, especially for
a man whose lungs are being consumed. For a brief moment in his work,
Novalis entertains the metallic God of immortality, who is undying only
because he is death itself. Hölderlin, in his Notes to *Antigone,* declares that
God now comes on the scene solely and inevitably—and that means absolutely—"in the figure of death" (2:373). Yet Novalis ultimately always takes
the part of life, and that means of mortality and mixture. He is anything but

oblivious of the air. For absolute purity, absolute density, is absolute asphyxiation and death, and Novalis—like his brothers Hölderlin and Schelling—prefers the death of all absolutes to the absolute of death.

Notes

My gratitude to Sonu Shamdasani of London for this reference to William James on "Hegelism." To all appearances, my essay has nothing to do with Hegel, so that James's remarks may seem out of place to my readers. Yet the shadow of what in a book entitled *Contagion: Sexuality, Disease, and Death in German Idealism and Romanticism* (Bloomington and London: Indiana University Press, 1998) I have called Hegel's "triumphant idealism," the idealism of the absolute, is cast over the three figures I want to invoke in this essay—F. W. J. Schelling, Friedrich Hölderlin, and Novalis (Friedrich von Hardenberg). None of them savored triumph, however, and each of them would have understood James's frustration.

A slightly altered version of this essay appears in *Research in Phenomenology*, vol. 32 (2002).

Allow me to note here my thanks to the students and faculty of the University of Western Ontario's Centre for the Study of Theory and Criticism, led by Tilottama Rajan, and to David Clark, who heard an earlier version of this essay and helped me to reconsider the matters discussed in this "Coda."

1. Luce Irigaray, *L'Oubli de l'air chez Martin Heidegger* (Paris: Minuit, 1983), now in an English translation by Mary Beth Mader published by the University of Texas Press (1999); Jacques Derrida, *Glas* (Paris: Galilée, 1974); trans. John P. Leavey Jr. and Richard Rand (Lincoln: University of Nebraska Press, 1986).

2. See Schelling, *Erster Entwurf eines Systems der Naturphilosophie* (Jena and Leipzig, Germany: Gabler Verlag, 1799), reprinted in *Schriften von 1799–1801* (Darmstadt, Germany: Wissenschaftliche Buchgesellschaft, 1975), 1–268; hereafter cited as EE. This is a photomechanical reprint of the 1858–59 edition by Karl Schelling, published in Stuttgart and Augsburg by the J. G. Cotta'scher Verlag. The new historical-critical edition headed by Hartmut Buchner is now underway, and the *Erster Entwurf* has recently appeared (too late, unfortunately, for my own work). A translation of this crucial text—the *First Projection of a System of Nature Philosophy* is regarded by most interpreters, myself included, as the most significant of Schelling's major texts on the philosophy of nature—is being prepared by Keith Peterson for State University of New York Press. Two earlier works are also vital to Schelling's view of nature, namely, his 1798 *Von der Weltseele: Eine Hypothese der höheren Physik zur Erklärung des allgemeinen Organismus,* in *Schriften von 1794–1798* (Darmstadt, Germany: Wissenschaftliche Buchgesellschaft, 1980), 399–637, which presents the entire text, and *Ideen zu einer Philosophie der Natur als Einleitung in das Studium dieser Wissenschaft,* first published in 1797, with a second edition in 1803, in *Schriften von 1794–1798* (333–97), which unfortunately contains only the introductions, not the main body of the text. There is an English translation of the entire work, *Ideas for a Philosophy of Nature,* by Errol E. Harris and Peter Heath (Cambridge, England: Cambridge University Press, 1988). Schelling's *Von der Weltseele* has not yet been

translated into English. For the essay on human freedom and the incomplete treatise on the ages of the world, see Schelling, *Abhandlung über das Wesen der menschlichen Freiheit und die damit zusammenhängenden Gegenstände*, in *Schriften von 1806–1813* (Darmstadt, Germany: Wissenschaftliche Buchgesellschaft, 1983); see also the useful, inexpensive edition by Horst Fuhrmans (Stuttgart, Germany Philipp Reclam Verlag, 1964), first published in 1809, and the 1815 *Die Weltalter, Erstes Buch*, edited by Karl Schelling for the *Sämmtliche Werke* in 1861, in *Schriften von 1813–1830* (Darmstadt, Germany: Wissenschaftliche Buchgesellschaft, 1976), 1–150. This text, along with the supplement attached to it, *Über die Gottheiten von Samothrake* (1815), while only tangentially related to the philosophy of nature, takes Schelling to the farthest reaches of his speculation—in which, however, nature is still extremely powerful. Even more impressive than the 1815 text is *Die Weltalter Fragmente*, edited by Manfred Schröter as a Nachlaßband to the Münchner Jubiläumsdruck (Munich: Biederstein Verlag und Leibniz Verlag, 1946). This volume presents the original versions of *Die Weltalter*, set in print (but not released for publication) in 1811 and 1813; the first half of the 1811 version is, I believe, of particular power and special interest. Jason Wirth, of Ogelthorpe University, has prepared an English translation of *Die Weltalter* (State University of New York Press, 1999). Finally, see also Schelling's *System der Weltalter: Münchener Vorlesung 1827/28 in einer Nachschrift von Ernst von Lasaulx*, ed. Siegbert Peetz (Frankfurt am Main, Germany: Vittorio Klostermann, 1990), which is a late formulation of Schelling's never-completed, never-published magnum opus.

3. On this *Hemmung der Lebenskräfte*, see Immanuel Kant, *Kritik der Urteilskraft*, ed. Gerhard Lehmann (Stuttgart, Germany: Philipp Reclam Verlag, 1966), 134, 187. The Reclam edition reproduces the B edition of 1793; in the *Akademieausgabe* of Kant's works, see 75, 129.

4. Schelling, *Erster Entwurf* (220); very similar wording appears (240). Alan White, *Schelling: An Introduction to the System of Freedom* (New Haven: Yale University Press, 1983), has recognized the importance of this passage. He cites it in his brief discussion of Schelling's text (53–54).

5. On the relation of trauma to Schelling's *Ages of the World*, see Krell, " '*Das Vergangene wird gewußt, das Gewußte aber wird erzählt*': Trauma, Forgetting, and Narrative in F. W. J. Schelling's *Die Weltalter*," in *Philosophy and the Discourses of Trauma*, eds. Linda Belau and Petar Radjanovic, in *Postmodern Culture* 11:2 (January 2001) at http://www.iath.virginia.edu/pmc/>. This recent essay expands on my analysis of the 1809 *Treatise* in Krell, "The Crisis of Reason in the Nineteenth Century: Schelling's Treatise on Human Freedom (1809)," in *The Collegium Phaenomenologicum: The First Ten Years*, eds. John Sallis, Giuseppina Moneta, and Jacques Taminiaux (The Hague: M. Nijhoff, 1989), 13–32.

6. Friedrich Hölderlin, *Sämtliche Werke und Briefe*, ed. Michael Knaupp, 3 vols. (Munich: Carl Hanser Verlag, 1992), 2:49–50. All subsequent references to Hölderlin are from this edition.

7. See Sophocles, Notes to *Antigone*, at 2:372, ll. 15–17, and 374, ll. 1–2, in context. Hölderlin everywhere sees Zeus, the Father of Time and the Earth, as the principal subject-object of epic and tragedy. The way in which tragedy brings the epic tradition to its fulfillment is suggested when Hölderlin remarks in a review that Homer's *Iliad* is "sung to honor Father Jupiter rather than Achilles or anyone else" (2:112).

8. On the issue of unification and dissolution in Hölderlin's interpretation of tragedy, see Krell, *Lunar Voices: Of Tragedy, Poetry, Fiction, and Thought* (Chicago and London: University of Chicago Press, 1995), chap. 2.

9. The notion of *Lebenslicht,* literally, "the light of life," is strange. Hölderlin refers to it in a number of late poems as well as in a letter to Casimir U. Böhlendorff, where he identifies it with a "savage martial" and "masculine" character, in which the "feeling of death" is experienced in "virtuoso" form (Hölderlin, *Sämtliche Werke,* 2:921). In short, the light of life is anything but debility in any usual sense, though it is shot through with a sense of mortality. See the editor's further references (3:402). Finally, one should recall that for the Schelling of the 1815 "Divinities of Samothrace" the original names for God designate not so much majesty and might as poverty and hunger. See notes 31, 36, and 47 (8:183–186, and 188–90).

10. See now Françoise Dastur, *Hölderlin: Le retournement natal* (La Versanne, France: Encre marine, 1997), which consists of two main parts, "Tragedy and Modernity" and "Nature and Poesy." See the discussion in Krell, *Lunar Voices,* 8–9 n. 9, 21–22 n. 21.

11. Hölderlin, *Hyperion,* 1:753; emphasis added. See the related passage in Hölderlin's translation of Sophocles' *Antigone* on Danaë's ticking or counting off the hours for Zeus (2:353).

12. See Douglas F. Kenney and Sabine Menner-Bettscheid, eds. and trans., *The Recalcitrant Art: Diotima's Letters to Hölderlin and Related Missives* (Albany: State University of New York Press, 2000).

13. See Krell, "A Small Number of Houses in a Universe of Tragedy: Aristotle's περὶ ποιητκῆς and Hölderlin's *Anmerkungen*," in *Philosophy and Tragedy: A Collection of Contemporary Essays,* eds. Miguel de Bestegui and Simon Sparks (London: Routledge, 2000).

14. In what follows, I will cite Novalis, *Werke, Tagebücher und Briefe,* eds. Hans-Joachim Mähl and Richard Samuel, 3 vols. (Munich: Carl Hanser Verlag, 1987), hereafter cited as WTB. I will make particular reference to volume 2, *Das philosophisch-theoretische Werk.* The Hanser edition is a relatively inexpensive hardbound edition based on the historical-critical edition initiated by Paul Kluckhohn and Richard Samuel. The Hanser edition, while not complete, contains most of the material that is in volumes 2 and 3 of the larger, far more expensive edition. Readers should nevertheless check important passages in volumes 2 and 3 in the larger edition, Novalis, *Schriften,* ed. Richard Samuel et al., revised by Samuel and Mähl, 5 vols. (Stuttgart, Germany: Kohlhammer Verlag, 1981).

15. Schelling notes that the culmination of God's every path, the *finis viarum Dei,* is embodiment in his *Ages of the World* (8:325). On Novalis's use of the *Mannigfach,* see 1:201, 205, 218–21, 229, and 347.

16. On the entire question of "hovering," let me once again (as I did in *Contagion*) recommend the study by Lore Hühn, "Das Schweben der Einbildungskraft: Zur Frühromantischen Überbietung Fichtes," *Deutsche Vierteljahrsschrift für Literaturwissenschaft und Geistesgeschichte* 70:4 (December 1996): 569–99. Hühn investigates the metaphor of the "hovering imagination," *schwebende Einbildungskraft,* in Fichte, Novalis, and in other early romantics. She argues convincingly that Novalis and others, such as Friedrich Schlegel, follow and even surpass Fichte in establishing

the imagination as the faculty that more than any other engages actuality. Moreover, the actuality engaged by the imagination, which hovers between being and nonbeing, is precisely "life" (593). Hühn's study is both wide-ranging in scope and precise in its detail; essential reading for this topic!

17. Jean-Paul Sartre, *L'Etre et le néant* (Paris: Gallimard, 1943), 678.

18. Georg Simmel, *Lebensanschauung: Vier metaphysische Kapitel* (Munich and Leipzig: Duncker und Humblot, 1918), 109. See the discussion in Krell, *Daimon Life: Heidegger and Life-Philosophy* (Bloomington and London: Indiana University Press, 1992), 94–95.

19. Krell, *Contagion,* 5.

20. Johann Wolfgang von Goethe, *Naturwissenschaftliche Schriften,* ed. Rudolf Steiner, 5 vols. (Dornach, Switzerland: R. Steiner Verlag, 1982), 2:5–7.

Schopenhauer's Telling
Body of Philosophy

Joel Faflak

. . . the intellect remains so much excluded from the real resolutions
and secret decisions of its own will that sometimes it can only get
to know them . . . by spying and taking unawares; and it must surprise the will in the act of expressing itself, in order merely to
discover its real intentions.

—Arthur Schopenhauer, *The World as Will and Representation*

I

It is a commonplace that Schopenhauer anticipates Sigmund Freud. Schopenhauer's will suggests Freud's *Triebe*, the dark materiality of the ego's substra-
tum fundamental to the psyche's makeup yet beyond its control.[1] Together
Schopenhauer's will and representation suggest Freud's primary processes
and secondary revision, the latter evoking a type of deceptive consciousness
of the former. For Freud, interpretation and the talking cure mitigate this
deception, just as his metapsychology is a theoretical *epoché* of the psyche's
empiricism. But for Schopenhauer the fundamental condition of being is
representation's inability to read the will's "real resolutions and secret decisions,"[2] as if psychoanalyzing a patient who invites yet pathologically resists
enlightenment. Embodying the Kantian idealism of the mind's representation

161

of the world, the will remains symptomatic. The subject's "immediate knowledge" (WWR 1:102) of the will is through his body, which anthropomor-
phizes the will as its most "immediate" representation of itself. However, the
idealism of this representation relies "parasitically" on the will as *"organism"*
(2:216). The will-as-body is representation's fundamental "condition" (1:102)
of being at the same time that it is vulnerable to this body's "every pertur-
bation" (2:216). Nurtured by the traumatic agitation of the intellect by a will
that the intellect would also cure, idealism offers the impossible enlightenment of psychoanalysis.

For Tilottama Rajan and David L. Clark, Schopenhauer's "deconstruction" of "Kant's idealistic insistence on the assertion of the mental
categories against the world of necessity . . . structurally anticipates the contemporary emphasis on the subversion of the subject of writing and the unconscious" at the same time that his "resistance to this deconstruction intimates
a survival of idealism."[3] This survival is the present essay's theme. David
Farrell Krell argues that a "crisis of reason" emerges from a tension between
a *"transcendental critique* of pure reason," authored in Immanuel Kant's
three Critiques, and a *"genealogy* of reason," suggested by his *Anthropology
from a Pragmatic Point of View.*[4] This is the crisis of a subject whose *sum*
depends on the epistemological ambivalence of the *cogito*, a shuddering in
the body of Reason as it encounters the uncanny doubleness of its psyche.[5]
Recognizing the willing subject as subject *to* the will's blind determinism,
Schopenhauer rethinks the cogito as the sum of its deconstructive parts. He
reads this uncanniness through a doubled and antagonistic self-positing: that of
representation's aesthetic imperative, through which the subject knows himself,
and that of the will's "immediate" manifestation of itself in the body, an other
self-positing at once essential and alien to enlightenment. Hence, Schopenhauer
puts an end to the aesthetic in the ascetic's end to knowing, which in turn
traumatically ends the subject. The ascetic, as we shall see, marks the symptom
of idealism's essential trauma: the idealist subject comes to know the will only
by setting aside this knowledge's traumatic impossibility.

Faced with this trauma, the (Kantian) idealism of philosophy's complete telling of itself is haunted by its own materiality, what I will call
philosophy's "telling body," which expresses the anatomy of idealism's interiority. *The World as Will* introduces into its writing the psychology of the
philosophical subject who is unable to speak of, and hence to comprehend the
body of, her own functioning. The text thus narrativizes within the body of
Reason idealism's promise of enlightenment as this body's undoing.
Schopenhauer inherits from Kant idealism's interminable struggle with the
fact that the subject is the "knower" yet never "the known" (WWR 1:5) of
his own consciousness. Freud's version of this idealism decodes the symptom's
cryptic body of evidence as if to put the body aside. But as the embodied

pathology of consciousness, the symptom is itself a reading of the psyche in the body that thwarts the patient's attempt to speak the symptom's meaning. The body speaks (for) the mind—the body *speaks* its mind—because the mind cannot speak for itself. In *Studies in Hysteria* Freud acknowledges how "psychical trauma . . . acts like a foreign body which long after its entry must continue to be regarded as an agent that is still at work." At this point Freud calls for the cathartic method of abreacting the *"strangulated affect"* cathected by trauma by allowing it *"to find a way out through speech,"* what he will later name the talking cure. Yet in searching for the "incubation and patho-genesis"[6] of hysterical symptoms, he encounters the unconscious fantasy of memory. This fantasy's unmanageable psychic growth leaves Freud's idealism divided against itself, unable to expose the kernel of traumatic truth in the form of the symptom's meaning.

Like the symptom that constellates its effects, trauma constellates psychoanalysis as an unresolvable epistemological dilemma.[7] Knowledge itself unfolds pathologically and repetitively rather than productively and progressively within idealism's heterogeneous organicism. For instance, virulent neuroses such as those associated with war trauma confronted Freud with the prospect of an interminable analysis without a cure. In Schopenhauer, however, interminability confronts its own chronic nature. Whereas in Freud interminability still intimates a desire for enlightenment's remedy, the *chronic* signifies an analysis fated to proceed in spite of its futility, the inescapable condition of being the subject must necessarily learn to accept. *The World as Will* is symptomatic of the trauma of idealism, then, because the text can never adequately give relief to the "strangulated affect" associated with its traumatic experience of the will as idealism's absolute. I am thus suggesting that *The World as Will* confronts psychoanalysis as endless trauma without the possibility of transformation. Idealism becomes the trauma of a psychoanalysis that idealism calls forth but from which it cannot then be released. Moreover, Schopenhauer's text does not presume to be enlightened about or by the failure of its own idealism. The text cannot surrender its idealism, which, like the psychoanalysis it calls forth, becomes the crucible of an existence from which the subject cannot be liberated.

Hence, in the cultural imaginary of psychoanalysis, Schopenhauer's *World as Will* narrativizes the philosophical unconscious of psychoanalysis to suggest the indeterminacy of psychoanalysis' own idealism. The will *embodies* philosophy itself as a necessarily failed attempt to account for the loss of its own idealism. The idealist corpus of Schopenhauer's text is desublimated by its own will as if by the Lacanian Real that "resists symbolization absolutely."[8] In turn, philosophy and psychoanalysis remain haunted by an idealism they cannot be said to supersede, yet to which they remain indebted: in Schopenhauer, that of a Kantianism haunted by its own absolute of pure reason; in Freud, that of an enlightened consciousness—also a type of Kantianism—which psychoanalysis by its very nature can never possess. Kant would make the categorical possibility of the subject's inner experience commensurate with his external empirical reality.[9] Yet he also argues that while the "thing in itself is indeed given, . . . we can have no insight into its nature."[10] Precisely by invoking reason's safe and definitive knowledge, he exposes a traumatic rift in the epistemology of being that this sublimation was meant to cover. Freud's unconscious similarly displaces the faculty of psychoanalysis to make the inner reality of psychic life commensurate with the outer terms of the patient's existence. Because psychoanalysis cannot authenticate the empiricism of the unconscious, enlightenment is never complete, and psychoanalysis can never deliver its promised cure. This failure signifies in contradictory ways. On one hand, psychoanalysis mourns the loss of its own promise of epistemological mastery. On the other, the failure encrypts mastery as if to avoid mourning its absence. Melancholy increasingly haunts Freud's writings after *Beyond the Pleasure Principle* as an inability to accept how the death drive prevents enlightenment. This melancholy links psychoanalysis back to a philosophical idealism over which Freud would claim precedence.[11] Schopenhauer's text struggles to internalize within philosophy's identity the specter of its own idealism. In philosophy's loss it gains psychoanalysis, but as a type of melancholic idealism unable to obtain the cure of enlightenment.

Schopenhauer speaks of the will as a *vis naturae medicatrix* (WWR 2:214) or "healing power of nature." But this cure is also toxic to the knowing subject, forcing him to suffer the will's "endless striving, . . . [e]ternal becoming, endless flux" (1:164). After Schopenhauer, Friedrich Nietzsche describes the cure as an experience of the Dionysian "excess of life": "after a forceful attempt to gaze on the sun we turn away blinded, we see dark-colored spots before our eyes, as a cure, as it were." This "cure" is the mask of Apollo, the "necessary effects of a glance into the inside and terrors of nature; as it were, luminous spots to cure eyes damaged by gruesome night." But enlightenment is also a dark curing or hardening of vision that registers enlightenment's trauma as the physiological symptom of its blinding effects. Nietzsche sees through the "sublime metaphysical illusion" of science.[12] For him Reason's madness is its attempt to correct itself *as* madness, so that the cure of enlightenment *is* its disease—Reason as the symptom of madness. Without Nietzsche's articulating mythography of Apollo's confrontation with Dionysus, however, Schopenhauer's seems a less determinate or acute encounter of representation with the will's "gruesome night." Yet the chronic nature of his resistance to surrendering idealism's absolute of enlightenment is more telling for its psychoanalytical pathos. *The World as Will* offers a philosophical *Bildung* of Reason in which the architectonic of Kant's critical method submits itself to psychoanalytic scrutiny. By submitting, philosophy confesses the radical limitations of its idealism as a type of false consciousness. However, psychoanalysis does not emerge from this confession as a way of overcoming these limitations by accepting them. In Schopenhauer's text, idealism ends up telling the story of the lost absolutism of pure reason, yet by resisting succumbing to the illusion of being enlightened by this loss. The next section will trace this story's unfolding in Schopenhauer's principal text, while the final section will explore the psychoanalytic form this unfolding takes.

II

When first published in 1818 *The World as Will* was largely ignored, as was a later 1844 edition.[13] This edition reprints the first and appends a second volume as a running commentary on, or supplement to, the first. Schopenhauer opens this volume by insisting that "philosophy is essentially *idealistic*" (WWR 2:5) and that "true philosophy must at all costs be *idealistic*": "everything of which [we have] certain, sure, and hence immediate knowledge, lies within [our] consciousness," although beyond this, "there can be no *immediate* certainty" (2:4). Writing against a rampant "Hegelism" (1:xxiv) that excluded Schopenhauer from its history of ideas, he is anxious to sustain this idealism. More tellingly, however, it expresses its own limitations, implicitly its inability to exorcize Kant. Chastising G. W. F. Hegel for forgetting Kant's lesson, Schopenhauer in turn demonstrates how Kant *could* not, as well as should not, be left behind. Caught between revering Kant as "the most important phenomenon which has appeared in philosophy for two thousand years" and exposing his system's "grave errors" (1:xv), Schopenhauer's text is typified by an "excessive preoccupation . . . with the Kantian philosophy" (1:xiv). The second volume confirms this return, not as a diagnostic revision of Schopenhauer's earlier thought, but as a symptomatic repetition of this thought's insistence on its own idealism.

Kant internalizes the mind's empiricism in advance of the world as if to determine its form a priori. But he also acknowledges that "nothing whatsoever can be asserted of the thing in itself" as representation, for "otherwise we should be landed in the absurd conclusion that there can be appearance without anything that appears."[14] However, for Schopenhauer Kant succumbs to precisely this absurdity by bracketing off the categories from empiricism— by abstracting Being from being.[15] Moreover, by setting aside the objective world as the inscrutable touchstone of empiricism, Kant suppresses how this contingency resists being subsumed a priori.[16] This resistance forms the kernel of Schopenhauer's idealism. For Schopenhauer, "nothing existing by itself and independent, and also nothing single and detached, can become an object for us." This describes his principle of sufficient reason, wherein "the pure *a priori* concepts . . . serve solely as *a priori* conditions of a possible experience"[17] without constituting this experience except as representation. Governing how consciousness functions *within* rather than *apart from* the world, sufficient reason prescribes idealism's limits lest it veer off into complete abstraction, as if to protect Kant from his own immanent Hegelianism.

But sufficient reason breeds its own disease by bringing the subject into immediate contact with the world as *will*, Schopenhauer's version of Kant's in-itself. In will, reason's sufficiency, more pragmatically than transcendentally idealistic, marks a problematic limit: the subject reenters from Kant's abstract world as the *principium individuationis*, the principle of individuation, but also as a mere appearance interminably contending with the will's mastery. The will is untiring and metaphysical, the "first and original thing" to which the intellect or representation, treated as physical and thus exhaustible, is a "secondary thing" (WWR 2:202), a "mere slave and bondsman to the will" (2:212). The will is a "blind irresistible urge" (1:275), not "subject to the principle of sufficient reason" in the world of representation, although the will mobilizes representation as its *"appearance"* or *"phenomenon"* (1:106).[18] Evoking a psychology at odds with Reason's abstraction, Reason's *dis*traction by the body of the will creates the subject as a "stable and unwavering phantom" (1:278 n.) at the fault line where will and representation mutually supplement and deconstruct one another. Book Two examines the will as an *urgrund* or originary ground anchoring the first book's representation of it. But the will finds a more ambivalent manifestation in the subject, who emerges as a troubled hybrid between two strains of the same ontology. The subject is the symptom of the will's disease, constituted by the very thing that subverts this constitution. This symptomatic subject bears the burden of proof for a body of evidence that is his own, yet also utterly alien to him. As "will become visible" (1:107), the body is both representation or "knowledge *a posteriori* of the will"—*embodied* will—*and* will or "knowledge a priori of the body"—*dis*embodied representation (1:100).

The will interiorizes the contingency between the subject and the world as an internal otherness or foreign body within the subject of philosophy itself. As Terry Eagleton writes, while Schopenhauer "privileges the inward in Romantic style, he nevertheless refuses to valorize it."[19] The will grounds the subject in the body of her experience through a type of romantic immediacy between the self and its interiority. However, only "presupposed" (WWR 1:5) by the forms of knowledge, the subject is then denied access to any definitive knowledge of this embodiment, so that interiority is radically displaced within itself, as if to reexteriorize or alienate itself. Inevitably, representation succumbs to its ceaseless effort to know the will, which appears as "a continual rushing of the present into the dead past, a constant dying" (1:311) or "constant suffering" (1:267). Representation is the fated repetition of the subject through the forms of his knowledge, the mere repetition of the will's endless striving as a drive toward the exhaustion of the knowing subject.[20] Rather than the enlightened, practical correction of a Kantian abstraction, then, sufficient reason becomes the symptom of Reason's traumatic inability to know the will. Although representation exists to know the will, "there is no permanent fulfilment which completely and for ever satisfies its craving" (WWR 1:362). The will is the "strong blind man" who carries the "sighted lame man" (2:209) of the intellect on his shoulders, so that insight illuminates a blindness essential to its own constitution. The will is both Reason as if yet without consciousness *and* Reason's unconscious, both the *prima mobile* of the subject's desire for enlightenment and a force utterly oblivious to this desire.

Once Book One's a posteriori effects of representation are subsumed by the a priori ground of these effects in Book Two's account of the will, a different story begins to emerge. As if compelled toward an insight it would both accept and resist, Book Two articulates how the "game" of "Eternal becoming" and "endless flux," although it reveals the will's "essential nature" through a "constant transition from desire to satisfaction," merely prevents the game from "showing itself as a fearful, life-destroying boredom, a lifeless longing without a definite object, a deadening languor" (WWR 1:164). The "subject of willing is constantly lying on the revolving wheel of Ixion, is always drawing water in the sieve of the Danaids, and is the eternal thirsting Tantalus" (1:196).[21] The first of these metaphors dominates here, in that it suggests a radicalization of the Freudian couch, which would otherwise articulate the phenomenology of the subject's experience of his own unconscious in the form of the narrative of his life story, the telos of which is the cure as an end to the text's tale of suffering. In Schopenhauer, however, the striving for knowledge itself leads to a kind of epistemological futility that marks this narrative as a self-making project predicated on the abyss of its own meaninglessness. The origin of idealism lies in its *need* for a psychoanalysis whose cure of enlightenment idealism must then surrender.

As if responding to this futility, the text's latter books would end the will's suffering by suspending the willing body in the end, rather than ends, of representation. In Book Three representation momentarily transcends itself through the aesthetic contemplation of the Ideas. Schopenhauer's Idea derives from that of Plato and from Kant's transcendental ideality of phenomena, but as if to demonstrate how these bracket themselves off from the reality they would represent. By subsuming within its unity representation's multivalent and repetitive phenomena, the Idea stages representation's finiteness as a type of absolute limit. Here the will appears to knowledge in the form least adulterated by the will's exhaustible iteration of itself via representation. Grasped intuitively as the gestalt of representation, the Ideas "lie quite outside the sphere of [the subject's] knowledge" (WWR 1:169) in a type of self-consciousness that transcends the desire for enlightenment. Book Three pursues this sublimation of idealism's contingency with its own interiority through a hierarchy of aesthetic epiphenomena ending in music. Music, like philosophy, expresses ths most immediate continuity with the will by abandoning the subject's body of representation as a contamination of the will's purity. In both philosophy and music, "knowledge tears itself free from the service of the will precisely by the subject's ceasing to be merely individual, and being now a pure will-less subject of knowledge" (1:178), an Idea expressing itself as if without the help of phenomena.

The aesthetic liberates the subject from empiricism itself via a wholly cognizant body which, paradoxically, suspends its own body of knowledge by "abolishing individuality in the knowing subject" (WWR 1:169). Therefore, the acme of the aesthetic in music and philosophy suggests the end of philosophy's telling body in more ways than one. The aesthetic poses an almost Hegelian solution to a Schopenhauerian problem by subsuming the body's contingency within the Idea's pure spirit of Reason. However, by wishing away the phantasm of the will's subjectivity as so many "vanished illusions" (1:164), the Ideas stage the subject's (dis)appearance as the symptom of a Kantian empirical dilemma for which the text, by staging this (dis)appearance, would account. Like Heideggerian *Schein,* wherein being is at once revelatory and illusory, or like the Lacanian gaze, wherein the cogito and its consciousness do not add up to the same subject, the apparition of the Idea marks a type of paralyzed mirror stage within Schopenhauer's idealism. Ceasing to be individual, the subject merely *appears* in a momentary retreat back into an imagined yet never sustained unity of Being.

As a cure for the will's suffering, the aesthetic offers an acute form of idealism's psychoanalysis. But the aesthetic's *knowing* epistemology remains acutely limited by its own philosophy by telling *how* philosophy overcomes representation. Philosophy thus remains susceptible to the endless striving for an absolute that is endemic to its existence as will. Schopenhauer's philosophy comes to realize, that is, that it is constrained by a *telling* body that is symptomatic rather than paradigmatic of the will.[22] Whereas Books One and Two deploy philosophy as objective critique, then, it emerges by the end of Book Three as this critique's untenable subject. As if to talk out this problem definitively, the text's fourth and final book meets in the telling body of the philosopher himself the will as the *ungrund* of philosophy to which its representation is ceaselessly fated to return. If, as Eagleton argues, the "aesthetic is what ruptures for a blessed moment the terrible sway of teleology, the tangled chain of functions and effects into which all things are locked, plucking an object for an instant out of the clammy grip of the will and savouring it purely as spectacle,"[23] Book Four is where the subject surrenders to this fate. Freud confronts in the death drive a desire to return to the end as absolute, wherein return suggests a repetition compulsion resisting enlightenment in the subject. Where Freud reads this return regressively, however, Schopenhauer attempts to account for it *as* enlightenment. For Schopenhauer Thanatos is not the absolute so much as is the elimination of death as an elimination of the desire for life. Death becomes the negative pleasure principle whose wish fulfillment lies with the elimination of desire itself.

Book Four targets the body as the site of the will's mortification (through fasting, chastity, etc.), a *"denial of the will-to-live"* (WWR 1:285) in order to attain pure knowledge of the will. Schopenhauer uses the example of the "holiness and self-denial" (1:288) of saints and martyrs, who eschew the will's striving as it *appears* to the subject as the *"affirmation of the will to live"* (1:285) in order to achieve the will-less calm of the will as if without its own need for self-consciousness. This asceticism *starves* or *suppresses* the will's appetite in the body, not in order to eliminate the body's phenomenon, as in suicide, but in order to *be* the will as a suspension of any desire for phenomenalization and thus for enlightenment. *Being* the will, as Schopenhauer articulates it, is not a matter of easy comprehension, for we are always ascertaining a being that denies its own need for knowledge. Self-renunciation brings the "unfulfilled and thwarted willing" (1:363) of how we think ourselves as phenomena of the will into direct contradiction with who we truly are as will, rendering any knowing embodiment obsolete. Book Four thus turns the idea of enlightenment entirely against itself. If the Idea is where "the will can reach full self-consciousness, distinct and exhaustive knowledge of its own inner nature," then "an elimination and self-denial of the will in its most perfect phenomenon [in the Idea] is possible" (1:288). The ascetic uses the Idea to "abolish the essential nature at the root of the phenomenon"—the striving of the will as the knowledge or *knowing* of representation—"whilst the phenomenon itself still continues to exist in time," and so "brings about a contradiction of the phenomenon with itself" (1:288). The "will turns about; it no longer affirms its own inner nature, mirrored in the phenomenon, but denies it" (1:380), as if "to think away the assistance of the intellect" (2:269). In this state, "only knowledge remains; the will has vanished" (1:411). What vanishes is idealism's illumination of the will through knowledge, a type of pure or direct knowledge wherein the will no longer desires to know itself as phenomena.

Placing the subject *beyond* the will to knowledge, then, asceticism offers a gnosis of the will that abandons knowledge. This gnosis is the most radical form of the text's psychoanalysis in that it dispels for the subject the "mere concepts and phantasms" (WWR 1:279) of his past and future so as to release him to the "real present" (1:279). Here he discovers himself as "his own work prior to all knowledge," which has been "merely added to illuminate [the will]," this 'illuminating' knowledge existing "merely in abstract thoughts" (1:293). These thoughts, because of their phenomenality, become the "cause of our pain as of our pleasure" (1:279) and are "often unbearable to us," as "in the case of intense mental suffering," because they "lie for the most part not in the real present" (1:299). Hence, the temporal form of the will's suffering in the body becomes the symptom of the mind's suffering, so that "we cause ourselves physical suffering in order . . . to divert our attention from the former to the latter" (1:299). But the return to the will also evokes a rather startling succumbing to it. To eliminate the body as the hysterical symptom of the mind's struggle to know the will is to eliminate the "absurd" idea that, "starting from reflection," the subject can "be something different from what he is; for this is an immediate contradiction of the will itself" (1:306). Liberation from the blindness of representation's "illumination," then, comes not by entering into the insight of the will, but by accepting our insight of it as a blind determinism: "We are like entrapped elephants, which rage and struggle fearfully for many days, until they see that it is fruitless, and then suddenly offer their necks calmly to the yoke, tamed for ever" (1:306). That the "will itself cannot be abolished by anything except *knowledge*" (1:400) means that we do not overcome the will through enlightenment, but rather by radically accepting the will in order to remain no longer susceptible to it. One engages in psychoanalysis, that is, not to secure its cure of enlightenment, but to put an end to its desire *for* enlightenment.

That the ascetic confronts self-knowledge as the most universal form of the will so as continually to renounce this knowledge produces no catharsis of the will's striving and thus no cure for its disease.[24] Ascesis is offered at the end of the text as the end of philosophy, yet also as the telos of philosophy's psychoanalysis. The text's idealism puts the philosophical analysand on the couch, as if suspended beatifically in the midst of his own suffering, in a moment of impossible enlightenment. The ascetic offers an acute acceptance of the will. But the internal mechanism of this acceptance is rather more chronic in nature, for the denial of the will-to-live "must always be achieved afresh by constant struggle" (WWR 1:391). The body's need for psychoanalysis is never satisfied, so that psychoanalysis becomes the yoke of the subject's existence. Indeed, the final passages of the fourth book marks the ascetic as an absurd absolute. That "only knowledge remains" when the "will has vanished" means that the world as representation is reduced to nothing in more ways than one: for those who are "still full of the will," this world appears as nothing; "to those in whom the will has turned and denied itself, this very real world of ours with all its suns and galaxies, is nothing" (1:412). The subject is suspended between the nothingness of being and the being of nothingness, a "negative knowledge" of a positive knowledge, neither of which he can possess: a moment of profound stasis that demands further psychoanalysis, but makes it further impossible. The ascetic thus stages the denial of the will-to-live as the subject's inhabiting of the trauma of idealism in the form of psychoanalysis. In Book Four Schopenhauer offers a chronic psychoanalysis whose own chronic nature must be set aside, but cannot.

Reading the ascetic back through the aesthetic, we can see how Books Three and Four express an impossible psychoanalytic subjectivity that Reason cannot enlighten. Both the illumination of the Idea in Book Three and its radical suspension in Book Four are moments of acute awareness meant to stay the text's otherwise chronic necessity for psychoanalysis. In either case, to meet the will on its own terms is to entertain an impossible state that is "higher than all reason," but as a kind of trauma of Reason that the philosopher is compelled to speak, yet as if never at all. Forever displaced from the absolute state of its existence, philosophy becomes an impossible telling: it must speak what it cannot know and, in telling, expose more than it knows without then having, or by no more desiring, access to this knowledge. The aesthetic and the ascetic suspend the will all the more pointedly to invoke its presence as a pathology resisting their cure. In either case, consciousness fails the subject. Rather than being the telos of any system, Books Three and Four are symptomatic of philosophy's ambivalent relationship with the interiority of its own idealism. Thus *The World as Will* evokes a representational crisis about philosophy's ability to *speak adequately of* this gap. Philosophy emerges from this crisis as a telling body that is the symptom of the disease of enlightenment with which the will infects the knowing subject, a symptom from which there is no relief. In the final section we shall explore the form this talking takes.

III

As the repeated articulation of a revised Kantianism, Schopenhauer's text unfolds narratively and palimpsestically rather than teleologically or architectonically. It continually reinforces the tenets of its own systematization, but as if to evoke the insufficient reason of their primary stating. This iterability signals a decided turn in the corpus of idealism.[25] Schopenhauer sets out his critique of Kant in his doctoral thesis, *On the Fourfold Principle of Sufficient Reason*, published in 1813, and it forms a crucial prolegomenon to his later work, an afflatus that sustains the consciousness of his later idealism.[26] This single-mindedness, I have suggested, is perhaps the most telling feature of Schopenhauer's system insofar as it works *against* its own architectonic coherence. This coherence is itself already problematic in that it depends on a will that resists and so never properly fits the organic whole of his system's representation of idealism. By prioritizing the will as a type of chemical 'free radical' within the larger structure of its own organicism, Schopenhauer's revision of Kant's system, seemingly against is own will, exposes the untenability of (Schopenhauer's) philosophy. Schopenhauer's resolution is divided against itself: he recognizes a profound otherness integral to his philosophy's identity; yet the attachment to Kant evokes a type of melancholic idealism, a longing to overcome the will despite its primacy. Schopenhauer writes against the grain of his own philosophy and thus against a Kantianism he both supplements and deconstructs, so that philosophy unravels into chronic psychoanalysis.

In the preface to *The World as Will*, Schopenhauer argues that "what is to be imparted by [his text] is a single thought" and explains that all elements of a "*system of thought* must always have an architectonic connexion or coherence": a "*single thought*, however comprehensive, must preserve the most perfect unity." But he continues, "If . . . it can be split up into parts for the purpose of being communicated, then the connexion of these parts must once more be organic." Unfortunately, "a book must have a first and a last line, and to this extent will always remain very unlike an organism, however like one its contents may be. Consequently, form and matter will here be in contradiction" (WWR 1:xii–xiii). To overcome this contradiction, Schopenhauer implores the reader to "*read the book twice*" so that he acculturates himself to the text's mode of being in order then to master or step outside of this interiority. Entering into the interior matter of the text's form, however, poses problems: "the earnest desire for fuller and even easier comprehension must, in the case of every difficult subject, justify occasional repetition. The structure of the whole, which is organic, and not like a chain, in itself makes it necessary sometimes to touch twice on the same point" (1:xiii). By introducing repetition, the organicism of Schopenhauer's system—the placing of a *single* thought within a *process* of thought—exposes itself to chronic analysis, a repetitive or pathological organicism that the text's "final analysis" attempts to negate in asceticism's denial of the will-to-live. In this sense, *The World as Will* is symptomatic of a talking cure for the disease of the will that unsettles the cure's rational imperative in advance of Freud. Schopenhauer's text seems fated to iterate the primal scene of its own Kantianism as the traumatic repetition of its desire to know the will, wherein the idealism of Kantian Reason becomes the trauma rather than the ideal dictating the text's unfolding.[27] Schopenhauer's text evolves as a repeated encounter with the trauma of idealism staged impossibly between philosophy and psychoanalysis, between Kant and Freud.

Schopenhauer argues that his text offers a "method of philosophizing which is here attempted for the first time" (WWR 1:xiv). His 1844 preface to the second edition refers to this method as *meditative* (1:xxvi), a word symptomatic of an anxiety about talking, wherein the philosopher is uneasy about confessing philosophy's interiority. The gesture is itself typically romantic. Jean-Jacques Rousseau begins *The Confessions* by calling it a work "without precedent,"[28] and William Wordsworth says of *The Prelude* that it is "a thing unprecedented in Literary history that a man should talk so much about himself."[29] In both statements the voice of revolution masks an uneasiness about nonoriginality and thus nonidentity. Talking betrays an other fear of losing the self in *too much* talk, a talking that is ambivalently chronic rather than determinately acute. Ironically, romantic literature's acknowledged burden of explaining itself frequently stands in place of its absent philosophical system. *The Prelude,* like Samuel Taylor Coleridge's *Biographia Literaria,* is written in place of the philosophical masterwork *The Recluse,* both symptoms of an inability to map the architectonic of Reason. Wordsworth produces instead a *Bildung* of Reason's "steadiest mood"[30] which, focused in his mental breakdown, is far from steady. And Coleridge encounters idealism by wandering in the "unwholesome quicksilver mines of metaphysic depths": contemplation errs pathologically from Reason's straight path, and the text unfolds as an "immethodical miscellany"[31] of thoughts without an efficient terminus. Thinking becomes unhealthy, and talking *about* thinking only produces more talking, too much talking becoming symptomatic of an inability to figure things out. This ongoing exposure of philosophy's interiority becomes chronically addictive, in the way that Schopenhauer's representation of the will reflects an addiction to speak of the will as the impossible real by which representation is infected as the primal source of its own constitution.[32] Ironically, Wordsworth never published *The Prelude* in his lifetime, as if unable to contain his excessive talking. As if to surmount Wordsworth's dilemma, Freud's talking cure suggests the acute cure not only *of* but *for* talking. One talks *just enough*, or in *just the right manner*, so that, rather than inventing psychoanalysis, Freud puts aside its disease as a resistance to becoming addicted to the very thing he invents.

Schopenhauer does not necessarily accede to this rationalism: "my philosophy does not allow of the fiction . . . of a reason that knows, perceives, or apprehends immediately and absolutely" (WWR 1:xxvi). Here meditation suggests the confession rather than the contemplation of interiority. In this respect *The World as Will* resembles Thomas De Quincey's *Confessions of an English Opium-Eater*. In De Quincey's text the writer interrogates his philosophical identity as the site where unreason chronically unsettles Reason. In the 1856 expansion of his original 1821 *Confessions*, De Quincey recalls "the slow and elaborate toil of constructing one single work"[33] of philosophical mastery. But the psychic and physiological disease of his addiction thwarted this work's organic growth. Up to his opium addiction, De Quincey's confession follows a straightforward developmental pattern, wherein the body of his suffering remains tranquil within the contemplative life of his mind. Opium disrupts this calm, however, by exposing the subject to the unconscious, compelling De Quincey to retrace its origins in the time before his addiction.

Yet the regressive thrust of this genealogy proliferates into a myriad of narrative and discursive forms, what De Quincey describes as a *"caduceus wreathed about with meandering ornaments or the shaft of a tree's stem hung round and surmounted with some vague parasitical plant."*[34] This "pathological" narrative turns a terminable autobiography into an interminable confession that is for De Quincey the other side of philosophy: the mind's contemplative pursuits are repeatedly distracted by their own body of psychosomatic evidence, in De Quincey's case the painful symptoms of his opium dreams. His analysis of the philosophical *anthropos* explores this *"Incommunicable"*[35] language of philosophy's unconscious. Here the subject is left alone to contemplate a mind tied irrevocably to the body's will, an encounter with the unconscious as the suspension of the philosopher's rational ability to understand it.

Schopenhauer's suturing between will and representation similarly marks the faltering of (self-)knowledge and thus of a subject who presumes to know himself according to a self-enlightening philosophical method that orders the empirical functioning of the body according to its intellectual representation. Schopenahauer thus offers an anatomy of idealism itself, wherein its body speaks as if displaced from its cogito, as if addicted to its own will. This body is both the corporealized will that manifests the unconscious of philosophy and the philosophical corpus that is repetitively compelled to speak this unconscious, so that the body of the text is also the body of the philosophical *anthropos* who speaks the text's unconscious will. The telling body of Schopenhauer's text pushes philosophy to the limits of its own idealism by the infiltration of a psychoanalytic discourse through which philosophy meditates upon its (in)ability to tell. As ruminative as it is cognitive, and therefore as much narrative and theoretical as it is philosophical, *The World as Will* constitutes a prolonged and repetitive telling of philosophy's identity, a self-positing of philosophy that takes into account the autonomous or deterministic nature of the will's own self-making imperative.

Robert Smith argues that philosophy is essentially autobiographical, telling its own identity in order to eliminate the chance or contingency that threatens the rational borders of philosophy's "conceptual organization." Chance is "what cannot be accounted for in advance" in the work of reason and is the work of unreason within reason which, paradoxically, makes reason possible. To eliminate chance from its rational operation, philosophy establishes its self-identity, yet "bought at the cost of total rational purity," for philosophy cannot *willingly* eliminate contingency. To eliminate chance philosophy must wait for it to erupt, thereby proving philosophy's authenticity and integrity. A "certain philosophical unconscious"[36] is thus staged within the philosophical method, and the anthromorphization of philosophy, its autobiographical identity, is realized by suppressing the psychic darkness of its own *anthropos*, what Smith calls the "poetics of reason." In Schopenhauer's *World as Will* this poetics, I would argue, produces the *Bildung* or literature of philosophy's account of its own interiority, which emerges within the contemplative exterior of its idealism to produce a psychoanalysis of philosophy. The organicism of a coherent intellectual system, which reads in the preface to the 1818 first edition as a romantic sublation of Kant's defects, is unsettled by this system's parasitic relationship to the unreason of its own will, a continual compromising of representation's immunity to the will.

Thus volume 1 of *The World as Will* evokes a repetitive philosophical narrative that returns upon the discontinuity between will and representation. In the preface to the second edition Schopenhauer then argues that volumes 1 and 2 bear a "supplementary relation to one another" (WWR 1:xxii), for "it would not do to amalgamate the contents of the second volume with those of the first into one whole." Volume 1 calls forth the second volume as both the cure and symptom of its own chronic nature. The first 1818 edition, then, emerges behind the 1844 excursus of the second volume as a kind of trauma to which the second edition anxiously responds. So much *more* talking in the second edition evokes a mourning for the failure of an Enlightenment empiricism whose crowning achievement is Kant's transcendental idealism. But this mourning falters. The ascetic, wherein one supposedly overcomes the feint of Reason's abstraction in the Idea, is a fate to be endured, less a terminus than a holding pattern of existence. Ultimately, Schopenhauer's text suggests a profound melancholy, and the subject's encounter with his willing body produces the chronic nature of philosophy as if addicted to its own psychoanalysis. The text's repetition compulsion turns hermeneutics into what Stanley Corngold calls a "prolonged meditation on death."[37] Mourning, the marking of the terminable limits of philosophy's identity that is also the triumph of philosophy's idealism, becomes melancholy, philosophy's iterated and chronic response to the will's death drive. The text both masters and is mastered by its melancholy, evoking a psychoanalysis of idealism which, while resisting its own finitude, also does not presume to know these limits as absolutes. This melancholy of the telling body of the text's idealism is its recurrent attempt to articulate the limits of its enlightenment. Yet within this fate it tells another story of this melancholic loss as the constitutive moment of the subject's identity. Even this moment, however, is melancholically divided against itself. The ascetic dramatizes the imagination's profound limitations of the subject's ability to *imagine* his own aesthetic enlightenment, the ascetic having the text's last word, but only in a type of endgame of existence.

Philosophy's complete telling of its own cogito is one form of the absolute in German idealism. But it is haunted by philosophy's telling body, which seeks the impossible cure for its having to tell or represent its own inability to know itself. As this impossible staging of the subject, *The World as Will* is a pivotal episode in nineteenth-century philosophy's encounter with the limits of its idealism. It marks within philosophy the emergence of a psychoanalysis with which philosophy remains ambivalently yet irrevocably complicit. In "My Chances/*Mes Chances*" Jacques Derrida writes, "the advent of psychoanalysis is a complex event not only in terms of its historical probability but in terms of a discourse that remains open and that attempts at each instant to regulate itself—yet affirming its originality—according to the scientific and artistic treatment of randomness. . . ."[38] The "greatest speculative power" of psychoanalysis is its "greatest resistance *to* psychoanalysis," a deconstructive gesture within enlightenment Reason that "remain[s] forever heterogeneous to the principle of principle."[39] In this respect Schopenhauer's text marks the trauma of the invention of psychoanalysis. It conceives of the end of philosophy as its collapse into psychoanalysis, a collapse that repeats philosophy's impossible encounter with its own idealism, so that psychoanalysis collapses back into philosophy. Freud, for whom the disturbing effects of his own countertransference with the very subject from whom he hoped to maintain objective distance radically unsettles the enlightenment impulse of his metapsychology, will repeat Schopenhauer's struggle. In this way, Freud himself is destined to repeat an encounter with Schopenhauer's fateful insight that, as Clark argues, "humankind can never wholly possess itself or live entirely within itself,"[40] although it remains compelled to speak as though it does.

Notes

I am greatly indebted to Tilottama Rajan and Arkady Plotnitsky for their comments and guidance on earlier versions of this essay. I also wish to thank Angela Cozea, whose generous invitation to present an earlier version of this essay at the Center for the Study of Theory and Criticism at the University of Western Ontario convinced me I was on the right track. I gratefully acknowledge that financial support for this research was received from a grant partly funded by Wilfrid Laurier University operating funds and partly by a SSHRCC Institutional Grant awarded to Wilfrid Laurier University.

1. See, for instance, Patrick Gardner, *Schopenhauer* (Bristol, U.K.: Thoemmes Press, 1963); and R. K. Gupta, "Freud and Schopenhauer," in *Schopenhauer: His Philosophical Achievement*, ed. Michael Fox (Sussex, England: Harvester Press, 1980), 226–35.

2. Arthur Schopenhauer, *The World as Will and Representation*, 2 vols., trans. E. F. J. Payne (New York: Dover, 1969), 2:209. Unless otherwise noted, all references from Schopenhauer are to this text, hereafter cited as WWR.

3. Rajan, and David L. Clark, "Speculations: Idealism and Its Rem(a)inders," in *Intersections: Nineteenth-Century Philosophy and Contemporary Theory*, eds. Rajan and Clark (Albany: State University of New York Press, 1995), 1–38. Although not

addressing Schopenhauer directly, Rajan treats poststructuralist psychoanalytic theory and nineteenth-century philosophy on equal footing in "Language, Music, and the Body: Nietzsche and Deconstruction," in ibid., 147–72.

4. David Farrell Krell, "The Crisis of Reason in the Nineteenth Century: Schelling's Treatise on Human Freedom (1809)," in *The Collegium Phaenomenologicum: The First Ten Years*, eds. John C. Sallis, Giuseppina Moneta, and Jacques Taminiaux (Dordrecht, Netherlands: Kluwer Academic Publishers, 1988), 15. Thomas Pfau describes this "crisis" as the "collapse of an autonomous, philosophical subjectivity" defined by "the traditional, ethically motivated agent of rationality and reflexivity, and thus as the origin and telos of philosophical cognition." See Pfau, *Idealism and the Endgame of Theory: Three Essays by F. W. J. Schelling*, ed. and trans. Pfau (Albany: State University of New York Press, 1994), 5.

5. See Slavoj Žižek, "The Cartesian Subject versus the Cartesian Theater," in *Cogito and the Unconscious*, ed. Žižek (Durham: Duke University Press, 1998), 247–74. Žižek argues:

> Kant himself makes this point quite clearly when he emphasizes how the subject is inaccessible to himself, not only in its noumenal dimension—I cannot ever get to know what I am for a Thing—but even phenomenally: the representation of "I" is necessarily empty. . . . Kantian self-consciousness . . . emerges precisely because there is no direct "self-awareness" or "self-acquaintance" of the subject: the Kantian self-consciousness is an empty logical presupposition that fills in the gap of the impossibility of direct "self-awareness." (262–63)

6. Joseph Breuer and Sigmund Freud, *Studies in Hysteria*, trans. and eds. James Strachey and Alix Strachey (London: Pelican Books, 1974; reprint, 1991), 56–57, 66, 92; emphasis in original.

7. See Cathy Caruth, Introduction to *Trauma: Explorations in Memory*, ed. Caruth (Baltimore: Johns Hopkins University Press, 1995), 4.

8. Jacques Lacan, *Seminar One: Freud's Papers on Technique*, ed. Jacques-Alain Miller, trans. John Forrester (New York: Norton, 1991), 66.

9. Immanuel Kant writes: "Pure *a priori* concepts, if such exist, cannot indeed contain anything empirical, yet, none the less, they can serve solely as *a priori* conditions of a possible experience." See Kant, *Critique of Pure Reason*, trans. Norman Kemp Smith (London: Macmillan, 1993), 129.

10. Ibid., 514.

11. This is the loss Freud feared in his bid for scientific respectability. In his case of the Wolf-Man Freud contemplates the speculative rather than constitutive nature of the primal scene and so confronts the theoretical viability of psychoanalysis itself. The case reads slightly in advance of the death drive Freud's sense of a force that forever threatens the self-transparent ego, the paradigm of the idealist project. See Freud, "The Case of the Wolf-Man: From the History of an Infantile Neurosis," in *The Wolf-Man by the Wolf-Man*, ed. Muriel Gardner (New York: Noonday Press, 1991), 238.

12. Friedrich Nietzsche, *The Birth of Tragedy* and the *Case of Wagner*, trans. Walter Kaufmann (New York: Vintage Books, 1967), 41, 67, 95.

13. Schopenhauer published a third edition in 1859, a year before he died.

14. Kant, *Critique of Pure Reason*, 87, 27.

15. Schopenhauer argues this point in a long appendix to the first edition entitled "Criticism of the Kantian Philosophy."

16. For Schopenhauer Kant reverts to perception only "in order to convince [himself] that [his] abstract thinking has not strayed far from the safe ground of perception, . . . much in the same way as, when walking in the dark, we stretch out our hand every now and then to the wall that guides us" (1:449).

17. Schopenhauer, *On the Fourfold Principle of Sufficient Reason*, trans. E. F. J. Payne (LaSalle, Illinois: Open Court, 1974), 42, 115.

18. Schopenhauer states: "No will: no representation, no world" (ibid., 1:411). The will is a "*groundless*" (1:106) grounding force, resistant to its own grounding. For instance, throughout the text the German *Wille* "merely" exists without an article to contextualize its syntax in relationship to the world.

19. Terry Eagleton, "Schopenhauer and the Aesthetic," *Signature* 1 (1989): 19. Eagleton reads Schopenhauer's text as immanently Marxist, a type of cautionary tale against the specter of a bourgeois appropriation of the "subject" as the privileged category exploited by a capitalist ideology championing the simulacrum of "individuality" while all the while manufacturing its sameness.

20. Eagleton writes that an "idealist philosophy which once imagined that it could achieve salvation through the subject is now forced to contemplate the frightful prospect that no salvation is possible without the wholesale abnegation of the subject itself, the most privileged category of its entire system" (ibid., 17). For Schopenhauer it is as "absurd to desire the continuance of our individuality, which is replaced by other individuals, as to desire the permanence of the matter of our body, which is constantly replaced by fresh matter" (See Schopenhauer, *World as Will*, 1:277). He shatters identity's permanence in the way that Freud in *Beyond the Pleasure Principle*, marks the death drive as a "matter of expediency" always returning the subject to a primal inertia: "an unlimited duration of individual life would become a quite pointless luxury." "We have," Freud continues, "unwittingly steered our course into the harbour of Schopenhauer's philosophy. For him death is the 'true result and to that extent the purpose of life,' while the sexual instinct is the embodiment of the will to live." See Freud, *Beyond the Pleasure Principle*, 1920, *The Standard Edition of the Complete Psychological Works of Sigmund Freud*, trans. James Strachey, 23 vols. (London: Hogarth Press, 1953–1974), 55, 59–60.

21. As Eagleton argues, Schopenhauer writes as a "scathing Juvenilian satirist" (Eagleton, "Schopenhauer and the Aesthetic," 4) for whom "[c]omedy is the will's' mocking revenge on the representation, the malicious strike of the Schopenhauerian id against the Hegelian superego," except that "the source of hilarity is also, curiously, the root of our utter hopelessness" (5).

22. As Rajan and Clark argue, "Schopenhauer is himself divided on the nature and goal of aesthetic representation, at once affirming art as a metaphysically independent category, a triumph over life, *and* demystifying art as a subliminatory fiction projected upon the abyss" (Rajan and Clark, "Speculations," 31).

23. Eagleton, "Schopenhauer and the Aesthetic," 13.

24. See Julia Kristeva, *Powers of Horrors: An Essay on Abjection*, trans. Leon S. Roudiez (New York: Columbia University Press, 1982). Kristeva speaks of psychoanalysis as an "indefinite catharsis" (208) as if infected by its own idealism for which it can offer no cure: "One must keep open the wound where he or she who enters into the analytic adventure is located. . . . [It is] a heterogeneous, corporeal, and verbal ordeal of fundamental incompleteness" (27).

25. The turn comes, Krell suggests, in Kant's corpus itself, wherein works such as the *Anthropology* compromise this body's organic critical mass. That the *World as Will* takes no explicit note of the *Anthropology* suggests that Schopenhauer's own corpus internalizes a rift within the Kantian system as Schopenhauer's radicalization of Kant, in that Schopenhauer's anthropomorphization of the will offers a full-blown account of a physiological anthropology that Kant sets aside as threatening to his own philosophy. Yet Schopenhauer also resists this radicalization by attempting to bring this body's heterogeneous shape within the contemplative range of its pragmatic form.

26. In the 1818 preface to the *World as Will* Schopenhauer writes: "[w]ithout an acquaintance with this introduction and propaeduetic, it is quite impossible to understand the present work properly" (1:xiv). Schopenhauer considered his 1851 *Parerga and Palimpemona*, his last major publication, as only "additions to the systematic presentation of [his] philosophy" (1:xxviii) focused in his early response to Kant.

27. Kant does not define the categories because "they would merely divert attention from the main object of the enquiry, arousing doubts and objections which, without detriment to what is essential to our purposes, can very well be reserved for another occasion" (See Kant, *Critique of Pure Reason,* 115).

28. Jean-Jacques Rousseau, *The Confessions* (Ware, Hertfordshire: Wordsworth Editions, 1996), 3.

29. William Wordsworth, *The Letters of William and Dorothy Wordsworth*, ed. Ernest de Selincourt, 2d ed., vol 1. *The Early Years, 1787–1805*, rev. Chester L. Shaver (Oxford: Clarendon Press, 1967), 1:586–87.

30. William Wordsworth, *The Prelude: 1799, 1805, 1850*, eds. Jonathan Wordsworth, M. H. Abrams, and Stephen Gill (New York: Norton, 1979), book 5, line 1, 1805 version.

31. Samuel Taylor Coleridge, *Biographia Literaria; or Biographical Sketches of My Literary Life and Opinions*, eds. James Engell and W. Jackson Bate (Princeton: Princeton University Press, 1983), 1:17.

32. The source of being is what Krell might refer to as idealism's "contagion." See Krell, *Contagion: Sexuality, Disease, and Death in German Idealism and Romanticism* (Bloomington: Indiana University Press, 1998). I borrow from Krell's account of German idealism in order to evoke Reason's lack of immunity to the contagion of the "dire forces of nature" (28). While Krell does not discuss Schopenhauer, one can read this contagion in terms of Schopenhauer's "crisis of representation." Schopenhauer argues that the "whole world of objects" as representation has "transcendental ideality," not as "falsehood or illusion," but insofar as these objects are "intelligible to the healthy understanding." See Schopenhauer, *World as Will*, 1:15. To lose representation, then, is to compromise the integrity of understanding as a type of pathology of consciousness. So, that Schopenhauer compares genius to madness in that its intuition

of the Idea, as the epitome of aesthetic contemplation, is a kind of leave-taking of representation suggests that the release from the will in genius is the sign of an unhealthy understanding, a lack of organic integrity.

33. Thomas De Quincey, *Confessions of an English Opium-Eater and Other Writings*, ed. Grevel Lindop (Oxford: Oxford University Press, 1985), 99.

34. Ibid., 120.

35. Ibid., 182.

36. Robert Smith, *Derrida and Autobiography* (New York: Cambridge University Press, 1995), 18–19.

37. Stanley Corngold, "On Death and the Contingency of Criticism: Schopenhauer and de Man," in *Intersections*, 364.

38. Jacques Derrida, "My Chances/*Mes Chances*: A Rendezvous with Some Epicurean Stereophonies," trans. Irene Harvey and Avital Ronell, *Taking Chances: Derrida, Psychoanalysis and Literature*, eds. Joseph H. Smith and William Kerrigan (Baltimore: Johns Hopkins University Press, 1984), 28.

39. Derrida, *Resistances of Psychoanalysis*, trans. Peggy Kamuf, Pascale-Anne Brault, and Michael Naas (Stanford: Stanford University Press, 1998), 86, 118.

40. David L. Clark, " 'The Necessary Heritage of Darkness': Tropics of Negativity in Schelling, Derrida, and de Man," in *Intersections*, 110.

Sacrificial and Erotic Materialism in Kierkegaard and Adorno

John Smyth

The relation to the opposite sex has also been made into the meaning
and earnest of life—into true Christianity.

—Søren Kierkegaard, *Journals*

Creation is a mistake that repeats itself.

—Kevilina Burbank, "Divorce"

A false alarm on the night bell once answered—it cannot be made
good, not ever.

—Franz Kafka, "A Country Doctor"

I

Idealism and *materialism* are tricky terms. Adamant materialists tend to
idealize matter, while idealists can sometimes produce thoroughly material
rabbits (or ducks) from ideal hats. The relationship between Søren Kierkegaard
and Theodor Adorno—both relating to romantic culture via, as well as contra,
G. W. F. Hegel—gains a good deal of its complexity from this kind of problem.

181

The sheer variety of uses to which Kierkegaard has been prostituted might raise the question of whether his seductiveness is not in inverse proportion to rigor. Consideration of his influences generalizes the problem to intellectual genealogy at large. If we begin with "existentialism" for instance, of which he is often called the founder, we find that his religious focus is frequently disposed of in both "left" and "right" existentialists (e.g., Jean-Paul Sartre and Martin Heidegger) by being either hygienically detached from his ethical and aesthetic "spheres," and/or recuperated in a way that remains ambivalent at best.[1] Today we find him in the guises of both theologian and proto-post-modernist, and sometimes both at the same time; and there have been attempts to rehabilitate his religious language in the light of both Wittgensteinian and Derridean so-called god-talk (conceived respectively as a language-game and a structure of subjectivity).[2] Despite his apparent distance from political theory, meanwhile, we can now sometimes even find him politically rehabilitated, to the extent of discovering him in one of the latest commentaries as a kind of mediator between Habermas and Vaclav Havel.[3] Situating Kierkegaard in his own period is no less confusing, beginning with notorious oscillations by commentators between Hegelian and anti-Hegelian as well as between romantic and antiromantic classifications. As putative founder of existentialism, supposed antidote to idealism, he is seen in the company of the likes of Marx and Nietzsche as a kind of turning point between romantic idealism and modernity. However, without here buying any particular view of intellectual history, and in deference to the title of this collection, we may begin with the narrower thesis that in formulating the absolute as (religious) paradoxy (i.e., in failing to affirm the absolute in a philosophical sense) Kierkegaard undoes the conventional equation between idealism and absolutism, producing—not so much an anti-idealist existentialism (a misapprehension astutely criticized, as we shall see, by Adorno)—but precisely *an idealism without absolutes*, which is also a materialism whose "logic" is sacrificial, a negation of the ideal.

My appropriation of Kierkegaard for the title of this volume may appear suspect, not least because many commentators, both religious and philosophical (like Sartre and Derrida), have insisted on applying the term *absolute* to Kierkegaard's concept of subjectivity.[4] Moreover, insofar as idealism and materialism signify by definition the absolute primacy of one concept over the other, "idealism without absolutes" is of course contradictory. The problem is complicated rather than resolved in dialectical thinking, since while dialectics relativize apparently contradictory principles in order to produce dialectical motion, they must also maintain a sufficiently absolute opposition to avoid collapse. Thus Marx and Hegel tend respectively, according to conventional wisdom, toward materialist and idealist syntheses, and Kierkegaard himself confirms that "basically, an unshakable insistence upon the absolute and absolute distinctions is precisely what makes a good dialectician."[5] This pronouncement, which seems to render null and void the thesis of "idealism without absolutes," is made in the context of a reproach against Hegelians for getting into the facile dialectical habit of "canceling the principle of contradiction," heedless to Aristotle's caveat that this can only be done by the same principle, "since otherwise the opposite thesis, that it is not canceled is equally true" (PF109). The context is further complicated by the fact that Kierkegaard's (religious) insistence on absolute contradiction is not in the service of dialectical absolutism, whether material or ideal, but of the hypothesis of absolute paradox inaccessible to dialectics from which the possibility of faith begins. Hence our nonabsolutist thesis can be defended by observing, first, that the "good dialectician" is committed to reading Kierkegaard's insistence on the absolute dialectically, and, second, that his lesson here is prefaced by a pointedly nondialectical warning: "Even if I were a better dialectician than I am, I would still have my limits" (108). The absolute that lies beyond dialectics is best represented, as his pseudonyms themselves represent it in the theological context, as a mere thought-experiment or even jest—"the god" of the *Philosophical Fragments* (where the pagan expression signifies its nonbinding character). Outside of a theology that is never arrived at—from a philosophical perspective, as Adorno has argued and as Kierkegaard's own pseudonyms confirm, Kierkegaard's major work can be most meaningfully characterized as that of a nonbeliever—we may be confident as any logical positivist in deducing that the absolute and the relative founder equally on "absolute paradox." Short of paradox, thus, we may be guided in this matter by Kierkegaard's well-known objection to Hegel's concept of absolute spirit: the hackneyed battle cry of existentialism that no existing spirit is absolute (unless it be god). As John Milbank puts it, Kierkegaard "admitted only pseudo-transcendental claims."[6]

Kierkegaard is an idealist in that he maintains a dialectical predominance of soul over body preserved in the term *spirit*, but his materialist relativization of spirit, I argue, leads to an ironization of the dialectic in which neither genuine synthesis nor duality can occur. In the *Concept of Irony* an absolute dissension of spirit and flesh is said to be first posited by Christianity—with consequences, to be sure, which are weighty (including the doctrine of the arbitrariness of the sign)—but short of the absolute paradox this positing is only relatively absolute, a product of history. More importantly, while every dialectical analysis of spirit in Kierkegaard can be superficially adduced against my thesis here, this only follows from the dictum that good dialecticians insist on absolutes and that even good dialecticians have their limits. Kierkegaard's dialectical power—his "philosophy" as such—is explicitly directed beyond dialectic: "Subjectivity moves dialectically in its affects; in them, however, blocked truth, itself enciphered, makes itself known. Clearly, this does not occur in the progress of the dialectic; but where the dialectic stops."[7] This is not Kierkegaard, but Adorno in his *Kierkegaard: Construction of the Aesthetic*. Notoriously difficult to summarize—partly because it is itself so thoroughly dialectical—Adorno's book nevertheless makes several general arguments that can orient us. The first is that Kierkegaard remains in part idealist and romantic in a pejorative sense, and that his debate with Hegel cannot be concluded on the idealist terms of either author. For Adorno, Kierkegaard's rejection of the Hegelian concept of mediation is eminently open to objection, particularly since his own "spheres"—the aesthetic, the ethical, and the religious—lack coherent mediation. It is in his affirmation of the existential reality of the spheres that Kierkegaard falls prey to an "archaic conceptual realism" whose basis is thoroughly idealistic, in which the spheres "rule like demonic abstractions" (CA 92). There can be no synthesis of the spheres because passage between them can be accomplished only by the notorious Kierkegaardian "leap" (of will or freedom) which is opaque to analysis. Whereas Kierkegaard attacks Hegel for incorporating the "leap" into logic, Adorno finds this critique "insubstantial" (90): "Kierkegaard's doctrine of existence could be called realism without reality. It contests the identity of thought and being, but without searching for being in any other realm than that of thought" (86). Questioning Kierkegaard's equation between "spirit" and "self" (79–80), Adorno concludes that the Kierkegaardian self, despite its putative unassimilability to systematization, is merely "the system, dimension-lessly concentrated in the 'point' " (80) (a mathematical metaphor frequent in Kierkegaard from *The Concept of Irony* onward): a microcosmic version simultaneously of Kant's transcendental synthesis and Hegel's "infinitely productive 'totality' " (80)—absolute idealism with a vengeance! Above all, "the absurdity of Kierkegaard's doctrine of the self relating relationship" (81), his definition of the self, requires to be rescued by the very kind of mediation that Kierkegaard so disdainfully satirizes.

Yet if Kierkegaard's "existentialist" doctrines, putatively opposed to idealism, are most thoroughly condemned as idealist myth, Adorno is also deeply sympathetic to Kierkegaard and sees in him a materialist grain that reaches far deeper than much twentieth-century existentialism. This explains not only what Adorno calls Kierkegaard's sympathies with materialist authors (CA 130) and his sensitivity to irony and comedy, and the kind of theorization they demand, but also at crucial moments his recognition of the deep interrelation of the aesthetic and religious—bypassing "the logic of the spheres" (105). Arguing that "natural life transcends itself in profoundest contradiction to the stated intention of Kierkegaard's spiritualism," Adorno cites his claim that "Woman because of her immediacy is essentially aesthetic, but just because she is essentially this, the transition to the religious is also direct. Feminine romanticism is in the very next instant the religious" (104–5).

For Adorno, atheist or not, there can be no question of bracketing the religious sphere, a strategy especially attractive to anyone who wishes to recuperate the psychology of the ethical and aesthetic without the embarrassment of their religious supplement. On the contrary, "the traditional, theological interpretation of Kierkegaard is more correct than the psychologically informed interpretation when it poses paradoxy as the highest theme and not the immanence of a 'spiritual life' whose systematic unity omits—along with the ultimate paradoxy—the cells of concretion" (CA 105). As observed by Robert Hullot-Kentor, the "Construction of the Aesthetic" is thus ambivalent, leaving it open whether this construction is Kierkegaard's or Adorno's; and Adorno's solution to Kierkegaard's idealism is "to fulfill it: to achieve the self-expression of the material" (xiv) by reclaiming the aesthetic sphere from its formal negation in the ethical and religious.

Adorno's second major argument concerns the sacrificial nature of Kierkegaard's portrayal of religion. This entails not just Kierkegaard's insistence on sacrifice as central to religion (most famously in *Fear and Trembling*), but also Adorno's insistence that while the theological interpretation of Kierkegaard is superior to the psychological one in recognizing the primary importance of his paradoxy, he must nonetheless be rescued from this paradoxy conceived "as the theological answer" (CA 105). "The task is rather: to reveal the structure of the paradoxy itself as dialectical and systematic and at the same time to construct its proper content," which becomes evident above all "in mythical sacrifice as it is represented in the reversal and ruin of Kierkegaard's idealism" (105). Adorno, like Kenneth Burke in *A Rhetoric of Motives*, thus accuses Kierkegaard of falling prey in the religious context to a sacrificial mythology whose mythical nature he recognizes clearly enough in context of art, eroticism, and the aesthetic sphere in general. Moreover, Adorno generalizes the sacrificial pattern from the religious (and autobiographical) domain to the philosophical: Kierkegaard stands accused—most obviously in such mantras as "truth is subjectivity," but more subtly elsewhere—of the sacrifice of reason and truth as such (106ff.).

This critique superficially resembles the familiar charge against Kierkegaard of mere irrationalism. But the fact that it situates his sacrificial mythology in terms of the reversal of his idealism, rather than identifying it as the mere deluded apotheosis of that idealism, signals one of the foremost distinctions of Adorno's approach, which remains faithful to Kierkegaard's situation of sacrifice at the juncture of the ideal and the material. Like Adorno's, my analysis will use Kierkegaard's texts against his tendency to overstep the bounds of his "idealism without absolutes," that is, his tendency to affirm the absolute paradox not as a matter of faith (as he claims), but philosophically (as he denies), by smuggling it into such opaque categories as "the self" and "the leap." But it will also use Kierkegaard against Adorno's critique as a way of clarifying not only their relation, but also the relation between the early Adorno of *Kierkegaard* (1933) and certain highly sacrificial formulations by the late Adorno of *Aesthetic Theory* (1970). I shall concentrate on *The Concept of Dread* (1844) because its theme is sacrificial psychology as such, focusing on sexuality conceived as the synthesis of body and psyche, material, and ideal.

Kierkegaard makes a distinction between the main body of the text, devoted to the science of psychology conceived (after Hegel) as "the doctrine of the subjective spirit," and its religious or dogmatic frame that presupposes the reality of sin and "the doctrine of the Absolute Spirit."[8] The former science is concerned with the study of possibility—here, more particularly, with the possibility of sin or freedom—whereas, contrary to modern stereotype, "With dogmatics begins the science which, in contrast to that science of ethics which can strictly be called ideal, starts with reality" (CD 18). Certainly this reversal of conventional views of the idealism of religious dogma in contrast to the realism of secular science is not without difficulties of a major order. Adorno, for instance, memorably condemns the introduction to *The Concept of Dread* (where these distinctions are proposed) as being wholeheartedly given over to "scurrilous methodological deliberations" (91) whose goal is to preserve the religious sphere from contamination, and as further evidence that Kierkegaard's overall doctrine of the spheres is fundamentally flawed. Without denying this latter point (since with Adorno I am arguing that Kierkegaard's religious can be secularized and divorced from the sacrificial theology of absolute paradox), we may nevertheless defend Kierkegaard by distinguishing between the religious dogma of absolute spirit or absolute freedom, the dogma that "begins with the real in order to raise it up into ideality" (18), and dogmatics that begins with the secular dogma of the actuality of relative freedom (a dogma presupposed, of course, by the ordinary concept of justice). Admittedly, Kierkegaard has reason to blur this distinction, just as his dialectical point that a relatively freely acting cause "definitively points to an absolutely freely acting cause" can be accused of religious tendentiousness. Indeed, his *secular* point that "freedom is never possible; as soon as it is, it is actual, in the same sense in which it has been said by an earlier philosophy [Leibniz's] that when God's existence is possible it is necessary" can be accused of a similar religious tendentiousness. But Kierkegaard makes no claim to demonstrate God's possibility, and "Freedom is never possible" merely means that if it is possible for me to act freely at this moment (a dogmatic claim), it is necessary that I am actually free.

For all of its superficial plausibility, Adorno's dismissal of the introduction of *The Concept of Dread* may thus be questioned as misreading the significance of its central point—a point about which Kierkegaard is confident enough to write: "The introduction may be correct while the deliberation

itself dealing with the concept of dread may be entirely incorrect. That remains to be seen" (CD 21).

II

Kierkegaard defines dread as an "intermediate determinant" between possibility and actuality (CD 44–45). But psychology *qua* science is idealistic: it
cannot deal with actuality or freedom as such, conceived as a synthesis of the
ideal and the material, but only with possibility—in this case, thus, the possibility of possibility and the possibility of actuality. This redoubling of the
argument, its attempt to calculate every concept to the second power, makes
The Concept of Dread a notoriously difficult text, one in which rigor is hard
to distinguish from sophistry. Just as the *Philosophical Fragments* conceives
history and freedom as a coming into existence within a coming into existence, a possibility within a possibility, so "dread is freedom's reality as a
possibility for possibility" (39). Hence Kierkegaard's psychology and its subject
matter stand in a specular relation. Psychology cannot explain either freedom
or sin (supposing these to exist); it can only posit their possibility. But this
is exactly how dread is defined: as first positing the possibility of freedom,
and then positing the further possibility of guilt as its consequence (41).
Dread, like psychology, is a *speculative* activity in which mind reflects on
itself. Dread defines a crucial aspect of the structure of *actual* speculation.

Because *The Concept of Dread* constantly speaks in religious language
and starts from the biblical account of the fall, it is tempting to dismiss its
claim to be "scientific" and psychological as opposed to dogmatic. But its
analysis of the structure of religious language and experience, as we shall see,
is devoted very largely to a deconstruction of the very kind of sacrificial
mythology that Adorno chides in his *Kierkegaard*, but that he also identifies
as the most important and deceptive "content" of Kierkegaard's paradox;[9]
and, since the text constantly denies that it is providing any kind of ethical
claim, it seems legitimate to regard it from a secular perspective as providing
an analysis of various manifestations of what nowadays would be called
"guilt-complex," as well as a cluster of related psychological and psychosomatic phenomena—including shame, sexual modesty, masochism, and superstition. It is notable that where Kierkegaard alludes directly to the New
Testament in his analysis of the "demoniac," he has nothing whatever to say
about possession by the devil or any purely spiritual doctrine or superstition,
but begins by alluding to such thoroughly psychosomatic disorders as "an
exaggerated sensibility, an exaggerated irritability, nervous affections, hysteria, hypochondria, etc." (CD 122). Though the text makes no claim to explain
these disorders as such or in detail, it does claim that they must be understood
in relation to the kind of sacrificial aberrations that are its primary focus. In

principle, then, I propose that it can be read in a similar spirit (though with a significantly different letter) to that in which Slavoj Žižek proposes we read Jacques Lacan: as an invitation to "sacrifice sacrifice."[10]

The Concept of Dread begins with the biblical fall and its consequence in sexual shame or modesty. But while it is emphatic about the significance of sexuality as an expression of spirit conceived as "a synthesis of the soulish and the bodily" (CD 39), it is careful to counter the "ethical misunderstanding of it as the sinful" (63)—"by sin sensuousness became sinfulness" (57)—ascribing this on the one hand to the idealist prejudice of rationalism (53), and on the other to the Christian positing of sexuality as "the extreme point of the synthesis" between body and soul (72). Nevertheless, "without sin there is no sexuality, and without sexuality no history" (44), and "the concept of bashfulness (shame)" derives its structure from its initial content as an ignorance that is oriented toward this knowledge (61). "In bashfulness there is dread" because spirit "is not merely qualified by relation to body but by relation to body with the generic difference" without this necessarily entailing any sexual impulse as such; hence "the dread in bashfulness is so prodigiously ambiguous" (61), a dread present equally in ignorance of the erotic and "in all erotic enjoyment" (64). In apparently dialectical terms (though we shall be forced to supplement these later on), we are informed "with Greek candor" that dread belongs to the erotic experience because the latter is constituted by spirit (as synthesis) while simultaneously excluding spirit from its "culmination" as though spirit were "a third party" compelled to hide itself (64). As synthesis, spirit expresses itself in the erotic experience as beauty; but as soon as it is posited as spirit per se "the erotic is at an end. Hence the highest pagan expression is that the erotic is the comical"; and "the spirit's expression for the erotic is that it is at once beauty and the comical" (62).

Certainly Kierkegaard may be accused again here of prevaricating between the dogmatic-religious and the merely historical senses of "spirit." It is well-known, for instance, that pagan or Socratic irony is supposed to give way to Christian humor acccording to the *Concluding Unscientific Postscript*; indeed this corresponds to the movement just cited from the pagan conception of the comedy of sex—illustrated by Socrates' claim that one should love ugly women, and his "ironic neutralization" of the erotic (CD 63)—to the Christian one that softens the comic and ironic by supplementing it with the beautiful, and that ultimately "suspends" the erotic, just as it famously "suspends" the ethical in *Fear and Trembling*, "because it is the tendency of Christianity to lead the spirit further" (63). But precisely this kind of argument lies open to Adorno's objections, both to the basic fuzziness of Kierkegaard's distinction between irony and humor (CA 96) and to the sacrificial structure of the spheres: "Abraham, as the subject of a 'dialectical lyric' [*Fear and Trembling*], is an allegorical name for the objective *(one might almost say physical*) dynamic of the spheres" (97, emphasis added). Odd as it sounds, Adorno's physicalist language is appropriate in this context. For just as *both* the religious suspension of ethics (conceived as rational ideality) and their religious return (as obedience to God) are portrayed in terms of Abraham's acceptance of physical sacrifice (of his son and the substitute ram respectively),[11] so Kierkegaard's sacrificial suspension of sexuality is in the service of its paradoxical—and physical—preservation in Christian marriage. Though supposedly won over "into conformity with the destiny of spirit" and transfigured by "love in a man in whom the spirit has triumphed in such a way that the sexual is forgotten and only remembered in forgetfulness," such that "sensuousness is transfigured into spirit and dread driven out" (CD 72), the paradoxy here is in reality at its most vicious. For all of its sacrificial insight—and arguably even as a consequence of it—*The Concept of Dread* not only posits a highly sacrificial view of the "spiritual destiny" of woman, but maintains the most vulgar sexual stereotypes attributed alternately to scripture and to romanticism: woman is more sensuous than man ("shown at once by her bodily organism"); "silence is not only woman's highest wisdom, but also her highest beauty"; "ethically regarded, woman culminates in procreation"; and so on (58–60). In this connection, Adorno's citation earlier concerning woman's immediate passage from aesthetic to religious spheres is arguably an index of her sacrificial status (rather than, as Adorno claims, a moment in which the sacrificial logic of the spheres is bypassed), and the "tedious vacuity" that Kierkegaard dialectically attributes to demoniac dread could hardly find more perfect expression than in these (fortunately brief) passages, which also betray—in their tendentious comparison of Greek and Christian conceptions of gender—all the aberrance Paul de Man attributes to Kierkegaard's historicism.[12]

The view of history and "spiritual destiny" proposed by his analysis of dread proper, however, is a different matter, providing a relentless critique of various modes of sacrificial ideology within as well as outside of Christian psychology. The pagan world, first, is analyzed in terms of its self-fulfilling confusion of history and fate, which "may mean two things exactly opposite, since it is a unity of necessity and chance," a unity "ingeniously expressed by representing fate as blind, for that which walks forward blindly walks just as much by necessity as by chance" (CD 87). "One can say therefore of fate as Paul says of an idol, that 'it is nothing in the world'—but the idol nevertheless is the object of the pagan's religiousness." Fate, like the oracle, is studiously ambiguous, though the oracular tragedy lies not in its ambiguity as such, "but in the fact that the pagan could not forbear to take counsel of it" (87). Whereas the concept of guilt does not "in the deepest sense emerge in paganism," since, if it had, it "would have foundered upon the contradiction that one might become guilty by fate" (87)—which would amount to a "mistaken concept of original sin" (88)—sin, nevertheless, is akin to fate in coming into being "neither as a necessity nor by chance, and therefore to the concept of sin corresponds providence" (88). Note that in this analysis the conceptual difference between fate and providence is strictly limited to the positing of guilt as the possibility of freedom (as neither necessity nor chance), and that any theological reification of providence in this context is therefore as unwarranted as that of fate itself.

Within the Christian world, "genius" represents the simultaneous perspicuity and aberrance of fate. Fate is nothing; it is the genius himself who discovers it, and the deeper his genius is, the more deeply he discovers it, for that figure is merely the anticipation of providence (CD 89).

Though Kierkegaard seems to leave room for a higher or theological form of providence by artificially confining his definition of genius to "immediate spirit, which genius always is (only that it is immediate spirit *sensu eminentiori*)" (CD 88), in reality this merely means that "genius is outside the general" (90), that is, that its positing of generality is always mediated by particular concretion, or that spirit is never posited beyond its definition as synthesis of the ideal and the material. However conceptually deep—and in proportion to the extent that concretion has previously served his genius—the genius is prone to be slave to the concrete: the military genius will fight only on the fourteenth of June "because that was the date of the Battle of Marengo" (89). Note, nevertheless, that this *immediate* mimetic subservience—exaggerated, in part, because Kierkegaard wants to deflate genius in the service of the spiritual—finds a definite *reflective* analogy in his own analysis of what it means to say that "original sin is growing" (47). It is growing because—while all sin requires a qualitative act of choice—quantitatively and "psychologically speaking," the "more" of sin that has come into existence since Adam has "a terrible significance," such that "the future seems to be anticipated by the past" (82). The reflective mimesis posited here, which is *inductive*, takes on the same form as the immediate mimesis of genius, which is in essence a repetition compulsion. Wholly abstractly formulated (as in the case of sensuality), "the instant sin is posited, the temporal is sin" (82); or in a psychological nutshell, "*dread of sin produces sin*" (65).

The inductive psychology of sin, a reflective or Christianized transformation of fate into a demonic sense of providence, conforms to the structure of what Rene Girard, in his mimetic theory of sacrifice, calls "masochist induction" or self-fulfilling prophecy. The mimetic structure here—no longer hidden by superstitious ciphers—is clarified in Kierkegaard's unpacking of the apparent psychological paradox concerning dread of sin: "Here the formula is: *The individual in dread, not of becoming guilty, but of being regarded as guilty, becomes guilty*"—"the utmost 'more' in this direction [being] that [an] individual from his earliest awakening is so placed and influenced that for him sensuousness has become identical with sin" (CD 67). Adorno, as we have seen, complains that Kierkegaard's critique of Hegel's logicization of the concepts of mediation and transition is merely in the service of an opaque and idealistic notion of "the leap"; but here the *actual* pattern of mediation (however much Kierkegaard appeals to the leap "beyond psychology") is clear: either one imitates others (the masochist sensualist) or one imitates oneself (the genius, whose "autonomy" is just as rich in masochist self-fulfillment). Genius "is great by reason of its belief in fate, whether it conquers or falls, for it conquers by itself and falls by itself, or rather both come about by fate," and "he is never greater than when he falls by his own act," when he "discovers the doubtful reading in the text and then collapses" (90). "A false alarm on the night bell once answered—it cannot be made good, not ever."[13]

The principle of mimetic mediation, we find, is everywhere in Kierkegaard's text the *actual* substitute for logical or dialectical mediation, and it everywhere appears where (as Adorno puts it) the dialectic stops. Dialectically corresponding to genius in the Christian age (genius is technically also "spiritless" because defined as immediacy), the "spiritless man" is superficially indistinguishable from the spirited one, "possess[ing] truth—not as truth, be it noted, but *as rumor and old wives' tales*" (CD 85, my emphasis) in a way "which corresponds exactly to pagan fetishism," except that "above all a charlatan is its real fetish" (86), that is, a fetish raised to the second power, a worship of the mimetic principle itself. Meanwhile, if "dread dialectically determined in view of fate" (86ff.) is thoroughly mimetic, "dread dialectically defined in view of guilt" (92ff.) is thoroughly sacrificial: "To the oracle of paganism corresponds the sacrifice of Judaism" (93). Indeed it is precisely the mimetic repetition of sacrifice that ultimately leads to "scepticism with respect to the act of sacrifice itself" (93), since the need to repeat the sacrifice betrays its inefficacy. The Judaic (and pagan) sacrificial principle is ultimately discredited as based on a primitive confusion between being thought guilty and guilt, between mimetic semblance and reality, and between self and other, whereas the "higher" (Christian) form of guilt should not be a fear of "being thought guilty . . . but fear of being guilty" (97). Nevertheless, we have just seen that the masochistic or self-sacrificial confusion of the two remains endemic to the Christian world, and the masochistic structure of sin remains fully operative in its properly Christian definition insofar guilt is said to be posited by moral freedom precisely as a lack of freedom: "the opposite of freedom is guilt [not necessity]" (97). Hence the "higher" dread of doing evil has its own pathologies, no less inductive in character than the "lower": notably, when "dread throws itself dispairingly into the arms of remorse" that in turn "discovers the consequence before it comes" and masochistically "interprets the consequence of sin as penal suffering." "In other words, remorse has become insane" (103). These, we are told, are some of *"the psychological states approximating sin"* (emphasis added) which do not pretend "to explain sin ethically" (105).

Whereas dread of evil "viewed from a higher standpoint, is in the good," and "the bondage of sin is an unfree relation to the evil," "the demoniacal [conceived as "dread of the good"] is an unfree relation to the good" (CD 106). Here Kierkegaard takes his departure from the demons of the gospels, which are either "legion" or mute, arguing that mimetic multiplicity and "shut-upness" (110) may equally signify demoniacal dread. But he is again careful to distinguish the demoniac conceived as a psychological state or mental pathology from sin, especially insisting that "we must give up every fantastic notion of a pact with the devil, etc." (109), which led formerly to a contradictory tendency to punish the sufferer. Accordingly, his exposition begins by juxtaposing the sacrificial severity employed in Christian tradition against the demoniac with the "therapeutic" purgations (powders, pills—"and then clysters!"[108]) employed by modern physicians. The former is explained (without being excused) as the result of a spiritual overidentification with the sufferer ("convinced that after all in the last resort the demoniac himself . . . must wish that every cruelty and severity might be employed against him"[108]), the latter by an over-physical and somatic, even genetic approach that underidentifies and hence also underestimates how "even divers of those men who want to deal with this phenomenon come themselves under the same category" (109). The prodigious ambiguity of the demoniac derives from the fact "that in a way it belongs to all spheres, the somatic, the psychic, the pneumatic," covering "a far greater field than is commonly supposed," and demonstrating how "a disorganization in one [sphere] shows itself in the others" (109).

Without claiming to comprehend the myriad psychosomatic modes of what we might nowadays call "mania," Kierkegaard's analysis concentrates on two modes of discontinuity, defined in terms of "shut-upness" or reserve, and "the sudden." Muteness or reserve expresses itself as an increasingly compulsive tendency to talk to oneself and ultimately to "involuntary revelation" (CD 114–15), a compulsion that can be triggered by the most trivial contact. Indeed the category of "revelation" (with all of its religious resonance) is here said to be "the same" (113) whether it entails the most sublime or the most ridiculous, since both derive from the sheer positing power of expression or communication as such: "Here applies the old saying, that if one dare utter the word, the enchantment of the magic spell is broken, and hence it is that the somnambulist wakes when his name is called" (113). Meanwhile, inasmuch as "communication is in turn the expression for continuity, and the negation of continuity is the sudden" (115), the latter is the temporal mode of that negation of continuity defined by reserve, a negation that precisely inasmuch as it recognizes that no law is an expression of unfreedom (116). In this connection, nota bene, mimesis is once more the principal category. Not only do we hear that "Mimic art is able to express the sudden, though this does not imply that this art as such is the sudden," and that "the suddenness of the leap . . . lies within the compass of mimic art" (a demoniac parody of the qualitative leap itself), but that "*Mephistopheles is essentially mimic*" (117, emphasis added).

Kierkegaard's mimetic definition of the devil explains much that would otherwise remain opaque in the text as a whole. His opening analysis of Genesis "associate[s] no definite thought with the serpent" (CD 43); indeed the lure to symbolic interpretation of the serpent is wittily regarded as itself a temptation of the serpent, a temptation specifically "to be *spirituel*" ("I am no lover of *esprit*" [43]). Roger Poole's analysis of this problem may be of help here. Chiding previous commentary for failing sufficiently to recognize the problem, his own solution is disarmingly simple: observing the frequency of *s* sounds in the Danish original at this and at other relevant points in the text, Poole suggests in deconstructivist and postmodernist fashion that we should identify the devil with this literal or textual hissing itself[14]—an interpretation of evil *à la lettre* with a vengeance! But this is instructive and misleading in almost equal measure. The insistence on the material letter does go some way toward explaining Kierkegaard's own pointed repudiation of "esprit" and the "spirituel" at this juncture—though Poole does not draw attention to this detail as such. What is misleading, however, is that his interpretation is presented as though it stood independent of Kierkegaard's own argument in general and, rather astonishingly, without any reference to the subsequent mimetic definition of evil in particular. By contrast, I claim that the refusal to be tempted by symbolic interpretation of the serpent follows directly from the mimetic definition of the devil, who might therefore in principle be represented in any form whatsoever, and must strictly speaking be represented by none. Precisely the temptation to externalize temptation as though "it come[s] from without" (CD 43) is at issue; or, more precisely (inasmuch as mimetic temptation *does* in one sense come from without), to essentialize and reify a mere form, to *spiritualize the material*. Poole is thus right in his insistence on material form, but misguided to divorce this materialism from the mimetic principle that indeed explains in precisely what sense, according to Kierkegaard, the "materialist" explanation of "spiritual" phenomena is precisely the right one. This illuminates not only such metaphoric details as where fate is called the "secret friend" of genius—as though fate were not merely something, but *someone* to be imitated—but also the entire conceptual genealogy of original sin. Rejecting the notion that Adam is tempted from without—either by the serpent or by God's prohibition ("even though it is certain both from pagan and from Christian experience that man's

desire is for the forbidden"[37])—Kierkegaard constructs his analysis on a
mimetic logic that mediates relations between external and internal along the
"materialist" lines just suggested. Thus his interpretation of Eve's mediation,
while maintaining that dread is more natural to woman than to man, denies
that this is an imperfection: "If there is to be any question of imperfection,
it consists in something else, namely, in the fact that in dread she seeks
support beyond herself in another, in man" (42). Similarly, Adam's first sin
derives from his reversal of this "natural" pattern of mimetic dependence; but
the argument from woman's natural weakness is only provisional since "Adam
and Eve are merely a numerical repetition" (42), entirely equal from the
perspective of spirit, and it is the pattern of repetition itself that is ultimately
decisive. Thus when the predisposition to sinfulness is located in the fact of
generation, the hackneyed issue of sexual desire (and the desire for the pro-
hibited, for transgression) takes backseat to quantitative or material reproduction as such: "*It is the fact of being derived which predisposes the individual*
[to sin], without for all that making him guilty" (43).

More strikingly still—especially since Kierkegaard here emancipates
himself altogether from the biblical myth (which is described as externalizing
what is internal)—when it comes to explaining in precisely what sense Adam
himself is neither tempted nor punished from without, we are told:

> This naturally has tormented many thinkers. The difficulty, however,
> is one we need only smile at. Innocence is indeed well able to talk,
> inasmuch as in language it possesses the expression for everything
> in the spiritual order. In view of this one need only assume that
> Adam talked with himself. The imperfection in the [biblical] ac-
> count, that another speaks to Adam about what he does not under-
> stand, is thus eliminated. Adam was able to talk. From this it does
> not follow that in a deeper sense he was able to understand the word
> uttered. This applies above all to the distinction between good and
> evil, which is made in language, to be sure, but is only intelligible
> to freedom. (CD 41)

We face in this passage a linguistic materialism that not only explicitly
divorces language from understanding, and is presented as the limit of psychological analysis (CD 41), but also explains why "the existence in this sense of
a thousand Adams signifies no more than one" (42). Kierkegaard's supposed
existentialist individualism is accordingly not (or at least not here) in any genuine contradiction with a collectivist or evolutionary conception of the origin of
language; on the contrary, Adam's language is explicitly compared both to "a
kind as imperfect as that of children when they are learning to recognize an
animal on the ABC card" (42) and to the mimeticism of the animal that "is able

to understand the mimic expression and movement in the speaker's voice, without understanding the word" (40–41). Hence too, like Kafka in "Investigations of a Dog,"[15] Kierkegaard rejects pseudoscientific talk of egoism as "dissolv[ing] into tautology, or else one resorts to *esprit*" in continuity with the kind of natural philosophy that "has found this egoism in the whole creation" (CD 70): "when one would explain sin by selfishness, one becomes involved in confusions, since on the contrary it is true that by sin and in sin selfishness comes into being" (71). Such selfishness is merely the dialectical equivalent of demoniac sociability, of collectivity, so that bondage to sin is compared precisely to "a game men play where two are concealed under a cloak, *appearing to be one person*, and while one speaks the other gesticulates without any pertinence to what is being said" (106, emphasis added).

With this image, we may allude to de Man's essay, "The Concept of Irony," where he at once praises Kierkegaard's book of that title as "the best book on irony that's available," and criticizes his aberrant historicism. One of de Man's main focuses is Friedrich Schlegel's philosophical allegory of "making the beast with two backs" (as the phrase goes), in a section of *Lucinde* called "A Reflection" that "got Hegel and Kierkegaard and philosophers in general, and other people too, very upset" (CI 169). De Man's point is not simply that Schlegel allegorizes philosophy as coition (since sexuality is fully "worthy of philosophical discourse"), but that he combines two "radically incompatible" codes, the material and the psychic, in a way that "represents a threat to all assumptions one has about what a text should be" (169). Here, however, far from sheltering history from the sacrificial randomness or "impertinence" of the relation of body and mind, gesture and voice, material and ideal, as de Man alleges, Kierkegaard squarely makes that relation into the origin of historicity.

III

Finally, to emphasize that Kierkegaard's mimetic-sacrificial analysis cannot be reduced to the language of nineteenth-century religiosity, I conclude by returning to Adorno. Adorno is of special interest here, not only for his early work on Kierkegaard, but also for his late work that essentially transfers the mimetic-sacrificial logic of Kierkegaard's psychology of sin to a thoroughly mimetic-sacrificial theory of aesthetics and to the work of art. Moreover, Adorno's insistence on the materiality of the work of art amounts not to a negation of the ideality and "spirituality" of art but on the contrary to a dialectical insistence on that ideality, to an "idealism without absolutes."

Whereas the early Adorno of *Kierkegaard* pits the materialist Kierkegaard against the idealist one, accuses the latter of being unable to free himself from a sacrificial logic, and remains generally silent about the relation of mimesis and sacrifice,[16] the late Adorno of *Aesthetic Theory* emphasizes this latter relation to the maximum extent, going so far as to define the "radical historicity" of aesthetic theory and even the quasinecessity of the artwork (359) in terms of sacrificial mimesis. Just as Kierkegaard may be called an "idealist" in that he constructs the role of the material from the dialectical perspective of spirit, yet remains an idealist without absolutes—and to this extent a materialist—in that the material mimetic element falls outside any absolute synthesis, so the late Adorno situates mimesis in the historical juncture (rather than the synthesis)[17] of matter and spirit, defending a conception of the objective "spirituality" of art from which the significance of its materiality must be constructed:

> If idealism was able to requisition art for its purposes by fiat, this was because through its own constitution art corresponds to the fundamental conception of idealism. . . . Art cannot be conceived without this immanently idealistic element, that is, without the objective mediation of all art through spirit; this sets a limit to dull-minded doctrines of aesthetic realism just as those elements encompassed in the name of realism are a constant reminder that art is no twin of idealism. (91)

As in Kierkegaard, this nonidealistic "spirituality" or nonabsolute "idealism" is *sacrificially constructed via a generalization of the principle of mimesis*:

> the spiritual element of art is not what idealist aesthetics calls spirit; rather, *it is the mimetic impulse fixated as totality*. The sacrifice made by art for this emancipation, whose postulate has been consciously formed ever since Kant's dubious theorem that "nothing sensuous is sublime," is presumably already evident in modernity [with the elimination of representation in painting and sculpture.] . . . (CD 90, emphasis added)

Adorno's sacrificial definition of art is summed up at its most abstract in his formula that "All that art is capable of is to grieve for the sacrifice it makes and which it itself, in its powerlessness, is."[18] But at the same time this abstraction cannot be comprehended without reference to a mimetic-sacrificial principle that has its origins both in real imitation between subjects—the "crowd" dynamics of fashion and collectivity in general—and in archaic violence:

> At the same time artistic expression enforces on itself history's judgement that mimesis is an archaic comportment . . . (CA 111). . . . [Unless it rises above regression] art deteriorates into a violent act

of spirit (93). The putative play drive has ever been fused with the primacy of blind collectivity. . . . In blunt opposition to Schillerian ideology, art allies itself with unfreedom in the specific character of play (317).

Just as Kierkegaard defines sin and guilt in terms of mimetic-sacrificial unfreedom, so Adorno associates mimetic play with the compulsions of "blind collectivity" and the archaic violence to which such mimetic collectivity can always regress. Mimesis, in modern terminology, is nothing but "fashion," whose bland comforts art characteristically claims to sacrifice, but that in this very act of pseudodifferentiation proclaims its necessary role:

> Fashion is art's permanent confession that it is not what it claims to be. . . . The disdain of fashion, however, is produced by its erotic element, in which fashion reminds art of what it never fully succeeded in sublimating. Through fashion, art sleeps with what it must renounce and from this draws the strength that otherwise must atrophy under the renunciation on which art is predicated. (CA 316–17)

In this erotic metaphor we are far from the early Adorno who chides Kierkegaard for consistently conceiving *passio* on the model of a sacrificial eroticism (CA 120); indeed, the late Adorno now generalizes the sacrificial element of eroticism by bluntly identifying it with the mimetic principle. The very rationality of the artwork, its self-definition as mimetic semblance— which as the work's "*materialis* [bears] the trace of the damage artworks want to revoke" (AT 107)—is accordingly linked by Adorno to social violence: "Reason, which in artworks effects unity even where it intends disintegration, achieves a certain guiltlessness by renouncing intervention in reality, real domination; yet even in the greatest works of aesthetic unity the echo of social violence is to be heard; indeed, through the renunciation of domination spirit also incurs guilt" (CA 134). It is now clear, I hope, just how systematically—though inexplicitly and perhaps partly unconsciously—Adorno transposes Kierkegaard's mimetic-sacrificial psychology of guilt to the theory of art, richly fulfilling his own early claim that Kierkegaard's aesthetics need to be rehabilitated in the light of his sacrificial paradoxy. Here indeed both domination and renunciation are sacrificially conceived, just as in *The Concept of Dread*, dread of evil itself leads sacrificially to guilt. Moreover, just as the "necessity" or "fate" discovered by artistic genius in *The Concept of Dread* is essentially mimetic and inductive—attesting to the crucial element of contingency in this necessity—so Adorno writes: "art does justice to the contingent by probing in the darkness of the trajectory of its own necessity. . . .Its immanent process has the quality of following a divining rod. To follow where the hand is drawn: This is mimesis as the fulfillment of objectivity. . . ." (CD 115). Similarly, Kierkegaard recommends that—instead of restricting himself to entirely detached and thus supposedly "objective" observation—the genuinely objective psychologist should actually produce the poetic semblance in himself of "every psychic state, which he discovers in another" (50), so that other, his subject, then further reveals himself in the mimetic interplay.

In *Aesthetic Theory*, as in *The Concept of Dread*, the history of sacrificial mimesis is raised to the second power inasmuch as the principle of mimesis itself, of *speculation* in the etymological sense, is caught up in the process of self-reflection. *Speculation* as mimesis is at once cognitive and material: "In his attempt to radicalize Marx's eleventh thesis, Adorno lets *natura* slip out of substance into an unceasing economimesis."[19] *Speculation*, whether artistic or philosophical, is relentlessly—almost comically—reduced by Adorno to a sacrificial mimesis of pain, so that not only does "artistic expression [comport] itself mimetically, just as the expression of living creatures is that of pain" (AT 110), but "one could almost say that the aim of philosophy is to translate pain into the concept."[20] Hullot-Kentor summarizes the sacrificial dilemma as follows:

> Adorno's aesthetics attempts to locate an image that would awaken history from its self-consuming progress as the compulsion to sacrifice. Such an image, however, would not be simple mimicry of the logic of sacrifice, but neither is it dialectically conceivable that the image would circumvent sacrifice. (CA xi)
>
> This might again recall Žižek's exhortation, written under a Lacanian banner, to "sacrifice sacrifice."

Lacan, of course, is famous for his theory of the "symbolic Other," toward whom all sacrifices are purportedly directed. Derrida, as mentioned earlier, similarly assimilates the Kierkegaardian god to the structure of subjectivity or interiority conceived in terms of relations to the "absolutely other," and conceives sacrifice in terms of the absolute instant of decision and the absolute sacrificial "leap" as illustrated by Abraham in *Fear and Trembling*.[21] As such, therefore, it is well worth noting that Derrida's (and Lacan's) notion of the sacred as a structure of absolute incommensurability, of absolute otherness, belongs firmly to that element in Kierkegaard that Adorno criticizes as a sacrificial mythology applied to reason itself, in which "the absolute difference of God is itself bound to the [illusion of] autonomous spirit as God's systematic negation" (CA 113). By contrast—but in full accord, nota bene, with the mimetic *commensurability* that properly belongs to the religious according to *The Concept of Dread*—Adorno claims that "*Ratio* without mimesis is self-negating. Ends, the raison d'etre of *raison*, are qualitative, and *mimetic power is effectively the power of qualitative distinction*" (CD 331).[22]

Finally, then, we see that despite his dismissal of the "scurrilous methodological deliberations" of the dogmatic introduction to *The Concept of Dread*, Adorno's emphasis on the generation of difference from similarity, the relative mimetic commensurability that underlies even qualitative distinction, falls squarely on the side of Kierkegaard's claims, inasmuch as a certain mimetic commensurability "paradoxically" must be—and thus actually *is*—assumed not only in judgments of guilt, but in any judgment or distinction whatsoever.

Notes

1. In "Thinking God in the Wake of Kierkegaard," in *Kierkegaard: A Critical Reader*, eds. Jonathan Ree and Jane Chamberlain (Oxford: Blackwell, 1998), 53–74, David Wood illustrates the ambivalence of Jean-Paul Sartre's thinking on the subject when he cites Sartre's judgment that "the *theoretical* aspect of Kierkegaard's work is pure illusion," while arguing that Sartre's appeal to the "*absolute* existence" of Kierkegaardian subjectivity marks "a logical/ontological distinction" (61). Wood also discusses Heidegger's view of transcendence.

2. Wood discusses both Wittgenstein and Derrida in this connection. See also Kevin Hart's "Jacques Derrida: The God Effect" in *Post-Secular Philosophy: Between Philosophy and Theology*, ed. Philip Blond (London and New York: Routledge, 1998), 259–80.

3. See Martin J. Bec Matustik, *Postnational Identity: Critical Theory and Existential Philosophy in Habermas, Kierkegaard, and Havel* (New York: Guilford Press, 1993).

4. See, again, Wood in *Kierkegaard*. (Derrida's essay in the same volume also repeatedly appeals to "absolute singularity," the "absolutely other," "absolute responsibility," etc.)

5. Kierkegaard, *Philosophical Fragments*, ed. and trans. Howard V. Hong and Edna H. Hong (Princeton: Princeton University Press, 1985), 108, hereafter cited as PF.

6. John Milbank, "The Sublime in Kierkegaard," in *Post-Secular Philosophy* (131–56, 148).

7. Theodor Adorno, *Kierkegaard: Construction of the Aesthetic*, ed. and trans. Robert Hullot-Kentor (Minneapolis and London: University of Minnesota Press, 1989), 101, hereafter cited as CA.

8. Kierkegaard, *The Concept of Dread*, trans. Walter Lowrie (Princeton: Princeton University Press, 1957), 21, hereafter cited as CD.

9. The tension between the sacrificial and the antisacrificial Kierkegaard is crucial to Adorno's analysis. In his "Sublime in Kierkegaard," Milbank makes a forceful case for the antisacrificial, arguing that "Kierkegaard sought to invent a nonsacrificial mode of communication." The paradoxy is opposed to the "philosophic *logos*, especially in its post-Cartesian guise" which for Kierkegaard "informs a murderous, sacrificial community" (141).

10. Slavoj Žižek, *Enjoy Your Symptom: Jacques Lacan in Hollywood and Out* (New York and London: Routledge, 1992), 165ff. Žižek forcefully discusses the problem of sacrifice in Kierkegaard in "Why Is Every Act a *Repetition*" (69ff).

11. Contra Adorno and many others, Milbank makes a brave and in some ways compelling argument for reading Kierkegaard's portrayal of "Abraham's sacrifice of Isaac as an anti-sacrifice because it is a completely pointless sacrifice . . . not at all a foundational sacrifice" in service of "the instition of the *polis*," "a self-cancelling will to sacrifice, since undertaken in the conviction that the moment of sacrifice will never arrive." See Milbank, "Sublime in Kierkegaard," 144. Nevertheless the moment of sacrifice *does* arrive for the surrogate ram.

12. Paul de Man, "The Concept of Irony," in *Aesthetic Ideology*, ed. Andrzej Warminski (Minneapolis: University of Minnesota Press, 1996), hereafter cited as CI.

13. Kafka, *Complete Stories*, ed. Nahum N. Glatzer (New York: Schocken Books, 1971), 225. For an indication of the mimetic-sacrificial structure of "The Country Doctor," see John Smyth, "Music Theory in Late Kafka," *Angelaki* 3:2 (1998): 169–81.

14. See the chapter on *The Concept of Dread* in Roger Poole, *Kierkegaard: The Indirect Communication* (Charlottesville: University Press of Virginia, 1993).

15. "I know that it is not one the virtues of dogdom to share with others food that one has once gained possession of . . . that is not selfishness, but the opposite, dog law, the unanimous decision of the people, the outcome of their victory over egoism, for the possessors are always in a minority" (Kafka, *Complete Stories*, 288).

16. A notable exception to this rule occurs in Adorno's treatment of the image of the crucifix in Kierkegaard, where he argues that "the later Kierkegaard's antagonism toward art cannot be simply reduced to the category of sacrifice." Rather, "Kierkegaard's material aesthetic itself indicates the theological concept of the symbol as the idea of an imageless self-presentation of truth. For this reason he entirely excludes from the verdict on art the children's storybook image of the crucifixion, which is as little subject to aesthetic semblance as to any law of form." See Adorno, *Kierkegaard,* 136. Here, problematically (as in late Adorno), the mimesis of sacrifice "indicates" the antimimetic and nonsacrificial.

17. "Art is not synthesis, as convention holds; rather, it shreds synthesis by the same force that affects synthesis. What is transcendent in art has the same [sacrificial] tendency as the second reflection of nature-dominating spirit" (ibid., 139).

18. Cited by Hullot-Kentor (ibid., xi).

19. Wilhelm S. Wurzer, "Kantian Snapshot of Adorno: Modernity Standing Still," in *The Actuality of Adorno: Critical Essays on Adorno and the Postmodern*, ed. Max Pensky (Albany: State University of New York Press, 1997), 147.

20. See Hullot-Kentor's citation (Adorno, *Kierkegaard,* xx).

21. See Derrida, "Whom to Give to (Knowing Not to Know)," in *Kierkegaard,* 150–74.

22. Compare Milbank's critique of Derrida and Žižek:

This preinscription of subjectivity within the text, such that marks of the text are also speaking "characters," articulated through the *activity* of mimetic repetition, is increasingly admitted by Derrida and his followers, and in another fashion by a Lacanian like Slavoj Žižek. Yet does this admission undermine the pure transcendental character of their sublime discourse? Its freedom from the taint of wager? If we are always already within the event of decision, then we can never unproblematically claim to see what is decided behind our backs. We cannot, especially, "see" that there is no finite/infinite, determinate/indeterminate proportion, which the tradition called "analogy" and Kierkegaard temporalizes as 'repetition' " (Milbank, "Sublime in Kierkegaard," 148).

Wood, in "Thinking God in the Wake of Kierkegaard" (66ff.), also pertinently criticizes Derrida's sacrificial reading of *Fear and Trembling*.

Absolute Failures: Hegel's *Bildung* and the "Earliest System-Program of German Idealism"

∾

Rebecca Gagan

Unprogrammed

In his discussion of Franz Rosenzweig's *Star of Redemption*, Ernest Rubinstein declares that the difference between Romanticism and Idealism is not "minute," but rather "infinitesimal."[1] To be sure, it is not new to suggest the complex interrelations between Romanticism and Idealism or to point out that the dividing line between the two is obscured. Yet Rubinstein's use of the term *infinitesimal* suggests a relatedness that is not simply obscured, but rather supplemental. Idealism's project, he argues, does not end with Romanticism but is rather supplemented by it and so continues to be expressed in and as Romanticism. To think of Romanticism as the supplement to Idealism is to return to Jacques Derrida's now famous discussion of Rousseau and supplementarity in his book *Of Grammatology*. If, as Derrida remarks, "there has never been anything but supplements"[2] and if we understand the supplement of Romanticism as that which was always inside Idealism, then it is not only that the separation between the two is "infinitesimal," but perhaps there is indeed no separation at all. The notion of a supplement signals the always already unfinished nature of a project. But, as Rubinstein points out, the supplement of Romanticism is also unfinished, incomplete. How then, does

203

one discern which episteme is being supplemented? Does Romanticism supplement Idealism or vice versa? Phillipe Lacoue-Labarthe and Jean-Luc Nancy suggest that "within the landscape of idealism in general" we can find the "horizon proper of romanticism . . . [t]he philosophical horizon of romanticism."[3] But of course, as anyone would know who had ever looked out at the horizon and wondered where exactly the land meets the sky, there is simply no way of knowing for certain. Rubinstein explains that "the true completion of the idealist movement is the romantic's infinitely hovering postponement of completion" (LA12). Put simply, then, if Romanticism has a supplemental relationship with Idealism—a relationship in which Romanticism's interest in incompletion and the incompletion of Romanticism itself "completes" Idealism—then, at the very heart of Idealism, there must be, too, only incompletion. Thus Idealism, it might be said, begins again in Romanticism, forever to be beginning.

In their discussion of Rosenzweig's discovery of the "Earliest System-Program of German Idealism," and of the relevance of this "fragment" to German Idealism, Lacoue-Labarthe and Nancy note the importance of this fragment as a "founding" text for Romanticism: a project dedicated to a programmatic systematizing of German Idealism that remains incomplete, and that serves not only as a symbol but as *the* theme or "exergue" for Romanticism and its embracement of ruin and incompletion (LA 29). For Lacoue-Labarthe, Nancy, and others, the "Program" is unfinished and fragmentary both in its articulation on paper, *and* as a "Program" or system of German Idealism. That is, as Lacoue-Labarthe and Nancy make clear in *The Literary Absolute*, the "System-Program" as a "Program" was never in fact completed by any of its potential authors (Schelling, Hegel, Hölderlin).[4] Simon Critchley suggests that the "System-Program" is "utterly improbable"—a failure precisely because of its utopian goals, its incompletion.[5] But what if, following Lacoue-Labarthe and Nancy, we read this incompletion, this failure of the "System-Program" to be completed, as the founding moment of Idealism? That is, as a moment that is entirely *un-Programmed*, a moment not of the Absolute, of finitude, and completion but rather a moment of loss, of failure even? The System-Program would then serve as a frame through which idealism itself could be viewed in all of its ruinous glory. For example, that the authorship of the "System-Program" remains undetermined—letters from Schelling (apparently overwhelmingly similar to the fragment) suggest his authorship while graphology reports suggest the fragment is in Hegel's handwriting—is important not only as a sign of how this "System" of Idealism remains open, vulnerable, and the property of no single thinker, but also as a performance of the very "ethics," of the "New Mythology" to which the authors hoped to give birth through their System-Program.[6] As a philosophical text that is unhinged both by its quasi-anonymous status and by its status as a "youthful" text, the System-Program always remains new, is always becoming and so is perpetually free. Moreover, that it fits into the oeuvres of Schelling, Hölderlin, and Hegel—H. S. Harris is careful to note in his study of Hegel that the "System-Program" changes nothing about Hegel's development (HD 249)—suggests that an Idealism without Absolutes is not simply adolescent thinking on the part of these Idealists, but rather is intrinsic to their works as whole.[7] For example, Allen Wood explains that Hegel's *Phenomenology of Spirit* is "a record of a long series of failures" while "at the same time it is . . . a record of the becoming of sciences as such or of knowledge."[8] Hölderlin, similarily, writes to Hegel's closest friend, Immanuel Niethammer, in 1796 (just a few months prior to the months in which the System-Program is thought to have been written) and declares that while Schelling and he did not "always speak in agreement" they "agreed that new ideas can be presented most appropriately in letter-form."[9] The letter-form, like the lecture form—a form in which, after 1816, many of Hegel's works would be presented—is a speculative, incomplete transmission that is akin to the fragmentary structure of the "System-Program" in its risking of nonclosure.[10] Lacoue-Labarthe and Nancy suggest, however, that after the "System-Program" Hegel went his own way, down the path toward the fulfillment of Idealism's goals (LA 37). How is it that German Idealism largely comes to be defined, not by the "founding" moment of incompletion that is the "System-Program," not by these so called youthful musings, but by the manifestation of a German Idealism that wills a *Bildung*, a process that disavows process, a movement toward ends and products and absolute knowledge? How did Hegel's "way" become the way of the Absolute?

I suggest here, that this particular vision of idealism is perpetuated, at least in part, in and through institutional histories—specifically that of the university. On the one hand, the university in North America has its "origins" in Kant's, Fichte's and Humboldt's writings about and plans for the university. Idealism's vision of the university is, as Bill Readings suggests, the "single moment of awakening of consciousness and the eternity of absolute knowledge."[11] For Readings, the university in the twenty-first century must counter the threat of Idealism's yearning for "epistemological master[y]" by recognizing that the "University is a ruined institution" (UR 171, 169). By "ruined," Readings means to indicate a university whose role, mission, and responsibilities are perpetually being negotiated. The university must be, Readings declares, "one site among others where the question of being-together is raised," a question that has been masked "for the past three centuries or so" (20). But is the ruined institution described by Readings newly ruined? Or is there a history of Idealism's "ruined" vision of the university that has been overlooked by theoreticians desiring a future for the university that is not contaminated by its past and by a certain notion of its Idealist origins? If the question of "being-together" must now be raised, then we must return to Hegel and to his discussions of the intellectual community. Hegel's writings—both youthful and otherwise—are filled with the question of what "being-together" means for intellectuals. He offers us not only a sense of intellectual work as always already ruinous and incomplete, but also, by connection, a vision of the university as a site in which the "being-together" of the intellectual community is itself defined by the unfinished, by vanishings. Hegel's thinking about the intellectual community—by way here of his *Aesthetics*, his *Philosophy of Mind*, and his *Phenomenology of Spirit*—challenges a landscape of Idealism that would put him on a direct path toward the Absolute and reveals, rather, a refusal of the fulfillment of the Absolute and the death of thought, community, and Spirit that such a fulfillment would bring.

Academia for Dummies

There are undoubtedly some who would see a comparison of a section of Hegel's *Phenomenology* with any book with the words *for Dummies* in the title as crude and objectionable. Indeed, Allan Bloom declared: "Hegel is now becoming so popular in literary and artistic circles, but in a superficial form adapted to please dilettantes and other seekers after depth who wish to use him rather than understand him."[12] Bloom's comments, which beg the questions, Who owns Hegel? Who owns philosophy? And even more generally, who owns thought? are questions which, ironically enough, inform much of Hegel's work and to which Hegel—unlike Bloom—offers no easy answers. The section of the *Phenomenology* entitled "The Spiritual Animal Kingdom and Deceit, or the 'Matter in Hand Itself' " *does*, I suggest, function as a kind of insider's guide to the academic community—a what to expect while expecting scholarly production condensed into a few brief pages.[13] It is here that Hegel attempts to articulate the challenges that the subject must endure as he attempts to find a place within the intellectual community. With, for example, the admonishment to "start immediately" and to not wait for a sense of how things will end, for confirmation of the end result, Hegel initiates his discussion of the importance of an investment in activity, in the process over the actual work itself (PS §401) One can never know what the "end" result will be since the ends and the means are completely implicated in the process. "Ends" as such are only realized through activity and will, inevitably, produce a result that could not be imagined—and certainly as many scholars know, a result that is far, far different from the initial glimmerings of a work. Hegel's primary aim in this section is to alert scholars and would-be scholars to the dangers of relying too heavily on the product of one's labor for a source of job satisfaction.

Just as Hegel's configuration of the "Absolute as Subject" in the preface to the *Phenomenology* is often understood as the *Absolute-Subject* and not as the Absolute itself as a subject that is unfinished, "self-moving" and incomplete, so too is it often assumed that Hegel is invested in "the book" and in the results or ends of labor (PS §18–23).[14] For Maurice Blanchot, for example, Hegel is the spokesperson for "the book" and for the completeness, the finality, and the totality that it represents.[15] Blanchot suggests that if philosophical thought is imaged by a philosopher's relationship to the university, then Hegel's position in a university chair at Berlin guarantees thought produced in conformity with the demands of this "magisterial form" (IC 4). But how then to understand Hegel's statement in this section of *The Phenomenology* that Alexandre Kojève, Lukacs, and most recently Gary Shapiro understand as a commentary on the intellectual community, that the work "obtains its truth in its dissolution" (PS §405)? Hegel in fact declares here that the work is something "perishable" that only "exhibits the reality of the individuality as vanishing rather than achieved" (PS §405). For Hegel, the work is not a coming to presence of the subject, not a model of completion or of absolute knowledge, but rather a sign of its absence. In his recent article on Hegel and academic work, Shapiro summarizes this notion of the vanishing work as follows: "Finished works are vanishing moments, ephemeral fulfillments at best. [As a scholar], if I thought to realize myself in such a work, I can be thrown into a profound self-doubt, for I see that I've not only misunderstood the character of work but must have had a faulty conception of myself to have expected completion and reconciliation from writing."[16] It is perhaps for this reason, the avoidance of self-doubt and disappointment, that Hegel himself had such trouble "finishing" his work.

Much to the frustration of the majority of his editors, both now and then, Hegel perpetually digresses, supplements, and defers the act of finishing. For example, in negotiations with a potential publisher over the manuscript that would become the *Phenomenology*, Hegel was contracted to receive eighteen florins per completed page with payment coming once the book was half finished. But, as Terry Pinkard notes in his recent biography of Hegel, determining when his book was half-finished proved an impossible task for Hegel, who could not see the end of his work.[17] The publisher eventually lost patience and refused payment until the complete work was submitted. That Hegel found difficult the task of delineating a halfway point in a project that perpetually exceeded its own boundaries is not surprising—not least of all because of the fear and reluctance that undoubtedly overwhelmed him at the moment he was asked to part with a piece of work that in his mind would never be finished. For Hegel then, it seems, it is in fact *not* "the Book," the work-object that counts, but rather the work-activity, the principle of work, the matter in hand (*die Sache selbst*; PS §409). Far from insisting upon the inaccessibility of the spirit (*Geist*) of the work, or the fixed nature of the work, Hegel is moving toward Blanchot's notion of "unworking," that is, toward an understanding of the work as that which cannot be revealed or fully realized since it is always in process. In Blanchot's words: "To write is to produce the absence of the work (worklessness, unworking [*désoeuvrement*])" (IC 424).

In the *Philosophy of Mind*, Hegel discusses the vanishing character of externalizations of the self, the "incorporeal corporeities" that are not at all unlike the products of academic labor. After discussing laughter and crying, Hegel moves on to a discussion of the voice about which he explains: "[It is] a material in which the internality . . . the self-existent ideality of the soul receives a fully correspondent external reality, a reality which immediately vanishes in its arising, since the propagation of sound is just as much the vanishing of it."[18] In a very strange but fascinating section of the *Phenomenology* on physiognomy and phrenology, the science of how the skull and the face express (or fail to express, as Hegel argues) the inner self, Hegel suggests that "speech and work are outer expressions in which the individual no longer keeps and possesses himself within himself, but lets the inner get completely outside of him, leaving it to the mercy of something other than himself " (PS §312). The idea that one's words or one's labor will always be subject to repossession by the Other, gets to the heart of the self-doubt, the fear of criticism that accompanies academic production and about that Hegel writes in the *Phenomenology*:

> The work *is*, i.e., it exists for other individualities, and is for them an alien reality, which they must replace by their own in order to obtain through *their* action the consciousness of *their* unity with reality; in other words, *their* interest in the work which stems from *their* original nature, is something different from this work's *own* peculiar interest, which is thereby converted into something different. (PS §405)

But while the subject is never fully revealed in "the Book," and while those who confront the Book find it to be an "alien reality" in which only their own interests are expressed, in which their own needs are met, Hegel interestingly suggests that it is precisely for this reason that the work remains important to the community more generally. To explain this, it is helpful briefly to return to Hegel's discussion of the voice. In the section of the *Philosophy of Mind* entitled "Anthropology," Hegel explains that this "vanishing voice," this incorporeal corporeality, is one of the most important externalizations of all because excessive talking at a funeral of a loved one, for example, allows for an objectification of pain that minimizes sorrow and comforts the mourner. These kinds of externalizations are for others perhaps more than they are for oneself. Through activity one is for oneself but the products of this activity, whether it be tears or an academic text, are for a community who will find themselves *not you* in these externalizations. Hegel seems to suggest that these externalizations are a literal self-sacrificing through which one is then able to connect with people (PM §401).

In the *Elements of the Philosophy of Right* Hegel suggests the importance of the product of work (and the reproduction of the work) to others in the intellectual community as property that "exists for other external things and is connected with their necessity and contingency."[19] In this sense, the academic community participates in the production of works with the understanding that a work is always already incomplete and that it will exist only as an empty container that others will come to possess and from which they will find and fuel their own work-activity. The academic community knows that the "matter in hand" is where it's at, that the work-activity is what counts. But Hegel's privileging of the "activity" of intellectual work is not only a result of his belief in the impossibility of realizing oneself in "the Book." It is also, I think, Hegel's contention that activity is a Habit (*Gewohnheit*) a way of "having or holding the self" (from the Latin *habere* meaning "to have") that helps one become an integrated community subject. The word *Gewohnheit* contains within it the verb to live (*wohnen*), which reveals much about Hegel's own use of the word *Habit*. For Hegel, habit is a means through which the intellectual can live in, or dwell with, ideas despite the "vanishing" nature of the work. Habit is a space of mediation (of which I will say more later) that dulls the sense of loss. Yet, Hegel's relationship to habit is extremely conflicted. If in the *Phenomenology*, Hegel seemingly charts a dialectical progression from a life of sensation to a life of habit, he is also, I argue, quite skeptical about habit's ability to produce "effective" people.

Habits of Highly "Effective" People

On the way to becoming a community subject, in this case a subject in an intellectual community, one must become integrated and move out of the realm of pure sensation or pure feeling (which Hegel configures as insanity) and into a life of Habit. As Hegel explains in the *Philosophy of Mind*, this integration into civil society is a "painful transition" that is "very distressing" and one in which hypochondria is not easily escaped by anyone (PM §396). Habit is the means through which one *attempts* to own one's thought. It is a way of coping with the illusions of ownership that I've just discussed, of striving to "be at home" with oneself. As Hegel explains in the *Philosophy of Mind*: "Habit is often spoken of disparagingly and called lifeless, casual, and particular . . . and yet habit is indispensable for the *existence* of all intellectual life in the individual, enabling the subject to be a concrete immediacy, an "ideality" of soul—enabling the matter of consciousness, religious, moral, etc., to be his as *this* self, *this* soul, and no other" (PM §410). Habit gives one the sense of being-at-home-with oneself and with one's ideas. It is a way to live in ideas without, on the one hand, slipping into the realm of pure sensation where one only feels and never has a sense of self-possession, or on the other, into what Hegel calls a state of "hyphochondria" where one is too inward, obsessed with one's subjectivity unable to come out of oneself—unable to leave the home so to speak. Friedrich Schiller, a contemporary of Hegel's and, as Rebecca Comay has recently suggested, a powerful influence on Hegel's thinking, describes the former state as follows.[20] First, though, it seems important to note that for Schiller the life of pure sensation and its opposite, pure rationality, are tempered by the category of the Aesthetic that approximates Hegel's notion of Habit in its capacity as a mediating sphere. In a certain sense, Schiller's *On the Aesthetic Education of Man* and Hegel's *Phenomenolgy* are parallel texts in their search for mediating categories. In Schiller's words:

> [H]is personality is suspended as long as he is ruled by sensation, and swept along by the flux of time. . . . For this condition of self-loss under the dominion of feeling, linguistic usage has the very appropriate expression: to be beside oneself, i.e., to be outside of one's own Self. . . . To return to self-possession is termed, equally aptly: to be oneself again, i.e., to return into one's own Self, to restore one's Person.[21]

To be "swept away" by sensation, then, is to leave one's dwelling, to neglect or refuse the home that Habit has built and to be beside oneself. But if, on the one hand, living in a world of sensation means, in part, never to be at home, to live elsewhere, everywhere, to be a transient, there are certain forms of insanity which, on the other hand, are induced by being too comfortable at home, by a reluctance to leave home. As Hegel explains in a letter to a friend in 1826:

> I define hypochondria as the affliction that consists in the inability to come out of oneself. I would know of many ways to come out of oneself, but the one I would advise is to reverse the position in which you place this demon relative to activity, not waiting on the demon's departure in order to allow this activity to occur, but rather driving away the demon precisely through activity.[22]

While Hegel doesn't discuss hypochondria directly in his quite lengthy discussion of insanity in the *Philosophy of Mind*, his definition of insanity in his letter to Karl Daub is very similar to his characterization of at least two forms of insanity that he does identify—distractedness and idiocy. Distractedness, in particular, is a form of insanity that is not uncommon among scholars who "desire to be universally esteemed" and in the process become immersed in their subjectivity and cannot come out of themselves (PM §408). The inability to come out of oneself results in an "unworking" of another kind—that is, an inability to act that is, nonetheless, a kind of intense work or labor itself. When Hegel suggests to Daub that he "knows" other ways to come out of oneself, he is undoubtedly referring to the following "cures" that he outlines in the *Philosophy of Mind:*

> [One] who held himself to be dead, did not move and would not eat, came to his senses again when someone pretended to share his delusion. The lunatic was put in a coffin and laid in a vault in which was another coffin occupied by a man who at first pretended to be dead but who, soon after he was left alone with the lunatic, sat up, told the latter how pleased he was to have company in death, and finally got up, ate the food that was by him and told the astonished lunatic that he had already been dead a long time and therefore knew how the dead go about things. The lunatic was pacified by the assurance, likewise ate and drank and was cured. (PM §408)

In *Madness and Civilization,* Michel Foucault labels this technique "Recognition by Mirror" and suggests it as just one of several normalizing "cures" for the insane.[23] While I don't have space here to engage Hegel's own relationship to Philippe Pinel and to the various other physicians working in the hospitals in France at the time, Hegel was au courant with the latest medical knowledge and, since his own sister suffered a mental breakdown, he was strongly invested in treatments for mental illness.[24] The most interesting "cure," however, and one that Hegel suggests as the most efficacious, is the placing of the patient on a seesaw—the seesaw movement induces giddiness in the patient and loosens the fixed idea (PM §408). I will return to this image of the seesaw and its relevance to Hegel's work in a moment. First, I want to turn to Hegel's own account of the hypochondria that apparently stayed with him for a period of ten years from the age of twenty-seven to thirty-seven— the period during which he was writing the *Phenomenology* (HD 265). You'll notice that Hegel's description of his own hypochondria reveals not a subject who has too tight a grip on his subjectivity, but rather, a subject who is beside himself, not holding onto thought but losing his train of thought altogether. This letter is a reply to Hegel's dear friend Karl Windischmann who, like Daub, wrote to Hegel complaining of a "profound hypochondria and semiparalysis." Hegel's reply is as follows:

> Health and serene mood—indeed a stable serene mood—are called
> for in no other field of work more than in this. Consider yourself

convinced that the frame of mind you depict to me is partly due to
this present work of yours, to this descent into dark regions where
nothing is revealed as fixed, definite, and certain; where glimmerings
of light flash everywhere but, flanked by abysses, are rather dark-
ened in their brightness and led astray by the environment, casting
false reflections far more than illumination . . . From my own experience I know this mood of the soul, or rather of reason which arises
when it has finally made its way with interest and hunches into a
chaos of phenomena but, though inwardly certain of the goal, has
not yet worked its way through them to clarity and to a detailed
account of the whole. For a few years I suffered from this hypochondria to the point of exhaustion. Everybody probably has such a turning point in his life, the nocturnal point of the contraction of his
essence in which he is forced through a narrow passage by which his
confidence in himself and everyday life grows in strength and
assurance. . . . Continue onward with confidence. It is science which
has led you into this labyrinth of the soul, and science alone is
capable of leading you out again and healing you.[24]

Just as the gentleman who thought he was dead was cured by being confronted with death, the cure for a hypochondria brought on by study is more
study. This notion of inoculation is a reiteration of Hegel's belief in activity's
curative effect. Because you'll never know where you're going or how to get
there exactly (this of course would be to see the means and ends as separate
from the beginning) you might as well just do it. It seems that for the academic, one must be careful not to hold on too tightly to one's subjectivity, or
to an idea, but at the same time one must find a way to be-at-home, to have
enough of a hold on oneself to be able to think without the burden of excessive feeling. The image of the teetering seesaw seems apt because it raises the
possibility of a balanced-off balancedness. A self-possession that is not too
possessive so as to become self-absorption, distraction, or hypochondria.
     But does one ever really leave this state of self-loss behind, or is it
simply managed somehow through Habit? More importantly, does Hegel really
believe that Habit is the end of self-loss, of those wanderings outside the self,
of the being beside oneself with giddiness or with grief, of the strayings from
home in which one does not know which path leads home or if one even
wants to go home at all? Does Habit set one free? As Hegel explains in the
Philosophy of Mind: "Although, on the one hand, habit makes a man free, yet,
on the other hand, it makes him its slave. In habit the human being's mode
of existence is 'natural,' and for that reason not free" (PM §410). As a "second Nature" habit is precisely not natural and thus inevitably restricts being.
Habit is something mechanical. As he briefly suggests in the *Science of Logic*,

habit, like certain forms of memory or action is mechanistic and divested of spirit. There is "lacking in it the freedom of individuality and because this freedom is not manifest in it, such action appears as a merely external one."[25] With this we've come full circle, it seems, and back to the tension between activity and the externalization of thought.

Hegel is uneasy with the idea of Habit because it threatens to empty activity of its self-realizing power and to limit the emergence of individuality, the becoming of the subject, which process encourages. In this sense, Habit might produce conformity of thought and thus an intellectual *community* in the very worst sense of the term—a community in which people are too comfortable at home. While Hegel *does* suggest in the *Phenomenology* that the community subject must come to realize his or her place in relationship to the universal, which is to say, how a particular kind of work connects to the whole, an idea that Schelling discusses in his book *On University Studies* (1798),[26] Hegel is not asserting that the transition, or birth, through the "narrow strait" into habit is an easy one and that one should, even if they could, disavow the realm of sensation. Hegel seems to suggest that the kind of "effective" person brought about by habit is one who is stripped not only of spirit, but also of the chance to be, themselves, a work in process. It is for this reason, perhaps, why Hegel returns again and again to a questioning of habit and to its imposed regularity, and to his search for a community, or a sphere in which production exists for production's sake—a production that is, as he explains in the *Aesthetics*, of "free activity." In the introduction to the *Aesthetics*, Hegel suggests that an escape from the "dark inwardness of thought," the "conformity to law," and the "fetters of rules and regularity" is made possible through the production of art. It is a place where we seek peace and enlivenment and forget the shadow realm of the Idea.[27] Art is a space of unworking, of the unfinished. It is, as Hegel suggests later, where one might leave behind the "world of finitude" (A 1:150). Art is where one can exist as a free subject "strip[ping] the external world of its inflexible foreignness" (31).

Through his discussion of the three types of art—symbolic, classical, and romantic—Hegel continues his thinking about habit, process, and the unfinished and articulates a movement from the symbolic to the romantic which, when read with his thoughts on the stages of life, suggests an emphasis on process that might otherwise go unnoticed. While it might seem as if Hegel is suggesting that romantic art sees the realization of the ideal in art and thus the end of a process that began with the disharmony and strife of the symbolic, it is important to understand that Hegel can't help but conceive of the stages of art in the same terms as he formulates the stages of life. This is not surprising, as Hegel tends always to be thinking of the fragments of past and forthcoming works through the lectures at hand (a testament to the very becoming of his own thought) and so questions from the *Philosophy of Mind* or the *Philosophy of Nature* are reinterpreted through, as is the case here, concerns in the realm of aesthetics. Thus, when Hegel describes the symbolic as a period of unrest in which the idea "bubbles and ferments" (A 1:76) and where "the Idea is presented to consciousness only as indeterminate or determined abstractly," (77), he recalls the stage of life in which youths experience the antithesis between self and world and rail against surrendering the ideal and passing, acting "against the current" of affairs, as discussed earlier, into a life of particulars, maturity, and habit. In youth, the "young man dreams that he is called and fitted to make the world over" and the passing into maturity is thus seen as a "sorry entrance into philistinism."[28] Like the symbolic in art that is, as Hegel notes in the introduction to the *Aesthetics*, a "struggling and striving," "a mere search" (A 1:76), youth is similarly described elsewhere as a stage in which one searches for self, for purposes, and is restless with a yet unrealized ideal which, Hegel is careful to explain, "inspires the youth's energy."[29] Classical art is represented by the stage of life in which one is mature and falls into a life of harmony and habit. But if classical art is the stage in which the ideal is perfectly realized and expressed through and also limited by, for example, the human form, it also for Hegel imperfect precisely because the inner and the outer do coalesce and thus collapse the vital energy that fuels youth. In his discussion of adulthood, Hegel explains that "it is just because his activity is so perfectly met and satisfied by his occupation—his impulses finding no opposition in their objects—it is because of this full development of his activity that the vitality of it begins to ebb. . . . Thus a man enters old age not only by the running down of the vitality of his physical organism, but also by the crystallizing of the spiritual life into habits.[30] This "classical" stage of adulthood is for Hegel a living death in which a focus on the "particulars" and a life of habit brings on a solidification of thought and a shutting down of that essential and life-giving energy of the symbolic.[31] Classical art is similarly restrained by the particular, that is, by the expression of the idea in the human form. In the *Aesthetics*, unlike in life, the classical stage, the seeming accomplishment of the adequate expression of the ideal, must be dissolved and the restfulness of classical art disturbed by the "absolute inwardness" of romantic art (A 1:519). That is, unlike a straightforward *Bildung* in which maturity and harmony are the ultimate goal, the *Bildung* of the *Aesthetics* is one in which the peace of the union of the inner and the outer is collapsed precisely because it signals for Hegel an Absolute peace that can only be akin to a kind of death of Spirit. *Bildung* for Hegel is a process that continually undoes itself so as to avoid the "processless habitual activity" of maturity.[32] It would seem, then, that Hegel is ultimately more interested in the questing and searching for the symbolic than in any other stage of life or art.[33] In romantic art process continues and, as Hegel describes in the *Aesthetics*, the idea is safeguarded from crystallization by the contingencies, accidents, and "adventures" of the external world that prevent a settling into particulars (A 575). Thus, it is significant that, unlike in Hegel's discussion of the phases of life in which man reaches maturity in adulthood and then moves toward death, romantic art, placed after the seemingly mature stage of classical art, grants a maturity to what is adolescent, unformed, in the symbolic. That it is *romantic* art, the final stage of art, which Hegel configures as incomplete and forever becoming, suggests that, while Lacoue-Labarthe and Nancy might set Hegel's project as the fulfillment of idealism, his project was, rather, always the postponement of idealism's accomplishment and the giving birth to a Romanticism that would not only emerge out of, but would also be inseparable from, an idealism without ends.

Absolute Failures

But there remains, of course, a desire not to read Hegel as a thinker interested in the symbolic, in unrest, but to read him as a "master"—as one who is always in control and moving always toward an end. As Harris emphasizes in his *Hegel's Development,* "Hegel suffered certainly, and he had fits of black depression; but he was always, probably, as much the master of himself as any man can reasonably hope to be—a fact that Hölderlin recognized when he called him a *ruhig Verstandesmensch* (calm, matter-of-fact person) and spoke of his cheerful attitude (HD 270). Harris doesn't mention that Hölderlin is said to have tried to comfort Hegel during one of his depressions by saying "soon you'll be the old man again." Can there not be a Hegel who is at once "at home" and also "beside himself?" We might think this distinction through Merold Westphal's discussion of the "published" Hegel that we "know and love" and the "unpublished" Hegel of the Berlin lectures (on the history of philosophy, the philosophy of history, the philosophy of religion, and aesthetics) (VH 270). But is the gap between the two Hegels really so wide? Are the Berlin lectures given late in his career—and transcribed by students, rewritten, supplemented, left unfinished—not a continuation of a program of idealism articulated at the commencement of his life as a philosopher? Is the open, incomplete, existential nature of the lecture form itself not an extension of the fragmentary, collaborative, loose form of the "System-Program"? In the "System-Program," the authors call for an idea of humanity that is not connected to "something mechanical"; only that which is free is called an "Idea" (A 155). The "unpublished" Hegel, like the Hegel of the System-Program, guarantees the freedom of the idea throughout his life and shields it from the mechanistic whether it be in the form of civil society, habit, classical art, or old age. Hegel knows that it is only through a continuation of process and free activity that one comes to knowledge both of the self and of the world. As Judith Butler explains in *Contingency, Hegemony, Universality,*

> In *The Greater Logic*, Hegel gives the example of the person who
> thinks he might learn how to swim by learning what is required before
> entering the water. The person does not realize that one learns to swim
> only by entering the water and practicing one's strokes in the midst of
> the activity itself. Hegel explicitly likens the Kantian to one who seeks
> to learn how to swim before actually swimming, and he counters this
> model of a self-possessed cognition with one that gives itself over to
> the activity itself as a form of knowing that is given over to the world
> it seeks to know. Although Hegel is often dubbed a philosopher of
> "mastery," one can see here . . . that the ek-static disposition of the self
> towards its world undoes cognitive mastery. Hegel's own persistent
> references to "losing oneself" and "giving oneself over" only confirm
> the point that the knowing subject cannot be understood as one who
> imposes ready-made categories on a pregiven world.[34]

To be beside oneself as a scholar is to allow the discovery that one is always
being given over to the world and to knowledge. From Hegel we learn that if
the scholar is a part of an intellectual community, and if the freedom of ideas
in that community is to be guaranteed, then it must be a community that is
invested in more than the "published." Perhaps if there is an intellectual community at all, it is not a community of readers, not a community of authors
either, but a community of the "unpublished," of "vanishing texts." Hegel's
intellectual community is one in which mastery and the attainment of the
Absolute is a sign not of Idealism's accomplishment, but rather, of its failure.

Notes

I would like to thank Tilottama Rajan and Jan Plug for their careful readings
and valuable responses to various versions of this essay. An earlier version of this
essay originally appeared in *European Romantic Review* 13, no. 2 (2002): 139–45.

1. Franz Rubinstein, *An Episode of Jewish Romanticism: Franz Rosenzweig's
The Star of Redemption* (Albany: State University of New York Press, 1999), 12.

2. Jacques Derrida, *Of Grammatology*, trans. Gayatri Chakravorty Spivak
(Baltimore: Johns Hopkins University Press, 1974), 159.

3. Phillipe Lacoue-Labarthe and Jean-Luc Nancy, *The Literary Absolute*, trans.
Philip Barnard and Cheryl Lester (Albany: State University of New York Press, 1988),
37, hereafter cited as LA.

4. See Lacoue-Labarthe in ibid.: "It is worth noting in advance that even
Schelling, the only person besides Hegel with the necessary will and power, will not
be able to follow this program through" (28).

5. Simon Critchley, *Continental Philosophy: A Very Short Introduction* (Oxford: Oxford University Press, 2001), 67.

6. "The Oldest System-Program of German Idealism," in *Friedrich Hölderlin
Essays and Letters on Theory*, ed. and trans., Thomas Pfau (Albany: State University

of New York Press, 1988), 154–56, hereafter cited as OSP. Pfau's notes indicate the fragment is now dated "somewhere between June and August 1796" (182). For a discussion of the authorship of the "System-Program" see H. S. Harris, *Hegel's Development: Towards the Sunlight 1770–1801* (Oxford: Clarendon Press, 1972), hereafter cited as HD.

7. See Julia Kristeva, *New Maladies of the Soul* (New York: Columbia University Press, 1995), for a discussion of the ways in which adolescence is a psychic space of incompletion and liberation rather than a stage of immaturity through which one passes and does not return.

8. Allen Wood, "Hegel on Education," in *Philosophers on Education: Historical Perspectives*, ed. Amélie Oksenberg Rorty (London: Routledge, 1998), 300–17, 303.

9. Pfau, *Friedrich Hölderlin Essays and Letters on Theory,* 132. See letter no. 117, February 24, 1796.

10. See Derrida, *The Postcard from Socrates to Freud and Beyond*, trans. Alan Bass (Chicago: University of Chicago Press, 1987). Here, Derrida discusses at length the ways in which, as an *envoi*, the letter is always vulnerable, open, and incomplete.

11. Bill Readings, *The University in Ruins* (Cambridge: Harvard University Press, 1996), 145; hereafter cited as UR.

12. Allan Bloom, "Introduction," Alexandre Kojève, *Introduction to the Reading of Hegel*, trans. James H. Nichols Jr. (New York: Basic, 1969), ix.

13. G. W. F. Hegel, *Phenomenology of Spirit*, trans. A. V. Miller (Oxford: Oxford University Press, 1977), §394–437. Hereafter cited as PS.

14. I am grateful to Tilottama Rajan for this insight.

15. Maurice Blanchot, *The Infinite Conversation*, trans. Susan Hanson (Minneapolis: University of Minnesota Press, 1993), 429, hereafter cited as IC.

16. Gary Shapiro, "Notes on the Animal Kingdom of the Spirit," in *The Phenomenology of Spirit Reader: Critical and Interpretive Essays*, ed. Jon Stewart (Albany: State University of New York Press, 1998), 225–39, 228.

17. Terry Pinkard, *Hegel: A Biography* (Cambridge: Cambridge University Press, 2000), 227.

18. Hegel, *Philosophy of Mind*, trans. Miller (Oxford: Clarendon Press, 1971), §401, hereafter cited as PM.

19. Hegel, *Elements of the Philosophy of Right*, trans. T. M. Knox (Oxford: Clarendon Press, 1958), 57.

20. See Rebecca Comay, *Mourning Sickness: Hegel and the Impossibility of Memory* (Forthcoming); and Merold Westphal *"Von Hegel bis Hegel*: Reflections on 'The Earliest System-Programme,' " in *The Emergence of German Idealism,* eds. Michael Baur and Daniel O. Dahlstrom (Washington, DC: Catholic University of America Press, 1999), 269–88 (hereafter cited as VH). Westphel explains that Hegel read Schiller's letters immediately upon publication and described them as a "masterpiece" (282).

21. Friedrich Schiller, *On the Aesthetic Education of Man*, in a Series of Letters, ed. and trans., Elizabeth M. Wilkinson and L. A. Willoughby (Oxford: Clarendon Press, 1967), 79–80.

22. Hegel, *Hegel: The Letters*, ed. and trans. Clark Butler and Christiane Seiler (Bloomington: Indiana University Press, 1984), 512–13.

23. Michel Foucault, *Madness and Civilization: A History of Insanity in the Age of Reason*, trans. Richard Howard (New York: Vintage Books, 1973), 262.

24. See *Hegel, Letters*, 561.

25. Hegel, *Science of Logic*, trans. Miller (New Jersey: Humanities Press, 1989), 711.

26. Schelling, *On University Studies,* trans. E. S. Morgan, ed. Norbert Guterman (Ohio: Ohio State University Press, 1966), 7.

27. Hegel, *Aesthetics: Lectures on Fine Art,* trans., Knox, 2 vols. (Oxford: Clarendon Press, 1972), 1:5; hereafter cited as A.

28. As quoted in Frederic Ludlow Luqueer, *Hegel as Educator* (New York: AMS Press, 1967),125. The following quotations from Luqueer's collection are from Hegel's *Philosophy of Mind* as well as Hegel's from addresses on education as rector of a gymnsasium in Nürnberg (*Gymnasilarede* 1810–12).

29. Luqueer, *Hegel as Educator,* 124.

30. Ibid., 119, 127.

31. Ibid., 125.

32. Ibid., 128.

33. See Rajan's essay in this volume for a discussion of Hegel's interest in the symbolic.

34. Judith Butler, Ernesto Laclau, and Slavoj Žižek, *Contingency, Hegemony, Universality Contemporary Dialogues on the Left* (London: Verso, 2000), 19.

Futures of Spirit:
Hegel, Nietzsche, and Beyond

~

Richard Beardsworth

Introduction

In the wake of Heidegger's "destruction" of metaphysical thinking, the continental philosophy of the last fifty years has increasingly placed the powers of human reason under suspicion. Central within the discipline of philosophy to this move has been a radical questioning of Hegelian thought and an affirmation of Nietzsche's oeuvre. The former has been considered *the* exposition of the concept, of the rational qua of the whole, of the identity of the real and thought; the latter *the* celebration, from underneath conceptuality, of affect, of the nonrational, of the difference between thought and becoming. The two judgments have moved together, suggesting that the philosophical tradition and its futures divide, as it were, between the two paths of thought that Hegel and Nietzsche propose. The alignment of continental philosophy with literature in the Anglo-American world continues to foster, with important exceptions, both this division and this future of continental philosophy. The opposing of Nietzsche to Hegel is, however, philosophically disempowering—for our understanding of the philosophical tradition, and, more importantly, for the rethinking today of the activity of philosophy in general. A reinvention of the manner, objects, and task of philosophy is needed. First, because the world is different from that from which twentieth-century continental philosophy emerged and had its immediate reasons for being, and this difference must be taken up by philosophy. Second, because, inversely, the world transparently needs philosophy today to help articulate its tendencies and laws so that new social transformation and construction are possible. Third, and finally, because the recent tribunal against reason's powers (whether it be more contra Hegel or more pro Nietzsche) is misplaced.

This essay rehearses a line of reflection within the modern German tradition of thought—Hegel, Nietzsche, Freud, and Marx—that redraws the postmodern opposition of Hegel to Nietzsche in order to begin to elaborate how power and title can be bestowed back upon the activity of reason in our contemporary world. The end that concerns me is the reconstruction of critical philosophy; the means to that end is, within the discipline of philosophy, the elaboration of a series of theoretical moves that reinvents the *gesture* of German thought, there where it remains powerful, from underneath its Heideggerian and French inheritance. This essay forms one such move, concentrating on the concept and development of *spirit*.

The essay is divided into three parts. The first part develops Hegel's notion of spirit and, from out of this development, considers what remains of import in Hegel's understanding of phenomenological experience and speculative thinking. The second part develops Nietzsche's understanding of spirit from out of his genealogy and "energetics" (theory of force) to suggest how Nietzsche's notion of spirit deepens the Hegelian insight into the activity of philosophy. In doing so, I will simultaneously propose an aporia of thought *between* Hegel and Nietzsche that can be configured in the idea of a *speculative materialism*. This speculative materialism is then taken up in the third part in specific gestures of thought within the thinking of Freud and Marx: namely, in how Freud accounts for religious form, and in how, crucially, Marx's phenomenological exposition of the capitalist economy is to be reinvented today as an articulation of spirit.

Hegel, Spirit, and Speculative Thinking

The past half-century's philosophical resistance to Hegel is both historical and substantial. The critiques of Hegelian rationality find common cause in the empirical fates of Marxism, and expression in the philosophical retracing of Marxian hubris to Hegel. Hegel has been questioned accordingly on at least four fronts: totality and the systematic, the identity of thought and being (together with the semantic saturation of the real), teleology (together with the resolution of contradiction and reconciliation), and the hegemony of the epistemological over the ethical. Whatever its particular form, this philosophical resistance has then looked to articulate, respectively, the essential openness of any system, the nonidentity between thought and being, the difference within and behind contradiction and alterity, and the radical alterity of the ethical to the philosophical. The wish to reinvent today a Hegelian-type gesture of philosophizing cannot brush these criticisms aside. Some remain pertinent and important. That said, *where* these criticisms have been oriented by a Husserlian and/or Heideggerian understanding of experience and of philosophy, they have lost the gesture of Hegelian thought *there where critical philosophy is still possible*. This gesture can be retrieved in Hegel's initial elaboration of spirit in the early theological writings and confirmed in his elaboration of the phenomenological method and of speculative thinking in the preface to the *Phenomenology of Spirit*.[1] Let me rehearse the first moment and then make my case.[2]

In the section of "The Spirit of Christianity and Its Fate" entitled in I. M. Knox's translation "The Moral Teaching of Jesus: Love as the Transcendence of Penal Justice and the Reconciliation of Fate" (SC 224–52), Hegel addresses two kinds of law: one posited, one experiential. His notion of spirit emerges from the second. In distinction to criminal law in which universal and particular are forever unreconciled, the law of the causality of fate reconfigures the universal and particular beyond the terms of their positedness. Hegel describes how an individual is alive, moving within the manifoldness and many-sidedness of life. This manifoldness is broken with the individual's destruction of life. Since, for Hegel, life cannot be destroyed in its indeterminate universality, life returns to persecute the murderer in the figure of a "hostile enemy," a ghost. The taking-away of life thus *creates its own law*—"the causality of fate"—that returns against the initial perpetrator *as* the removal of her life. Through the "inversion" of life in the form of a ghost, fate constitutes the realization on the part of the transgressor that she has taken her *own* life. Hegel writes: "Destruction of life is not the nullification of life but its diremption (*Entzweiung*), and the destruction consists in its transformation into an enemy . . . life lets loose its Eumenides . . . for life is not different from life, since life dwells in the single Godhead" (229).

This essential continuity of life constitutes the condition for life's inversions *and* reformations. The feeling of disruption of life on the part of the murderer becomes "a longing for what has been lost," which lack "is life known (*erkannt*) and felt as not-being" (SC 230). This rediscovery, recognition, appears next within the individual as the *love* of life (232). Love constitutes in affective, sensible form the realization that *apparent differences form parts of an essential "whole" (life)*. Whereas in posited law a fragment remains fragmentary, the transgression that issues from life reveals the whole *through* the loving recognition of its fragments *as* divisions of life. As Hegel puts it, in love, "justice is satisfied" (232): chasing "differences and devising unifications ad infinitum," it turns to "the whole manifold of nature in order to drink love out of every life" (307). Love completes the law of fate, signaling both the return of the trespasser to the life that it initially separated and, through the inversions of misrecognition and recognition of this life, the newfound desire to grasp the essential manifoldness and many-sidedness of life that it had missed, rediscovering in so doing its own humanity as part of life. Hegel looks to the message of love and forgiveness of sins in the New Testament for an account of this recognition and finds it in the notion of *spirit* as *spirit*. Christ's grace lies in his recognition that acts against the law are undone if the other has recognized life. The sinner's recognition finds concrete form in her heart's recognition, above law and fate, of Christ *as* Christ, a concrete love acknowledged in turn by Christ through the forgiveness of her past. "Faith is a knowledge of spirit through spirit; only like spirits can know and understand one another; unlike ones know only they are not what the other is" (239). The act of forgiveness enacts spirit because it reconfirms *what life was* prior to its differentiations. It thus constitutes a process of recognition (of the spirituality of life) that *comes through* error and illusion. In such experiential recognition life becomes spiritual.

Hegel then argues, crucially, that this law of the "causality of fate" is not just revealed by the killing of life. Murder constitutes an example that reveals the movement of fate to be a *general structure* of life. Since life is manifold and many-sided, since it is made up of differences in its nonconceptual unity *as* life, life is *always* injured. A life cannot not injure life. Thus one's humanity is not just rediscovered through the causality of fate. The causality of fate presents a dynamic particular to humans as *emergent subjects*. Spirit is thus *the structural potential of humanity to re-find life*.

"The Spirit of Christianity and Its Fate" has been carefully criticized by Jacques Derrida for its "onto-theo-teleology," that is, with respect to the argument just outlined, for presupposing life as a unity from which the original separations and consequent reconciliation ensue.[3] This presupposition appears in the naming of life as 'the Godhead,' behind which Derrida ultimately inscribes, following the later Heidegger, the radical difference of the gift of being.[4] Derrida's gesture is exemplary of the contemporary mode of continental philosophizing. I believe it misplaced regarding the formulation of spirit here offered for these reasons.

First: the causality of fate points to a phenomenological law of experience through which the human subject *as* subject can always in potential run. This law is one of the recognition of one-Self as part of a greater complexity of relations that are revealed through the "illusions" of misrecognition. The Hegelian distinction between life in its unity and in its diremption is retrieved out of the philosophical recognition that the specificity of experience for human subjecthood lies in this spiritual nature. This nature is neither given nor presupposed: while "always there" qua the manifold unity of life, spirit develops *through* history and through the inversions of sensibility consequent upon hominization. That Hegel reads this development out of religion, in terms of religious categories and divisions, should not shroud the fact, therefore, that he aims at what is particular to human formation as such, a particularity re-marked by *all* religious categories *to the degree* of this formation. Christianity recognizes this particularity more than other religions because, with the historical emergence of subjectivity *out of* the community, this experience begins to *appear as such*. The message of Christ is historically specific and exemplary because the loss of inter-humanity emerges with the formation of the subject, which inter-human relation *returns* in the rediscovered feeling of love for life. Here Hegel anticipates the comprehension of the relations between religion, law, and property in the *Philosophy of History*.[5] Contemporary philosophy's judgment that this rediscovery of life and humanity is metaphysical (nostalgic for a prior unity) cannot thereby exposit what is specific to the human in its historical formation, what is specific to life in its historical generality (causalities and connections always beyond the categories of causality and connection particular to misrecognition and recognition), and what is specific to the religious (the constant remarking of the *historically formed* diremptions of life).

Second: for Hegel, determinate life's necessary conflict with indeterminate life means that "we are all sinners." Qua life, determinate life cannot not do injustice to life. The causality of fate reveals the essential law of life as a differential unity of justice and injustice. On the one hand, life must be determined for life to be life: difference must be articulated. On the other hand, this very determination, while just, is unjust, will necessarily create differences that will have to be reconfigured. The unity of justice and injustice is, in other words, a *speculative* unity, one that is the law of *all* determination. The law of spiritual experience, the inversions of misrecognition and recognition, translate therefore: at *a phenomenological level*, an ontology of the essential unity of life as the essential *difference* of life; *at an epistemological level*, the *absolute* requirement of life that life forms and shapes itself, suffers from such shaping, but demands, again, such shaping; and, consequently, the *speculative necessity* of (1) *seizing the real in thought* in order to respect difference, and (2) of expounding the *historical* fates of such seizure in its necessary misrecognitions (inversions of life).

The recent move away from Hegel into a quasi-ontological or ethical (quasi-"Judaic") thinking of the "remainder of thought" loses here the *risk* of reason to determine difference *and* the exposition of the essential justice and injustice of this very determination. It thereby loses an exposition that leads philosophy, necessarily, to a *historical* manner of philosophizing, one in which the speculative unity of the religious, the historical, and the social is expounded.

Third: this exposition should not be seen simply as the "painting" of "grey on grey,"[6] that is, as the retrospective tracing of the diremptions of life from out of an ever-present but nonconfigurable manifold of life qua spirit. The rediscovery of life and humanity is the rediscovery of a web of relations in which one forms a part. To determine life, and through determining it, to merge further into it and to comprehend all the more its differences—what Hegel calls, following religion, "love"—is a *formative* recognition of human life. The rediscovery of humanity as the recognition of life means that this recognition *works toward* ever-greater inclusivity in its determination of difference. In Hegel this work takes on teleological proportions as if the end is presupposed, the horizon of such work closed. To criticize Hegel in these terms is right; but, again, such criticism misses the gesture of his thinking: to determine the difference of life in such a way that these differences can become as *transparent* as possible *from within* the inversions of recognition and misrecognition. Gillian Rose's strong Hegelianism is right to suggest, therefore, that Hegel's subsequent work on law is read most creatively as attempts to figure, from out of the historical separation between modern law and social life, "a just society."[7] Hegel's comprehension of the difference of life leads philosophy not only to retrospective exposition, but also to the *risk* of reason *as* the venture of *construction*. This lesson of spirit holds for future philosophical activity.

In the preface to the *Phenomenology of Spirit* spirit as the phenomenological experience of life in its manifold unity is reconceived as the "speculative" nature of thought. In two notorious passages Hegel writes:

> That the true is actual as system, or that Substance is essentially Subject, is expressed in the representation of the Absolute as Spirit. . . . The spiritual alone is the actual; it is essence (*das Wesen*), or that which relates to itself and determines itself, other-being and being-for-self . . . and in this determinateness remains with itself; in other words it is in and for itself.[8]

> Self-recognition in absolute other-being . . . is the ground and soul of *Wissenschaft*. . . . What is separated and non-actual is an essential moment . . . for it is only because the concrete does divide itself and make itself non-actual that it is self-moving. The activity of dissolution is the power and work of the understanding . . . but that an accident as such, detached from what circumscribes it, what is bound and is actual only in its context with others, should attain an existence of its own . . . is the tremendous power of the negative. . . . Death, this non-actuality, is of all things the most dreadful, and to hold fast to what is dead requires the greatest strength. . . . But the life of Spirit is not the life that shrinks from death and keeps itself untouched by devastation, but rather the life that endures it and maintains itself in it. Spirit is this power only by looking the negative in the face and tarrying with it.[9]

The notion of spirit constitutes the comprehensive attempt to recognize what has been separated within a whole. *Speculative thinking* forms the attempt to recognize differences in their separateness and, in so recognizing them, articulate the movement of which they are a part. Recent criticism of Hegelian systematics is justified in response to the discursive conceptuality of these passages. It loses, however, the drive behind their notions of spirit, reason, and the *phenomenological* difference between essence and appearance: that of building up the differences of the actual into a network of connections emerging from the development of these differences' posited appearance. This building of the actual into relations of causality misrecognized in our initial knowledge of them is what Hegel calls the "concrete." Not to force a distinction—with regard to the difference between *Vernunft* and *Verstand*—between Hegel's evident idealism and the *gesture* of speculative thought deprives philosophizing of the arms of *conceptual* thinking. To place such speculation, as recent thought has, exclusively within the realm of meaning and to place *outside* it radical notions of differential alterity (the gift, the other, death, and matter) that can either only be alluded to analogically (Levinas, Derrida, Lyotard) or experienced nonscientifically (Deleuze) is: (1) to renounce the ethical *work* and *risk* of rational thought to determine differences, and (2) to justify this renunciation as epistemological modesty. As a result, philosophy curtails its speculative powers of reason to *open things up*. This leaves differences in the world unarticulated either for fear of determining difference or in the understandable joy of celebrating the singular. The recent turning from Hegel leads consequently to philosophical and political stasis. For, in renouncing the work of differentiation, it ironically abandons those who suffer from the lack of such opening and articulation. Such abandonment forms the *fate* of philosophical concentration on the remainder of life. This fate is to be redressed given that life increasingly takes shape today through forces that have force, precisely, *by forcing essential connections apart* (world capitalism). Philosophy needs, therefore, to regain its speculative titles in order to expound the diremptions of this predominant economic culture and to seek therefrom new ways of articulating the differences of life. By not doing so, philosophy will continue to lose the relation between thought and suffering qua the separated and isolated and thereby forego the immanent relation Hegel saw in speculative thinking between knowledge and the construction of humanity. Retrieving the gesture of the speculative reforges, in other words, the relation of life between philosophy and the city.

Nietzsche and Spirit

The opposing of Nietzsche to Hegel finds great strength in the former's explicit dislike for systematic thought, his destruction of religion, and his concomitant search for overhumanity. These moves ignore in part or in full

Nietzsche's own thinking of spirit from the "Trilogy of Free Spirits"[10] to the insistent idea of spiritualization (*Vergeistigung*) in his book *On the Genealogy of Morality, Beyond Good and Evil, Thus Spoke Zarathustra*, and *The Antichrist(ian)* (which is a better rendition of Nietzsche's title).[11] Between these works, Nietzsche deploys his major concerns: (1) that philosophy move behind the Kantian modern subject to trace, through genealogy, the origins of subjectivity, reason and their divisions; (2) that out of this "historical philosophizing" emerge the terms of the "transvaluation" of what this history posits; (3) that genealogy leads immanently to an ethical thinking beyond the terms of the modern subject and its exclusions; and (4) that these terms reconfigure, beyond the reactive, the values of Christ and Caesar.[12] These concerns constitute lessons of spirit in the Hegelian sense. Hence, beneath the surfaces of Nietzsche's text, it is important for philosophy to seize the similarities between Hegel and Nietzsche, after Kant, as it comes to understand its own predicament and powers. These similarities are most evident in the *Genealogy*. I will focus on two instances of spirit in the second essay: the emergence of promising and the sovereign individual (GM 2: §1–3) and the formulation of the extramoral or supramoral strong community (2: §10), concluding with the Self of love in *Thus Spoke Zarathustra*. In the first we see how Nietzsche deepens Hegel's understanding of spirit; in the second two we see Nietzsche confirming spirit while transvaluating the terms of religion. This will lead to a figure of aporia from out of which I will define, between Nietzsche and Hegel, a *speculative materialism* of spirit.

In the first paragraph of the second essay of the *Genealogy* Nietzsche specifies the human as the ability to makes promises and writes:

> A promise . . . is [not] a passive inability to be rid of an impression . . . it is an active *desire* not to let go . . . it is the *will's memory*: so that a world of new things, circumstances and acts of will may be placed in between the original "I will," "I shall do" and the actual discharge of the will, its *act*, without breaking this long chain of the will. But what a lot of preconditions there are for this! In order to have that degree of control over the future, man must first have learnt to distinguish between what happens by accident, and what by design, to think causally, to view the future as the present and anticipate it, to grasp with certainty what is end and what is means, in all, to be able to calculate, compute—and before he can do this, man himself will really have to become *reliable, regular, necessary* . . . so that he, as someone making a promise, is answerable for his own *future*! (GM 39)

The paragraph succinctly enacts a genealogy of Kant's ethical and epistemological categories in the first and second *Critiques*.[13] The will of Kantian sovereignty and Enlightenment practical reason is redeveloped as a particular configuration of forces that give rise over history to the power to promise and to the person who embodies that power: the "sovereign individual" with the 'right' to make promises (GM 40). Through this history humanity learns to shape its world and itself in terms of the necessary and the accidental, cause and effect, ends, and means and ultimately, the moral and the immoral. In the following paragraphs these forces are then genealogically situated in a violent history of the technological civilization of affect (a historical "technique of mnemonics:" 41) from which the self-responsibility of humanity (saying "yes" to oneself) emerges. This history is what Nietzsche calls "spiritualization" in a reinscription of the classical understanding of spirit to mark a dialectical process of civilization between the human organism and its *Umwelt* (§5). The end result of this process so far is "The free man who has his own standard of value," who "gives his word as something which can be relied on" since "he stands upright in the face of fate," and whose awareness of himself becomes his "dominant instinct," his "conscience" (40). Nietzsche's philosophical method and the objects that this method delivers are eloquently demonstrated here.

First, the destruction of metaphysics qua the genealogy of moral value situates categories of theoretical and practical reason within history and its interconnecting constellations of force (those of technology, corporality, and affect). From out of this genealogy the sensible (in Kantian terms) is *expanded*, above and beyond its metaphysical determinations, into a series of differentiations from which categories of reflection emerge. The energetic and material disposition of promising, the forces composing this disposition and the terms of reflection upon this history are all historical differentiations of the sensible, turning within the history of human complexification/civilization. The terms of this expansion need to be clear: they announce the specificity of Nietzsche's philosophical gesture.

For Nietzsche, metaphysics consists in reversing the order of these differentiations and inverting their priority. Thus, Kant's move in the second *Critique* and in *Religion within the Boundaries of Mere Reason*[14] to place a pure will outside of time and space and to bring it into relation with sensibility as an incomprehensible instance that precedes sensibility inverts the sequence of events. The historical result of spiritualization (a sovereign individual) is removed from out of the realm of sensibility and placed back as the a priori horizon to which humanity is beholden. Kant thereby argues that the modern subject is divided between a will interested in the moral law and a will subordinated to the propensity of evil. Nietzsche calls this gesture "the reversal of cause and effect."[15] What is an effect, the provisional end of a historical process, is retrospectively placed back as the origin of this process. Derived from this origin that stands outside it, the process is thereby reduced

in its complexity and mediated history. The Nietzschean inversion (*Umdrehung*)
of this metaphysical move is not therefore to reduce the transcendental to the
empirical (as Heidegger argues[16]), nor is it simply to resituate the empirical
and the transcendental in history. By bringing both the "transcendental" and
the "empirical" back into their history of emergence, Nietzschean genealogy
develops the separation into two distinct instances *as* an inversion and accompanying simplification of the *differentiations* of *historical sensibility*. It is this
field of historical differentiations that emerges out of the philosophical "destruction" of the Kantian distinction between a pure and impure will. Nietzschean
genealogical method leads, then, to a specific way of philosophizing and a
specific philosophical object of reflection: the comprehension of the categories
of formal subjectivity within a history of spiritualization (from the biological
to the sovereign). It leads, that is, to a vast differentiation of Kantian sensibility
that must be expounded historically in order to be grasped.

Second: rewriting the Kantian moral conscience from out this history of
spiritualization, Nietzsche shows that only through such historical philosophizing can the *immanent* relations between history, knowledge, and ethics be
established. The recent anti-Hegelian wish to separate epistemology from
ethics loses Nietzschean method here. But the point goes further. This genealogy not only accounts for Kantian moral conscience in terms of a sensible
complex of historically differentiated forces: Only through such historical
philosophizing can it deliver *the terms by which this conscience is transvaluated*. The sovereign individual is not simply the Kantian moral subject.
Comprehended historically and materially in terms of force, this individual
looks forward to the "digestive power" of the overman so aware of himself
in his relation to his *Umwelt* that "wanting to take a many-sided and thorough
view of things," he can nevertheless stand decisive "in the face of fate."[17] This
sovereign embodiment (*Einverleibung*) of force delivers *amor fati* [love of
fate]. Consequently, within the terms of this history of spiritualization, Enlightenment reason and subjectivity are not, as often argued, an obstacle to
Zarathustra's children; rather, they form the very precondition of going beyond the Enlightenment in the first place. The account of the promise does
not reduce subjectivity to force; on the contrary, as *Beyond Good and Evil*
puts it, this "moral" stage of Kantian subjectivity is given its "full, if provisional rights,"[18] but awaits transvaluation into the "extramoral" through
rerelating it to *what the modern subject excludes*.

My commentary on the Nietzschean promise points to a powerful
materialist account of spirit: (1) it historicizes spirit in terms of the complexity of force in order to get at the modern subject's exclusions, thereby ex-
panding our understanding of sensibility and deepening our need to differentiate
amid life; (2) it places spirit and its categories of reflection within this history

in order to configure new relations between what is included and excluded; and (3) it points to the future of spirit through the comprehension and embodiment of this history.

These points suggest how close Nietzsche's and Hegel's philosophical gestures are. Both work from out of the abstractions of modern subjectivity bequeathed by Kant to philosophical modernity. Both work to undermine these abstractions and to place the subject on a more expansive, more accountable and, therefore, more humanly just footing through historically tracing the formations of subjectivity and their exclusions. Both call this footing "spirit," and understand spirit in terms of the *mediations* of history. Both see philosophical activity, in its mediations with the real, as seizing and rerelating that which is *separated out* by the powers of subjectivity, calling this drive for the knowledge of differences "spirit." Both seek to overcome the diremptions of life in terms of a notion of free spirit that has superseded the difference between Kantian autonomy and heteronomy. And yet both are aware as modern subjects—resentfully and nonresentfully—that such supercession can always fall back into one of its sensible differentiations. From this perspective, the opposition of Nietzschean force to Hegelian reason not only makes no sense. It obscures the intimate relation between history, epistemology, and ethics that constitutes the object of their philosophies. It is therefore important that present philosophizing reengage with this tradition of spirit.

The differences within the terms of my comparison are also clear. Nietzsche's notion of *Geist* radicalizes Kantian sensibility by reinverting it back into history qua a differentiated evolution of forces that includes conscious and unconscious motivation. Nietzsche's notion of what precedes and mediates the modern subject's *unknown* relation to itself and its environment constitutes a deepening of the terms of life with which Hegel's phenomenology of consciousness historically works. In this sense the concept of spirit is more differentiated in Nietzsche than in Hegel: which is why much postmodern thought has turned to the first to think the relations between mind and body while disavowing that these terms work within spirit. The materialist, energetic reformulation of the Hegelian "concrete" can be seen from this perspective to *further* the speculative seizure of difference behind Hegel's *specific determination* of spirit and the diremptions of life. To deepen this determination is not to curtail reason's powers; it is, precisely, to enlarge them.

That said, this perspective of radical materialism cannot account for the necessity of the religious in the way Hegel's notion of spirit does. Nietzschean genealogy analyzes religion in terms of the fear of the human organism toward its *Umwelt*. The psychological deduction of religion misses what Hegel understands by retaining the transcendence of religion over matter: religion constitutes the form in which interhuman and interliving relations return out of life's diremptions; its values are those of that return. Diremption and return are continuous with life, "eternal" in this sense. Whether one believes or not (and this is not my philosophical interest), there is thus a limit to the material, energetic deepening of Hegelian spirit and of the Nietzschean drive to seize difference nonsubjectively and nonphenomenally. This limit is to determinate life's essential inability to comprehend the manifold unity of life: that is, in abstract terms, the *speculative unity of the justice and injustice of life*. It leaves us, necessarily, in an aporia between Hegel and Nietzsche's comprehensions of subjectivity. On the one hand, Nietzsche deepens the seizure of what is excluded by subjectivity in the modern diremption of life *at the genealogical risk* of reducing the manifold of life to the law of active and reactive force. On the other hand, Hegel comprehends the relation between the manifold of life and religion *at the idealist risk* of covering over sensible differences that demand further differentiation. It is philosophically impertinent to wish to resolve this aporia. It is *the* aporia of spirit, that which makes spirit a recurrent object of philosophical reflection and invention beyond the schools of idealism and materialism. The two authorships of spirit in the work of Hegel and Nietzsche need, rather, to be thought in their differences and similarities within this aporia, which aporia is therefore *formative*. This means, contra recent philosophies of aporia that celebrate the impasse of reason, that differences should be expounded and constructed within the *speculative* identity of spirit and matter: whether one begins in life from the side of religion à la Hegel, or from the side of material force à la Nietzsche. This venture is one of *speculative materialism*.

The identity and difference of spirit between Nietzsche and Hegel emerges tellingly later in the second essay of the *Genealogy*. The moment provides my second example of Nietzschean spirit. I will conclude this section upon it.

Following the terms of the history of spiritualization Nietzsche proceeds to fill out Kantian moral conscience in terms of the historical differences of economic force (e.g., §4, 5, and 8). Guilt (*Schuld*) stems from debt (*Schulden*), and debt derives from the early history of creditor/debtor relations. These relations are transferred from the economic to the legal realm, and from the legal to the moral. The equivalence between credit and debt is mirrored in the parity between deed and punishment. Crime remains within the economy of blood-debt and revenge, where punishment is celebrated as the inverse of the initial violence. Three moments of law are then elaborated: the prelegal moment of law (revenge), the stage of the legal system and the supralegal moment of "mercy" (§5, 6, 7, 10, and 11). These three moments of law mirror those of the premoral, moral, and extramoral morality (§32 of *Beyond Good and Evil*). In the prelegal only the *consequences* of the deed have import for the society in which the lawbreaker has perpetrated his or her deed: the question of justice remains one of security, of duties to the community, not of rights to the individual. In the "moral" stage of penal legality, categories of legal judgment have emerged with those of subjectivity. The "wrongdoer is shielded" from the revenge of the injured and the community through the separation of doer and deed, subject, and act. In the supralegal moment, society is figured as one that has "attained such a consciousness of power that it could allow itself the noblest luxury possible to it": letting the criminal go unpunished. Nietzsche continues:

> Justice which began by saying "Everything can be paid off, everything must be paid off," ends by turning a blind eye and letting off those unable to pay—it ends like every good thing on earth by sublimating itself [*sich aufhebend*]. The self-sublimation of justice [*diese Selbst-Aufhebung der Gerechtigkeit*]—we know what a nice name it gives itself—*mercy* [*Gnade*]: it remains of course the prerogative of the most powerful man, better his way of going beyond the law [*sein Jenseits des Rechts*]. (GM 50–51; SW 5: 308–9)

This description of the development of law is Hegelian in method and logic: law is traced through historically in its separations (custom and subjectivity) to the point where a figure of law emerges that supersedes these separations. This *Aufhebung* is ironically described in semireligious terms: those of mercy. Nietzsche cannot not present this apex of legal spiritualization, however, except in terms that collude with the religious and the spiritual. To go beyond positive law (*Recht*) is to go beyond the modern subject and its rights and interests, bringing the political and moral (in Kantian terms) into an identity that finds its precipitate in the legislator's supermoral act of grace. This act is only possible because of the community's own strength: it is therefore not simply the deed of individual will to power, of an aristocratic overman; rather, it forms the individual actualization, the individual *embodiment* of the community's potential strength. This identity of the political and moral in the legislator's mercy is nevertheless contingent: the premoral can *always* return, and security as the legal counterpart to the premoral can become again the spirit of a community in a spiral of violence. This act of mercy refers, then, to a community of spirit in which the morality of religion *has not been destroyed*, but *aufgehoben* (negated, conserved and superseded).

This *Aufhebung* of the law returns Nietzsche to the necessity of religious categories as much as it transvaluates these categories: it is *one and the same* gesture, re-cognizing philosophically what the eternal return of the "religious" mis-recognizes—life. The same *Aufhebung* is found in those sections of *Thus Spoke Zarathustra* where Nietzsche speaks of the Self as a transformation of the distinction between spirit and sense, ego and body, and of the bestowing gift of love as a transformation of the distinction between egoism and altruism ("Of the Despisers of the Body," "Of Love of One's Neighbor," and "Of the Bestowing Virtue").[19] These passages carefully underline the ethics of transvaluated love, conjoining with this account of overhuman mercy, which emerge from the history of spiritualization.

> Sense and spirit are instruments and toys: behind them lies the Self. The Self seeks with the eyes of the senses, it hears with the ears of the spirit.[20]

> You compel all things to come to you and into you that they may flow back from your fountain as gifts of your love.
>
> Truly such a bestowing love must become a thief of all values; but I call this Selfishness healthy and holy. . . .
>
> Our sense is upwards, from the species to the over-species . . . your body is elevated and resurrected; it enraptures the spirit with its joy, that it may become creator, evaluator, lover and benefactor of all things.[21]

The loving Self is the *Aufhebung* of Christian love: coming from behind the New Testament distinction behind spirit and sense, it refashions and exceeds in materialist energetic mode the distinction between spiritual selflessness and corporal self-love, inverting the one into the other and moving, in thought and act, beyond the inversion. The loving Self is an individual so aware of him and herself, so aware that he and she embody forces beyond their ego *as* him and herselves that he and she are able to give to others. The love of the other rests upon this rich *Selbst-sucht*, the fruit of long labor. It is the same rich selfishness that takes the legislator beyond positive *Recht* and makes possible the promise of the sovereign individual, a promise that emerged first in the external constraint of premoral cruelty. The beyond of positive law fulfills, in genealogico-energetic vein, those of Christian love.

Nietzsche's genealogy of spirit is rational and aporetic. It is rational because it looks for differences, articulates them, and it relates the various fields of human activity from out of this articulation within the spiral of spiritualization, forging *thereby* relations *between* epistemological differentiation and ethical construction. It is aporetic because, first, genealogy must recognize *from within* religious disposition (mercy, love, and spirit) the supra-ethical disposition of emergent free spirituality, and, second, *qua* (the disposition of) philosophy, it knows it does not *embody* it. Genealogy expounds nevertheless that this supra-ethics is immanent, historical, and that the spirit of mercy grows out of its other, cruelty. It expounds that this growth is divided within itself, slow to heal, and always contingent. In other words, Zarathustra names no "*reverse* experiment" (GM 70), but an historical experiment, worked at and shaped *from out of modern subjectivity and its exclusions.*

Thus, in its specific historical constellation, Nietzsche must repeatedly figure, as the hard repetitions of *Thus Spoke Zarathustra* make clear, the future of ethics from out of the transvaluation of the Christian values of mercy and love.

In this sense, the philosophical similarities and differences between Hegel and Nietzsche just underscored meet in the chiasmatic figure of spirit (love of life). In this figure, the articulation of difference, deep within life, is not eschewed; it is the privileged object of philosophy in its attempt—as a sober, but joyful determination of life—to open up a relation between the knowledge of the human and the love of the human. Since, for both Hegel and Nietzsche, but from different ends of the spectrum of spirit, life is never complete, but always present, this opening of life will always occasion further inversion and diremption. Hence why this knowledge and this love are for both, simultaneously, *beyond* the human—*amor fati*.

Freud, Marx, and Spirit

It is in these similarities of historical method, object, and end that present philosophy needs to refind the gesture of thought that allows for critical intervention in the world. For it is only through comprehending the exclusions of the modern subject out of history that the future of this subject can be sought. In this third part, I look at two crucial gestures to do this, those of Freud and Marx, on the basis of the figure of speculative materialism to which the work between Hegel and Nietzsche's notions of spirit takes critical philosophizing.

It is clear that Freud furthers Nietzsche's articulation of difference behind the modern subject and what it excludes. The unconscious constitutes the psychological precipitate of civilization's diremptions. Freud thereby reinforces the spiritual concept of life (as an historically dirempted manifold) and the need for critical thought to confront this "ever-present," but nonconceptualizable life from out of its diremptions. Freud's place within the post-Kantian tradition of spirit is located in his rerelating of the unconscious with the conscious qua life. Deepening further Nietzsche's enlarged genealogy of sensibility, individual, and mass psychologies are Freudian names for the identity and difference between the human organism and its *Umwelt*. Freud's exposition of the unconscious presents a phenomenology of what are the inversions of exclusion and return in predominantly modern subjectivity. An account of such inversions leads to a series of metapsychological and cultural papers in which what is excluded and included is reconfigured as the process of the human organism's historical growth. Freud is thus seen to develop Nietzsche's genealogical, energetic materialism (spiritualization) by further elaborating the terms of this growth and further differentiating the affective expressions of it.

Given this, Freud also understands the spiritual "values" of guilt and conscience in terms of the evolution of the human organism. He argues in *Civilization and Its Discontents*[22] that this history is one of the *internalization* of force and that the civilization of the individual (Nietzsche's history of responsibility) is at one and the same time the invention of the subject and the deepening of guilt. For Freud also, moral freedom and guilt are inseparable, two sides of the same coin of interiorization. The desire to break from civilization to offload one's conscience is the *necessary* underbelly of modern subjectivity. Freud's differentiation of the affective distinguishes itself from Nietzsche's genealogy of conscience, however, in the account of this interiorization. This difference is important for pursuing further a material notion of spirit because it attempts to comprehend the place of the religious in collective life there where Nietzsche consigns it too quickly to the reactive. This is where I am interested in the Freudian gesture.

For Freud, the biological organism is driven by two opposing drives: that toward increasing growth, that toward death (an earlier state of things). The more an organism grows, the more it also regresses. Freud's hypothesis is written in speculative mode.[23] With more recent work within physics and biology on the metabolic principles of animate and inanimate systems, Freud's hypothesis can be predicated on the theories of entropy and negentropy. A biological organism is one that "lives" off a constant source of energy; without such a source biological life returns to matter. The drive to return to an earlier state of things is, in this light, a resistance to the further differentiation of matter consequent upon new sources of energy. All life moves within a fundamental tension between entropic and negentropic forces. Freud interpreted this tension within human biological organisms as that between the drive to death and the tendency to life. Life is therefore from the beginning in tension with itself: it cannot be reduced, as Nietzsche wishes, to pure activity.

Moral conscience is accordingly not the internalization of an initial active force that returns upon the subject and therefore aggresses it. Since life is from the first dualistic, conscience constitutes the internalization of a force that was initially *within the organism* as an internal biological tendency. This force, the death drive, is projected out as aggression and then reinternalized as conscience. Conscience is thus the inheritance of the death drive within the instances of the subject. This offers a more radically materialist account of spirit than Nietzsche's *affective* account of conscience affords. It seizes the spiritual values of conscience and guilt *within* a biological theory of life that *at the same time* allows for the Nietzschean process of spiritualization (the history of conscience and responsibility as a movement between organism and *Umwelt*). Freud thereby supplements Nietzsche's historical seizure of differences, tracing how the living organism is from the beginning divided within itself, and expounding how this division will have a necessary influence on the dialectic that emerges between the organism and its environment. The example of religion brilliantly shows this.

Religion is, for Freud, the receptacle of guilt: it is a form of spiritual life that embraces the death-drive in the human organism. The division between eternal life and sin, between a good will and an evil will in Christianity, constitutes, therefore, a *highly spiritualized derivative* of the *biological tension between the drive to growth and the drive to an earlier, more quiescent state of things*. This tension between two "selves" within the living organism accounts for the importance of the figure of Christ and his religion. What Christ promises is redemption from the self-inflicted violence of the death drive ("guilt"). Nietzsche's account of life, however mediated *qua* spiritualization, misses this "biological" dimension to religion since his notion of force is not differentiated enough internally. Consequently the form of religion (not, as we have seen, its values) is reduced to a simplistic psychological mechanism of fear and is disregarded in *The Antichrist(ian)* as unable to account for the complexity of reality.[24] Freud shows us however from within the spirit of Nietzsche's own biological materialism that the form of religion may be understood as, precisely, addressing the forces of the human organism. He thereby not only offers further differentiation to Nietzsche's development of historical energetics, he grasps the highest spiritual *forms* from within that development *there where* Nietzsche's unitary understanding of the source of affective force cannot. The further development of the religious in these terms of the collective unconscious is called for by the contemporary return of religious form from out the diremptions of twentieth century life. It points to where Freud's depth psychological comprehension of the individual and collective diremption of life will always allow for the return of the religious, redeploying the aporetic tension between Hegel and Nietzsche's expositions of spirit: *further* differentiation of the sensible *within* the nonconfigureable manifold of life.

The return of religious form in contemporary life is due in part to the Marxist suppression of the religious in the twentieth century consequent upon the nineteenth century's critique of religion *qua* alienation. Marx's own version of this critique[25] is one with his philosophical move to stand Hegelian dialectic on its head and reroot spirit in matter. Given my exposition of the continued force of speculative thinking for critical thought today and of the importance of the further differentiation of substance for the future of ethics and politics, it is clear that this essay cannot but end with Marx. My exposition points to what Marx we inherit for the construction of the future.

The first section suggested that the lack of speculative thinking today in the culture of contemporary philosophy is all the more serious given that present economic force keeps things apart. Marx's inheritance of the phenomenological method in *Grundrisse* and *Capital*[26] constituted the first attempt in modern history to expound the autonomization of modern socioeconomic life in such a way that its tensions and contradictions could be seized for critical intervention and transformation. These works remain the model of critical philosophy as I understand it at the beginning of this essay. Contemporary philosophy has often turned away from this model because of the "metaphysics" within this method and the ontology of labor and political practice (the subject of the proletariat as a universal social agency) that dog it. My retrieval of speculative thinking and spirit from Hegel and Nietzsche's understandings of philosophy has delivered up a method, a historical way of rehearsing this method and an ethical end to this activity. The critical method of *Grundrisse* and *Capital* work strongly within the parameters of this retrieval if one eschews their economism and productivism. This means that philosophy needs to take up again Marx's *gesture* of thought.

This gesture consists in seizing the object of philosophy *as* the economy (the economic continuum of sensibility) and speculatively expounding—through its history—its relations, exclusions, and contradictions with regard to life as a whole. In doing so, the contemporary organization of the economic (both theoretical and practical) will be recognized immanently as fragmentary understandings of experience and law and thereby lifted into a larger understanding of social life from which critical transformation is again possible. This critical project of Marx has been abandoned in recent years for reasons just intimated: the fates of Marxism, the reductionism of Marxian materialism, the saturation of civil society in totalitarian "communism," and Marx's ontology of labor. Such abandonment confuses the *gesture* of the critical project with classical philosophical and economic traits within it. Much contemporary philosophy has committed this confusion on the basis of its nonspeculative understanding of the comprehension of difference. It is time not to repeat Marx, but to reinvent Marx's gesture so that it can speculatively work on contemporary economic tendencies of capital and contemporary diremptions of life (society, culture, religion, and the collective unconscious) from out of their historical and present formations. In terms of the speculative development of world capitalism(s), this implies, schematically put, two moves:

On the one hand: it means, first, holding onto Marx's historical materialism there where he works economic sensibility up into the terms of modern life, and deriving from present economic rationality and irrationality developed laws of economic causation across the human, the social, and the natural. It means, *second*, so tracing these laws that those who suffer from their lack of articulation are empowered by this knowledge. In this sense philosophy should reengage with the Marxian gesture of thought to work towards the greater transparency of difference, toward a "just society." It also means, therefore, holding to the Marxian value of social democracy as a horizon of sociality and spirit that is uncovered through the modern diremptions of life under capital.[27]

On the other hand, it means speculatively rethinking the Marxian gesture through, and beyond, the *relevant* objects and tools of analysis of modern economic reflection. As far as I am aware, this had not been done *in comprehensive, speculative fashion*: it is indeed a very large project. Philosophers are nervous about entering the domain of the economy today, keeping rather their critical attention to the cultural and the aesthetic, and becoming thereby more abstracted from their fellow citizens (human life!). Economists are, inversely, wary of comprehending economic force in general given (1) the intense specialization and division of intellectual labor in economics, and (2) the economic parameters of scarcity and growth in a highly integrated world economic system. As a result, people are increasingly split between the utopianism and/ or voluntarism of justice and the inhuman complexity of the economic system. *Only* in seizing the matter of the economy as a fragmented part of life will new thoughts and new strategies emerge to change this situation. This is the lesson of spirit that I have rehearsed here. It is most telling today with regard to rerelating, in the Hegelian and Nietzschean sense, spirit, and the economy. Such a critique needs a large space of interdisciplinary investigation between, at least, economics, history, international political theory, sociology, anthropology, and the environmental sciences. Interdisciplinarity presents a provisional step to this space, but the telling gesture will be to hold these connections *within* a concrete spiritual sense of knowledge, community, and individuality. This gesture has yet to be invented. Teased out of the increasing command of the economy and of its dissipative powers, the university could become again the place, and places, of such speculative thinking. Without the latter, displaced social agents, militants, and citizens may remain disinherited. This project would thereby rerelate knowledge, responsibility, and citizenship in a transformation of the Marxian insight toward the reconstruction of ethical life and spirit.

Notes

1. G. W. F. Hegel, "Spirit of Christianity and Its Fate," in *Early Theological Writings*, trans. T. M. Knox (Philadelphia: University of Pennsylvania Press, 1971), 182–301, hereafter cited as SC; Hegel, *Phenomenology of Spirit*, trans. A. V. Miller (Oxford University Press, 1977).

2. The following essay, breaking with my sense of philosophy in *Derrida and the Political* (London: Routledge, 1996), works with the arguments of the "strong" Hegelianism of the late British philosopher Gillian Rose toward a speculative exposition of contemporary economic life. See her reading of Hegel in *Hegel Contra*

Sociology (London: Athlone, 1981) and her speculative developments of law in *The Broken Middle. Out of Our Ancient Society* (Oxford: Blackwell, 1992); and Rose, *Judaism and Modernity. Philosophical Essays* (Oxford: Blackwell, 1993).

3. Jacques Derrida *Glas*, trans. John P. Leavey Jr. and Richard Rand (Lincoln: University of Nebraska Press, 1986), 34–93.

4. Ibid., 238–45.

5. Hegel, *Philosophy of History*, trans. J. Sibree (New York: Dover, 1956).

6. Hegel, *Philosophy of Right*, trans. T. M. Knox (Oxford: Oxford University Press, 1981), 13.

7. Rose, *Hegel Contra Sociology*, 65–69.

8. Hegel, *Phenomenology*, 14.

9. Ibid., 18–19.

10. Friedrich Nietzsche, *Human, All Too Human. A Book For Free Spirits*, 2d ed., trans. R. J. Hollingdale (Cambridge University Press, 1996); Nietzsche, *Daybreak. Thoughts on the Prejudices of Morality*, trans. R. J. Hollingdale (Cambridge University Press, 1982); Nietzsche, *The Gay Science*, trans. W. Kaufmann (New York: Random, 1974).

11. Nietzsche, *Thus Spoke Zarathustra*, trans. R. J. Hollingdale (London: Penguin, 1961); Nietzsche, *Twilight of the Idols/The Anti-Christ*, trans. R. J. Hollingdale (London: Penguin, 1968); Nietzsche, *Beyond Good and Evil. Prelude to a Philosophy of the Future*, trans. Hollingdale (London: Penguin, 1974); Nietzsche, *On the Genealogy of Morality*, ed. K. Ansell-Pearson, trans. C. Diethe (Cambridge University Press, 1994). *Genealogy* is hereafter cited as GM. Subsequent German references are to the *Sämtliche Werke. Kritische Studienausgabe*, eds. Georgio Colli and Mazzino Montinari (Munich: DTV, 1988), hereafter cited as SW.

12. These themes are developed in unaporetic fashion in Richard Beardsworth; *Nietzsche* (Paris: Les Belles Lettres, 1997); and Beardsworth, "Nietzsche, Nihilism and Spirit," in *Nihilism Now. Monsters of Energy*, eds. K. Ansell-Pearson and D. Morgan (London: Macmillan, 2000).

13. Immanuel Kant, *Critique of Pure Reason*, trans. Norman Kemp Smith (London: Macmillan, 1929); Kant, *Critique of Practical Reason*, trans. T. K. Abbott (New York: Prometheus Books, 1996).

14. Kant, *Religion within the Boundaries of Mere Reason*, trans. Allen Wood and George Di Giovanni (Cambridge: Cambridge University Press, 1998).

15. Nietzsche, *Twilight of the Idols*, 58–65; Nietzsche, *Genealogy*, §11 and 12.

16. Heidegger, *Nietzsche*, vols. 1–4, trans. D. F. Krell (San Francisco: Harper, 1991).

17. Nietzsche, *Beyond Good and Evil*, 141–42.

18. Ibid., 47.

19. Nietzsche, *Zarathustra*, 61–63, 86–88, 99–104.

20. Ibid., 62.

21. Ibid., 101–2.

22. Freud, *Civilization and Its Discontents*, in *Penguin Freud Library*, vol. 12 (London: Penguin, 1991), 243–340.

23. Freud, "Beyond the Pleasure Principle," in ibid., vol. 10 (London: Penguin, 1991), 269–338.

24. Nietzsche, *Anti-Christ*, §46 and 47.

25. Marx, "A Contribution to the Critique of Hegel's Philosophy of Right," in *Early Writings*, trans. Rodney Livingstone (London: Penguin, 1975), 243–57.

26. Marx, *Grundrisse*, trans. Martin Nicolaus (London: Penguin, 1973); Marx, *Capital*, 3 vols., trans. Ben Fowkes and David Fernbach (London: Penguin, 1976–81).

27. "On the Jewish Question" in Hegel, *Early Theological Writings*, 211–42.

Conclusion: Without Absolutes

∿

Arkady Plotnitsky

The title of this volume, "Idealism without Absolutes," is a conjunction of two apparent opposites, idealism and the lack of absolutes accompanying it, since idealism is customarily conjoined or even defined by one or another form of absoluteness. As, however, the essays here assembled argue, individually and collectively, the opposition is only apparent, at least in certain, but, philosophically and culturally (including politically), arguably decisive, circumstances. Indeed these circumstances make idealism without absolutes not only possible but also rigorously inevitable. The same argument may also, and correlatively, be made concerning the other pair of apparent opposites that define the argument of this volume, idealism and materiality, if not materialism. This opposition is more common and persistent but is also more radically *subverted* by this argument. (I would be hesitant to speak of deconstruction in this case, although certain deconstruction[s], in their various senses, are involved in this subversion.) It may be recalled that *materiality* itself is broadly defined by this volume as the subversion (it can take diverse forms) and the ultimate suspension of absolutes, idealist, or materialist, or at least *absolute* absolutes, since certain limited, relative absolutes remain inevitable and some of them useful and effective.

The volume's title is also a peculiar but (this case would be easier to argue) inevitable mixture of history and philosophy, with culture and specifically Romantic culture added on courtesy of the subtitle, "Philosophy and Romantic Culture" (a similar mixture of its own) and further complicating the mix. More rigorously, one ought to speak of a cluster or mixture of mixtures. For each of these denominations—history, philosophy, and

241

culture—is already a mixture, including, as Hegel taught us, by virtue of ineluctably involving two other terms of this triad. The mixing and denominative expansion hardly stop there, however, and are ultimately uncontainable. Most immediately, "idealism" is an historical reference to a certain post-Kantian or post-Cartesian philosophical tradition, usually named "idealism," or "German Idealism," also known as critical philosophy. The latter is arguably a better name, especially if one fundamentally links, as this volume does, the critical force of this philosophy to materiality, with or without matter (as the readers of this volume would know, it may be both). There are, however, good reasons for the using the name "Idealism" for this tradition, although it is also used, indeed more often, for wrong reasons as well. So much depends here on how one conceives of idealism, in particular whether it is defined as being with or, conversely, without absolutes, and on how one reads the key figures involved. "Idealism without absolutes" is primarily a philosophical concept or set of concepts, collectively developed in this volume, including in Gilles Deleuze and Felix Guattari's sense or concept of (philosophical) concept, introduced in their book *What Is Philosophy?* which defines philosophy itself as invention of new concepts.[1] From this perspective, this volume is both an exploration and a practice of philosophy, and I would like by way of conclusion to outline the structure or architecture of the concept of "idealism without absolutes" here developed as I see it.

It is fitting to begin by observing that, as must be apparent from the foregoing essays (beginning with the introduction), the dissolution of absolutes is where critical idealism and critical materialism, indeed many a critical materialism and many a critical idealism, interactively work together or against each other, but always, jointly, against absolutes. In the idiom of this volume, they are joined in a certain form of *materiality*, rather than materialism, unless the latter involves the same type of materiality as well, in other words, is coupled to idealism without absolutes. The plurality just invoked is essential and ultimately irreducible (Jacques Derrida would speak of dissemination) and is part of the critical force of idealism(s), materialist idealism(s), and idealist materialism(s), without absolutes. Whatever the initial term or cluster of terms (e.g., that of *ideality* and *materiality*), the workings of this irreducible multiplicity inevitably bring other terms into play and, equally inevitably, prevent any actual or potential conceptual or phenomenal (en)closure. Such an enclosure would inevitably reinstate an absolute, however (humanly) inaccessible it might be.

One can put it more strongly and rigorously as follows. Once we suspend absolutes, the irreducibly multiple also entails and possibly results from the irreducible loss in knowledge in all our theorizing and indeed in all cognition. This loss in knowledge or, to use Georges Bataille's term, this unknowledge (*nonsavoir*) inhabits and inhibits any possible knowledge.[2] It even affects knowledge concerning the impossibility of knowledge, since neither what can nor what cannot be known can any longer be guaranteed. Under the conditions of knowledge and/as idealism without absolutes (idealist or materialist, divine or human, or inhuman, say, those reducing the world to some ultimate constituents of nature, some [absolutely] elementary particles), the unknowable becomes irreducible not only in practice, which may be the case once absolutes are in place, but also and most fundamentally in principle. There is no knowledge in principle available to us, now or ever, which would allow us to eliminate the unknowable and replace it with some conception of actually or possibly knowable reality behind it. Nor, however, can one postulate a structured and especially causal economy of this reality, as unknown or even unknowable but existing, in and by itself, outside our engagement with it, which economy would, in any event, involve an implicit modeling on something that we know. This second prohibition (correlative to the suspension of metaphysical realism, idealist or materialist, at the ultimate level of description) is crucial. For some forms of absolutist idealism, or materialism, in philosophy or elsewhere, in mathematics and science, for example, allow for, and are often defined by, this type of assumption. By contrast, the unknowledge that I invoke here is not only unexplainable in practice and in principle but is also irreducible in practice and in principle, irreducible to any unconditional (absolute) reality or necessity, knowable or unknowable. It follows that, rigorously, this unknowable cannot be named "unknowable," or "unnamable," anymore than Samuel Beckett's "unnamable" in *The Unnamable*. In sum, this unnamable unknowable—unnamable even as unnamable, unknowable even as unknowable—coupled to the irreducibly multiple, is ineluctable in all our theoretical or cognitive processes. And yet it is also essential to any knowledge we might have and to the very possibility of knowledge.

This type of argument was crucial to the work of the key twentieth-century figures defining the argumentation of this volume, from Nietzsche on. It was also at least made inevitable, if not actually made, by Kant (perhaps especially on the sublime, a great inspiration for twentieth-century anti-absolutist thought) and Hegel. Their thought, especially once amplified by that of their fellow idealist philosophers or that of Romanticism, still governs, albeit not absolutely, the landscape of modern and then postmodern and, by now, post-post-modern philosophy and culture, in part by shaping the genealogy of the concept of unknowledge and the argument concerning its role, as just outlined. The degree to which this type of concept and argument is actually developed by the major representatives of Idealism themselves is a matter of complex interpretive decisions and argumentation. Accordingly, that some versions of this argument in the essays assembled here or in certain works, such as those of Derrida and Paul de Man, that these essays consider would sometimes use Kant and Hegel, or other Romantic and Idealist figures, against each other is hardly surprising, and adds strength, complexity, and richness to the argument itself in question. One could trace the effects and the very workings of this argument throughout the present volume at all levels. They extend from what de Man called "dismemberment [or disarticulation] of language" and "dismemberment of the body," and their many interactions (including those defined by, and defining the interplay of, phenomenality and materiality) to the multiple-heterogeneously interactive and interactively heterogeneous-fields and disciplinary crossings or mixtures.[3] The very question of language or the body, or, one might add, technology, and of the relationships among them, would require and has received a radical reconsideration from this viewpoint, including in de Man's own work, although many other figures, beginning, again, with Nietzsche, may be mentioned here, such as Jacques Lacan or Derrida. De Man, it may be observed, opens his "Phenomenality and Materiality in Kant" (in AI) with remarks on the relationships between critical philosophy and ideology, extending from the eighteenth century to our own time. The question of these relationships is far from closed. It may be argued, however, that it is also the question of idealism or materialism with absolutes (ideology?) versus those without absolutes (critical philosophy?), which could be traced to de Man's earlier juxtaposition of symbol and allegory. In any event, a different form of theoretical or, ultimately, all cognition, and of conceptual and (they are never absolutely dissociable) linguistic organization is at stake.

Rather than "organic," as in the case of "symbol," whereby the parts and the whole are harmonized together within and by the same law, this organization may be seen as "allegorical" in de Man's sense. As such, it is juxtaposed to all classical organicism, including that of conceptual or discursive organization, just as de Man's allegory is juxtaposed to the (absolutist) organicism of the symbol. Symbol is arguably the primary trope of organicism, or of aesthetic ideology, roughly from Winckelmann, Goethe, and Schiller on, and is one of de Man's main targets from his pioneering "Rhetoric of Temporality" on. In commenting on Coleridge in "The Rhetoric of Temporality," de Man writes: "The symbol is the product of organic growth of form; in the world of the symbol, life and form are identical. . . . Its [symbol's] structure is that of the synecdoche, for the symbol is always part of the totality that it represents. Consequently, in the symbolic imagination, no disjunction of the constitutive faculties takes place, since the material perception and the symbolic imagination are continuous, as the part is continuous with the whole."[4] De Man sharpens this argument in addressing Hegel's more subtle and rigorous view, the view ultimately problematizing the absolutes of Hegel's and of all idealism, in "Sign and Symbol in Hegel's *Aesthetics*" and elsewhere in *Aesthetic Ideology* and in other later works. The essence of the argument, however, remains in place, and may be *translated* into the idiom of the present discussion as follows. This idiom and hence also conceptualities are, admittedly, not de Man's own, and this difference must be kept in mind. Hence I speak of "translation" here.

The organic totality of the whole, continuity, causality, nonarbitrariness of representation, and so forth are all concepts enabling and governing the epistemology of absolutist idealisms (or absolutist materialisms). The suspension of absolutes, taken to its rigorous limits (which are also those of de Man's allegory), inevitably fissures this epistemology. Indeed it often does so (deconstructively) from within the concept or inscription of the ideal or the absolute (e.g., that of the symbol), since, as de Man shows, such an inscription, once rigorously pursued, is never able to escape this fissure, or allegory. Nor, as a result, can the (customary) hierarchy of symbol and allegory ever be unambiguously maintained even by the greatest and the most rigorous theorists of the symbol, and especially by them, since their rigor prevents them from doing so, even if against themselves. "The Rhetoric of Temporality" sets de Man's program in motion: "Whereas the symbol postulates the possibility of an identity or identification, allegory designates primarily a distance in relation to its own origin, and, renouncing the nostalgia and the desire to coincide, it establishes its language in the void of this temporal difference" (BI 207). One might cite a number of epistemologically parallel passages in other authors, from (and before) Nietzsche on, whose work is key to the present volume. Some, such as Jean-François Lyotard, or de Man himself, would link this type of epistemology to that of Kant's sublime. At a certain point the distance and, as it were, disidentification of allegory or of idealism without absolutes in general inevitably, ineluctably invades the field of the symbol or of the ideal, without, however, dissolving this field (in either case), but rigorously delimiting and limiting it.

The discursive and theoretical organization or disorganization (later de Man will speak of "disfiguration") becomes subject to the same radical fissure. Thus, for example, according to de Man, in Hegel, "aesthetic theory and art history are the two *complementary* parts of a single *symbolon*" (*Aesthetic Ideology*, 93, emphasis added). It would be difficult to ascertain whether de Man also had in mind here Niels Bohr's complementarity, his interpretation of quantum mechanics, defined by the same type of fissured epistemology, in which complementary "parts" never add up to a single whole, rather than an organicist one, where they do. It would, however, also be difficult to think that he did not have something like it in mind, given (beyond the fact that he was familiar with the epistemology of quantum theory) where this view eventually leads him, namely, to the workings of allegory, invading Hegel's project. This trajectory extends to "Hegel on the Sublime" (AI 105–18). In "Sign and Symbol in Hegel's *Aesthetics*" de Man closes as follows:

> We would have to conclude that Hegel's philosophy, which, like his *Aesthetics*, is a philosophy of history (and of aesthetics) as well as

a history of philosophy (and of aesthetics)—and the Hegelian corpus indeed contains texts that bear these two symmetrical titles—is in fact an allegory of the disjunction between philosophy and history, or . . . between literature and aesthetics, or . . . literary experience and literary theory. The reasons for this disjunction . . . are not themselves historical or recoverable by way of history. To the extent that they are inherent in language, in the necessity, which is also an impossibility, to connect the subject with its predicates or the sign with its symbolic significations, the disjunction will always, as it did in Hegel, manifest itself as soon as experience shades into thought, history into theory. (AI 104)

In other words, even if Hegel aims (a complex question) at the symbolic "complementarity" harmonizing the parts within the whole of his immense project, he ends with an allegorical, irreducibly disjunctive, complementarity, which experience and history inevitably bring into his thought and his theoretical project. This is not to say that this allegorical complementarity is disorganized, any more than quantum theory is vis-à-vis classical physics. Instead at stake is a different form of organization, which, I argue, defines de Man's own, even if not Hegel's, discursive practice, as it does those of other major figures here invoked, from Nietzsche to Derrida, and beyond, and, following them, those of the essays of this volume.

To give a brief summary (I can do no more here) of this fissured, allegorical organization, the particular elements involved (e.g., those of aesthetics, rhetoric, epistemology, politics, or of reading) interact and are organized: that is, we may meaningfully consider collective configurations of them as having structure or order. This organization, however, does not govern (as the symbolic or other forms of classical wholeness would) these elements in their individuality or particularity, at the limit—ultimately to the point of defying any attempt to define them by any denomination and thus making each unique or singular. Accordingly, the same dynamic is found already among particular elements within any given denomination, to the degree that each can be contained within itself. The theories and readings here assembled continuously submit to and enact this dynamic, and expose it in the works read in this volume. They do so even as, and by virtue of the fact that, they equally submit and pursue that which escapes even this (far-reaching) dynamic or, for that matter, anything and everything; that which is irreducibly inaccessible, indeed inaccessible even as inaccessible or as "that." Once our idealisms or our materialisms—our materialist idealism, our idealist materialism—give up as they must, all absolutes, the efficacity of the interplay of the (organized) collective and (singular) particular elements or "effects," or of each effect in question, to begin with, may also be irreducibly inaccessible in the same sense. In other words, as I have stressed here, it precisely brings together the irreducible multiplicity and the irreducible incompleteness of knowledge. But it also makes them the conditions of all knowledge, thus always irreducibly without absolutes, always irreducibly inconclusive. "The difficulty of allegory," de Man argues, "is . . . that [an] emphatic clarity of representation does not stand in the service of something that can be represented" (AI 51). Indeed it may be said to stand in the service of that which cannot be represented by any means, is intolerant of attribution of any properties, and is ultimately beyond any conception or phenomenalization, while, at the same time, having the irreducible multiplicity of concepts as its ultimate effect.

In other words, allegory is defined, specifically as against symbol, jointly or reciprocally, by both unknowledge and multiplicity, interactive, and yet heterogeneous—interactively heterogeneous and heterogeneously interactive. Part of the argument of this volume is that this concept of allegory (in this specificity, for it can be and have been conceived otherwise, along with and through different types of reading de Man's work) applies to Idealism, or we may now say (given this phrase a new meaning), Romantic Idealism. In particular, Romantic interdisciplinarity becomes defined allegorically in this sense, for example, through multileveled translations of disciplines from within and from without, rather than their (absolute) synthesis.

This view has major historical significance and major conceptual and cultural implications. I have already mentioned the "complementarity" (which is another name for the relationships in question) of aesthetic theory and art history in Hegel invoked by de Man. We may extend or (in either sense) *complement* it by considering, following some of the essays of this volume such as those by Jan Plug and Andrzej Warminski, by considering the way in which history, first, that of Romanticism and/as Romantic interdisciplinarity, becomes related to, and understood through, art history in this allegorical matrix. Historically, this juncture is, as we have seen, crucial as well, in particular given the question of the relationships between symbol and allegory in Winckelmann, Goethe, Schiller, and elsewhere in Romantic culture of the time, and then in Hegel's *Aesthetics*, as considered by de Man. The irreducible allegorical structure of Romantic interdisciplinary does not and cannot aim at a "symbolic" *Gesammtkunstwerk* [total artwork]. As a result, the relationships between history and art history, and, again, between either or both with aesthetic theory, become heterogeneously interactive and interactively heterogeneous, under the general conditions of unknowledge, rather than subsuming one another (in either direction) or being both subsumed within a larger economy of (absolute) synthesis, dialectical, or other. It is this type of argument, at various junctures and on various scales, that the key Idealist and Romantic figures considered in this volume bring to bear, sometimes against their own grain, on what we would now see in terms of interdisciplinarity, as Hegel does, for example, in exploring the relationships between history and philosophy, with which I began here. But then much more is at stake (conceptually, disciplinarily, terminologically, and still otherwise) in each of these denominations and, this is the main point, in the relationships between them and the efficacious allegorical dynamics of these relationships.

One of the premises and the arguments of this volume is that this type of allegorical organization and its practice at whatever level (conceptual, discursive, disciplinary, or still other) are epistemologically, philosophically, and culturally Romantic. Indeed it may be argued to define Romanticism and Romantic culture. By the same token, this argument (with its full scope defined by this volume in mind) gives the concept of Romantic culture a new historical and philosophical meaning, which extends this denomination from its pre-Kantian past to our own culture and beyond, without, at the same time, depriving it of its historical genealogy in Idealism and its confrontation with absolutes. Accordingly, I would like, by way of conclusion, a conclusion to a conclusion, to turn from "cold philosophy" to Romantic poetry and Romantic culture, in this case the poetry and culture of John Keats (from whom I borrow the phrase "cold philosophy"), even though philosophy, poetry, and culture may come much closer, including in Keats's own work, than he is willing to allow. Keats famously writes in *Lamia*:

> . . . Do not all charms fly
> At the mere touch of cold philosophy?
> There was an awful rainbow once in heaven:
> We know her woof, her texture; she is given
> In the dull catalogue of common things.
> Philosophy will clip an Angel's wings,
> Conquer all mysteries by rule and line,
> Empty the haunted air, and gnomed mine. . . .
> Unweave a rainbow. . . .
>
> *(Lamia)*

Keats may well be right about fleeing charms, although the loss of charm alone may not be the greatest sacrifice here. The remainder of the passage, however, has proved to be, at least for the moment, among the least prophetic of Keats's insights, although he might delight in his failure. But only "might," since he might not want cold philosophy to ever arrive, however slowly, where poetry gets so quickly, by being content in its negative capability with half-knowledge and guided by beauty, obliterating all [philosophical?] considerations. Here, as Keats has both Isaac Newton and especially René Descartes in mind, philosophy is also natural philosophy or science, or what we now call "modern (and specifically mathematical) science." As, however, is clear from the poem itself, more than only science and indeed primarily philosophy, is, reciprocally, a model for and is modeled on this science. Descartes, both a paradigmatic modern philosopher and (along with Francis Bacon, Galileo, and Newton) a paradigmatic modern mathematician and scientist may here be read as also a sign and even the sign for this conjunction of philosophy and science (mathematics included) in modernity. This unweaving of the rainbow does not, however, appear to be possible, at least as far as nature goes, and nature perhaps can go no further. This is what mathematics and physics, and their cold philosophy, have ultimately revealed to us as they arrived to relativity and quantum physics, for now at least, the ultimate theory of light and hence of the rainbow. Light cannot ultimately be cataloged in terms of common or any other things, which are reduced to the known, simple constituents, of the kind that Democritean atomism (or classical, linear, or wave, optics) would envision, and indeed, it may be shown, it cannot be envisioned. Its mystery cannot be conquered by rule or line, which, let me reiterate, does not prevent knowledge, in physics and philosophy, or poetry, alike, but instead enhances it and even makes it possible. It is the responsibility of cold philosophy, its commitment to the maximal possible rigor (which, it follows, cannot ever be absolute or serve as absolute, anymore than anything else), to *show*, to *demonstrate*, this, let me risk the word, *fact*, this cold fact of nature, physical or human, alike. There is a tremendous lesson in this for all our knowledge, including ethical knowledge, and one does not need quantum or any other physics to learn this lesson, the lesson of the role and the necessity of the unknowable in all our knowledge, of the absence of absolutes in all our idealisms (in either sense). Accordingly, rigor and philosophy, even cold philosophy, become possible in the absence of absolutes and rigorously require this absence.

The rainbow—her "many-colored scarf," a great example and image of the multiple, as Percy Bisshe Shelley called it (perhaps with Keats's passage in mind, as he also invokes "cold light" in line 468) in *The Triumph of Life* (357)—can be explained, within the limits of classical physics, in terms of its decomposition into a gray matter, as it were, of identical atomic entities. As an allegory (in de Man's sense) of quantum physics, however, or of philosophy, cold but without absolutes, it tells us such a decomposition of the multiplicity into the identical, or more rigorously and more powerfully, of the multiplicity of the particulars into the multiplicity of identities is impossible. (It is thus also an allegory of allegory in de Man's sense, defined by this impossibility.) The epistemology of this physics and this philosophy is, by and large, the same, and it may also be explored in terms of spectrum-spectral figurations (ghost, guest, *Geist*, spirit, the apparition, light and appearance, etc.), so prominent in recent discussions. These figurations also conjoin the figures (allegories) of rainbow and apparition in the way they are in Shelley's *The Triumph of Life* or in Keats's *Fall of Hyperion* (or again, *Lamia*).

This science and this philosophy both tell us that the irreducible multiple of the particular could only dissolve (if such as in the word) into the mystery of the unknowable, mystery without mysticism. This mystery is defined by the fact that something irreducibly beyond the limits of the theory or any possible explanation, or even beyond any possible conception, is at the same time essentially responsible for all that we can conceive of or know. In this sense, our knowledge is irreducibly inconclusive; one can never close it; one can never dot all the *i*'s, cross all the *t*'s, anymore that I can do so in this inevitably inconclusive conclusion. The situation is mysterious in the sense that the emergence of the conceivable and the knowable or/as the multiple (of the irreducibly different particulars) is irreducibly unexplainable. This mystery is, however, without mysticism in the sense of assuming some unknown (divine or otherwise metaphysical) single agency behind such predictions, for example, on the model of the so-called mystical or negative theology (which postulate an unknowable divine, to which no human attributes could be possibly assigned, forgetting, naturally, the human nature of such an "unknowable divine"). In other words, insofar as it must dismantle all theology and all ontotheology (any theological-like economy of determination), cold philosophy may indeed have to "clip an Angel's wings" (although this would require far more than mere touch). But it does not unweave the rainbow. Instead, it tells us that the rainbow—the multiplicity of its colors, its divergent, spectral harmonies, its abysses, above and below—cannot be unwoven. The rainbow is ununweavable, except into (insofar as we can get hold of it) another rainbow, or a rainbow of rainbows. This is the nature of Romantic knowledge or, one might say, of Romantic Enlightenment, which must live without absolutes and *knows* how to do it.

Notes

1. Gilles Deleuze and Felix Guattari, *What Is Philosophy?* trans. Hugh Tomlinson and Graham Burchell (New York: Columbia University Press, 1993).

2. It would be difficult to contain this concept in Georges Bataille by any reference or even by a set of reference short of near totality of his text. See Bataille's *Inner Experience*, trans. Leslie Anne Boldt (Albany: State University of New York Press, 1988) may be mentioned among Bataille's better-known relevant works. Some of among the key texts elaborating the concept are assembled in Bataille, *The Unfinished System of Nonknowledge*, ed. Stuart Kendall, trans. Michelle Kendall (Minneapolis: University of Minnesota Press, 2001).

3. Paul de Man, *Aesthetic Ideology* (Minneapolis: University of Minnesota Press, 1996), 89, hereafter cited as AI.

4. de Man, *Blindness and Insight* (Minneapolis: University of Minnesota Press, 1983), 191, hereafter cited as BI.

Contributors

Richard Beardsworth is Professor of Philosophy at the American University of Paris. He is the author of *Derrida and the Political* (Routledge, 1996) and *Nietzsche* (Les Belles Lettres, 1997), has written extensively on continental philosophy, and is editor of *Tekhnema: Journal of Philosophy and Technology*. His translation of Jean-François Lyotard's *Confession of Augustine* won the Modern Language Association Aldo and Jeanne Scaglione Prize for Translation of a Scholarly Study of Literature (2001).

Joel Faflak is Assistant Professor in the Department of English and Film Studies at Wilfrid Laurier University in Ontario, Canada. He has edited, with Julia Wright, a collection of essays, *Nervous Reactions: Victorian Recollections of Romantic Writers* (State University of New York Press, 2004), is editing Thomas De Quincey's *Confessions of an English Opium-Eater* (Broadview Press, forthcoming), and is finishing a book, *Burden of the Mystery: The Scene of Romantic Psychoanalysis*. He is the recipient of a John Charles Polanyi Prize and a Governor General's Gold Medal for Research Excellence.

Rebecca Gagan is a doctoral candidate in the English Department at the University of Western Ontario. She is currently completing a dissertation on Romanticism and intellectual work.

Gary Handwerk is Professor of English and Comparative Literature at the University of Washington, Seattle. He is the author of *Irony and Ethics in Narrative: From Schlegel to Lacan* (Yale University Press, 1985); coeditor of *The Scope of Words: In Honor of Albert S. Cook* (Lang, 1991); and has translated Nietzsche's *Human All Too Human* (Stanford University Press, 1997). He has written articles on Samuel Beckett, Godwin, James Joyce, Schlegel, nineteenth-century political narratives, and Romantic historiography.

David Farrell Krell is Professor of Philosophy at De Paul University, Chicago. He is the author of *Postponements: Woman, Sensuality and Death in Nietzsche* (Indiana University Press, 1986); *Intimations of Mortality: Time, Truth, and Finitude in Heidegger's Thinking of Being* (Pennsylvania State University Press, 1986); *Daimon Life: Heidegger and Life-Philosophy* (Indiana University Press, 1992); *Lunar Voices: Of Tragedy, Poetry, Fiction, and Thought* (University of Chicago Press, 1995); *Infectious Nietzsche* (Indiana University Press, 1996); *Archeticture: Ecstasies of Space, Time, and the Human Body* (State Univeristy of New York Press, 1998); *Contagion: Sexuality, Disease, and Death in German Idealism and Romanticism* (Indiana University Press, 1998); and *The Purest of Bastards: Works of Mourning, Art, and Affirmation in the Works of Jacques Derrida* (Pennsylvania State University Press, 2000). He has edited and translated a wide range of books by Martin Heidegger, including *Basic Writings, Nietzsche, and Early Greek Thinking.* He has written extensively on the Presocratics, Plato, F. W. J. Schelling, G. W. F. Hegel, Friedrich Hölderlin, Novalis (Friedrich von Hardenberg), Friedrich Nietzsche, Luce Irigaray, Martin Heidegger, and Derrida.

Arkady Plotnitsky is Professor of English and University Faculty Scholar at Purdue University, where he is also Director of the Theory and Cultural Studies Program. He is the author of several books and numerous articles on critical and cultural theory, continental philosophy, British and European Romanticism, and the relationships among literature, philosophy, and science, in particular *In the Shadow of Hegel* (University of Florida Press, 1993), *Complementarity: Anti-Epistemology after Bohr and Derrida* (Duke University Press, 1994), and most recently *The Knowable and the Unknowable: Modern Science, Nonclassical Thought and the "Two Cultures"* (University of Mighigan Press, 2002).

Jan Plug is Assistant Professor of English and also teaches in the Centre for the Study of Theory and Criticism at the University of Western Ontario. He is the author of *Borders of a Lip: Romanticism, History, Language, Politics* (State University of New York Press, 2003) and the translator of a number of books and articles including Marc Froment—Meurice's *That Is To Say: Heidegger* (Stanford University Press, 1998) and Derrida's *Who's Afraid of Philosophy?: Right to Philosophy 1* (Stanford University Press, 2002) and (with others) *The Eyes of the University: Right to Philosophy 2* (Stanford University Press, forthcoming). He has also published articles on Samuel Taylor Coleridge's visionary languages, Immanuel Kant and the political, and Heinrich von Kleist, language, and politics.

Tilottama Rajan is Canada Research Chair in English and Theory and former Director of the Centre for Theory and Criticism at the University of Western

Ontario. She is the author of *Dark Interpreter: The Discourse of Romanticism* (Cornell University Press, 1980); *The Supplement of Reading: Figures of Understanding in Romantic Theory and Practice* (Cornell University Press, 1990); and *Deconstruction and the Remainders of Phenomenology: Sartre, Derrida, Foucault, Baudrillard* (Stanford University Press, 2002). She has coedited *Intersections: Nineteenth-Century Philosophy and Contemporary Theory* (State University of New York Press, 1995), *Romanticism, History and the Possibilities of Genre: Reforming Literature 1789–1832* (Cambridge University Press, 1998); and *After Poststructuralism: Writing the Intellectual History of Theory* (University of Toronto Press, 2002).

Jochen Schulte-Sasse holds a joint appointment in the Department of German, Scandinavian and Dutch and the Department of Cultural Studies and Comparative Literature at the University of Minnesota. He teaches and writes about eighteenth- and twentieth-century German literature and culture, European intellectual and cultural history, and theoretical issues such as psychoanalysis and literature. He has published widely on aesthetic theory and history, media history, and the institutionalization of art. A co-editor of the journal *Cultural Critique*, he is currently working on the conceptual history of the imagination in the sciences and the humanities from ancient Greece to the present.

John Vignaux Smyth is Professor of English at Portland State University, Oregon. He is the author of *A Question of Eros: Irony in Sterne, Kierkegaard and Barthes* (University Press of Florida, 1986), *The Habit of Lying: Sacrificial Studies in Literature, Philosophy, and Fashion Theory* (Duke University Press, 2002), as well as of articles on modernism, continental philosophy, and literary theory. His poetry has appeared in *Grand Street* (2003).

Andrzej Warminski is Professor of English and Comparative Literature at the University of California, Irvine. He is the author of *Readings in Interpretation: Hölderlin, Hegel, Heidegger* (University of Minnesota Press, 1987), and of the forthcoming *Material Inscriptions*. He has edited Paul de Man's *Aesthetic Ideology* (University of Minnesota Press, 1996) and coedited de Man's *Romanticism and Contemporary Criticism: The Gauss Seminar and Other Papers* (Johns Hopkins University Press, 1993). He has also published articles on Romanticism, theory, and American narrative.

Index